HANDBOOK OF
CHRISTIAN SPIRITUALITY

HANDBOOK OF CHRISTIAN SPIRITUALITY

Michael Cox

1817

HARPER & ROW PUBLISHERS, SAN FRANCISCO
Cambridge, Hagerstown, New York, Philadelphia
London, Mexico City, São Paulo, Singapore, Sydney

First published 1983. Revised and expanded 1985.
HANDBOOK OF CHRISTIAN SPIRITUALITY.

FIRST HARPER & ROW EDITION

Library of Congress Cataloging in Publication Data

Cox, Michael, 1948–
    Handbook of Christian spirituality.

    Bibliography: p.
    Includes index.
    1. Mysticism–History   2. Spirituality–History.
I. Title.
BV5075.C676   1985   248.2'2   84-48236
ISBN 0-06-061601-6

85 86 87 88 89 10 9 8 7 6 5 4 3 2 1

In memoriam
T.R.H.

'For not what thou art, nor what thou hast been, seeth God with His merciful eyes, but what thou wouldst be.'

The Cloud of Unknowing

'Thou hast made us for Thyself, and our heart is restless until it rests in Thee.'

St Augustine, *Confessions*

Contents

PART THREE: ASPECTS OF MYSTICISM SINCE 1600

Preface

THE aim of this book is a modest one: to offer the 'general reader' a starting point for a deeper acquaintance with the Christian mystical tradition. It is intended to be no more and no less than this – a first step on the road to understanding that tradition and its continuing significance for us all, whether we be Christians, nominal or active, or frank agnostics. Brevity has been essential in such a short compass; but with this undoubted virtue has gone the sin of omission, and I regret very much that space has not permitted me to treat a great many matters, and a great many fascinating and important mystics, in more detail.

My interest in Christian mysticism must be confessed immediately to be an amateur one, arising from a long-standing fascination with the *testimonies* of those who over the centuries have claimed a personal knowledge of God and with what those testimonies mean for the rest of us, rather than from an interest in the historical development of mystical theology. If this book primarily addresses itself to the non-specialist reader it is because I am one myself. It is not, therefore, a book for the professional theologian or historian, and such specialists must forgive the inherent imprecision of generalities. It is for ordinary readers who, like me, find the fact of claimed mystical experiences, and the implications of such experiences, acutely compelling both as documenting the tenacity and richness of the religious instinct in man and as providing momentous food for thought.

This will probably seem to some to be an intolerably uncritical position to assume in the face of experiences and phenomena that are in every respect, and in every sense, extraordinary. Mystical experience, it may be justly argued, is not in the least self-evidently valid. But I have thought it better in an introductory book to let the mystics speak for themselves as far as possible and to refrain from critical analysis, which can only be undertaken, and understood, after long and intimate knowledge of the vast corpus of mystical literature. My approach has been to let my readers hear, in a concise form, what Christian mystics since the Patristic Age have said of their experiences: I have not thought it a proper part of my task to indicate what should be made of these depositions.

On the other hand, it would be wrong to pretend that I have written this book in a spirit of complete objectivity and detachment. For the record, I believe that the sheer weight of testimony debilitates and neutralizes scepticism, which is a healthy and essential attitude to take up when dealing with anomalous phenomena such as Unidentified Flying Objects, which have an undoubted relationship with psychological processes, but which is something of a blunt instrument when one is dealing with the entirely different phenomena of mystical – genuinely mystical – experience. No one, in my view, can be long acquainted with Christian mystical literature without sensing that at its core are apprehensions that completely realize the strict and generally accepted definition of mysticism – that is, the direct personal experience of Ultimate Reality, of God. Eccentricities, aberrations and psychological malfunctions abound in the Christian tradition as in any other; but this core remains, for me, inviolate and immune to both cynical dismissal and reductionist analysis.

I make only the merest apology for concentrating solely on the Christian mystical tradition, although this is not meant to imply a disparagement of the mysticism of other cultures. It is simply that, in common with the spiritual traditions of the West in general, both orthodox and unorthodox, Christian mysticism has been somewhat overshadowed by its Eastern counterparts. We have an immensely rich and varied spiritual tradition in the West, and the specifically mystical part of that tradition has much to offer to the great company of 'seekers' that the turmoil and materialism of the twentieth century have created.

Yet this concentration on Christian mysticism also embodies a personal bias, and I have constantly had at the back of my mind the words of F. C. Happold in the introduction to his excellent anthology of mystical writings: 'While I am reluctant to apply to Christianity such concepts as "final" and "truer than", since neither can be logically demonstrated as valid (they partake of the

truth of faith rather than of the truth of reason), I do . . . recognize
in Christianity a quality of "uniqueness", something which I do
not find in any of the other higher religions.' I share this
reluctance, and this recognition.

The problem of selection has been a difficult one, particularly
with regard to later figures and to the subject of mystical thought
in literature. I am aware that some readers will find the text
weighted too much in favour of pre-Reformation mysticism, but
the concentration on the period from the Church Fathers to the
end of the sixteenth century has been a deliberate one. By the time
of St Teresa of Avila and St John of the Cross the structure and
language of the contemplative life are firmly established – indeed
in both St Teresa and St John of the Cross they find classic
expression – and the mystics that come after the Carmelite saints,
both Catholic and Protestant, draw on a deeply-rooted tradition.
In an introductory book of limited length, therefore, it seemed
best to focus primarily on what might be called the classic phase of
Christian mysticism. Protestant mysticism, dealt with briefly in
Part Three, really requires a book to itself and I have had to
content myself with the briefest of outlines.

My indebtedness to previous writers on the history of
mysticism will be apparent: no one who writes on the subject can
avoid the shadows of such as Evelyn Underhill, Rufus Jones and
W. R. Inge. I am grateful to Dr Grace Jantzen of King's College,
London, for her help and advice, to Mr R. A. Gilbert for his
valuable suggestions, and to the Revd Canon Anthony Duncan
and Fr Christopher Bryant SSJE, Editor of *New Fire*, for allowing
me to quote the account that concludes Chapter 10.

Finally, I must acknowledge a less apparent debt: to Thomas
Rice Henn, my Director of Studies at Cambridge, who conveyed
to all his pupils the notion of proving great literature 'on the
pulses'. If we cannot easily apply that excellent principle, as the
mystics themselves have done, to the study of mystical
experience, for to do so would entail a life of renunciation and
discipline few are capable of, we can at least accord the greatest
possible respect to those few in every age who tell us with childlike
simplicity that they have, in their various ways, proved God upon
the pulses.

MICHAEL COX
Feast of St Matthew, 1984

PART ONE: FOUNDATIONS

1. The Nature of Mysticism

MYSTICISM, wrote Coventry Patmore, is the science of ultimates.

It is a science in an absolute sense, being the passionate and all-consuming quest for supreme and perfect *knowledge,* for the Ultimate Reality philosophy calls Truth and theology acknowledges as God.

The brief transforming sensation, the shattering moment of vision, can transfigure and elevate, however fleetingly, the most ordinary human life. In some degree many of us have experienced such moments, be they triggered by love, a landscape or great art. These visionary flashes serve no evolutionary function: they partake of an inexplicable 'otherness'. They seem almost to be imposed on us; indeed, they may be seen as violations of the mundane, exalting us but at the same time briefly upsetting the tranquil undemanding rhythm of our everyday lives.

Such a feeling of profound disturbance in the midst of rapture was an element of Wordsworth's great vision:

> And I have felt
> A presence that disturbs me with the joy
> Of elevated thoughts; a sense sublime
> Of something far more deeply interfused,
> Whose dwelling is the light of setting suns,
> And the round ocean and the living air
> And the blue sky, and in the mind of man:
> A motion and a spirit, that impels
> All thinking things, all objects of all thought,
> And rolls through all things.[1]

The joy that disturbs, that disrupts and throws into sharp and often disquieting relief the pettiness of our self-centred existence, that *demands* a new response from us to the implication of our experience – this indeed is a component of the true mystical experience. Why should a mountain peak, a sonata, a painting or a sonnet inspire such patently irrational sensations? It may be – it is – pointless to inquire. We know only the compulsion, only the irresistibility of the experience.

In these fleeting experiences of unity we approach the borders, though only the borders, of the mystical state. Deep aesthetic perceptions can uplift us and with such perceptions there comes the feeling of identity between the mind and the thing it perceives. In some especially acute experiences this harmony is total: the mind and its object of perception are indeed one, and to this extent such experiences may loosely be called mystical. But in comparison with the experiences this book is principally concerned with these are but shadow images of the real thing.

For the true mystic, the element of vagueness and incoherence, and the inability truly to apprehend the nature and significance of his experience are swept aside in a veritable torrent of certainty. His sensations and reactions are focused by supreme and inalienable certitude and he is uplifted by the utter authenticity of his vision. The mystic therefore tells his story with absolute assurance: he *knows* what others simply believe.

What is Mysticism?

The need to define our terms, or at the very least to sketch in the boundaries of our enquiry, is necessary at the outset, for mysticism is a much misused and abused word. On the one hand it is used indiscriminately to describe a motley gallery of vaguely spiritual or psychical experiences; on the other it is linked in the popular imagination with the darker aspects and lunacies of the western esoteric tradition, so that a newspaper report can refer to a 'mystical cross' used by self-styled Satanists. This semantic misappropriation was commented on sixty years ago by Dom Cuthbert Butler in his classic book *Western Mysticism*:

> [Mysticism] has come to be applied to many things of many kinds: to theosophy and Christian science; to spiritualism and clairvoyance; to demonology and witchcraft; to occultism and magic; to weird psychical experiences, if only they have some religious colour; to revelations and visions; to other-worldliness, or even mere dreaminess and impracticality in the affairs of life; to poetry and painting and music of which the motif is unobvious and vague. It has been

identified with the attitude of the religious mind that cares not for dogma or doctrine, for church or sacraments . . . And, on the other hand, the meaning of the term has been watered down: it has been said that the love of God is mysticism; or that mysticism is only the Christian life lived on a high level; or that it is Roman Catholic piety in extreme form.[2]

German, unlike English, gets round this problem to some degree by using the word *mystizismus* for psychical or occult phenomena and *mystik* for what is generally taken as authentic mysticism. The latter begins in a fundamental consciousness of a beyond, of a Reality, changeless and eternal, that permeates and gives meaning to the world and experiences of finite creation. The mystic in all cultures apprehends a truth that is beyond the grasp of the rational intellect: his consciousness is extended so that, in a state of inexplicable sublimity, he grasps the abiding unity of all things, perceiving the co-immanence of the eternal and the temporal. For the religious mystic, which in the context of this book means the Christian mystic, this apprehension becomes the direct experience of the Presence of God. This is one of the simplest as well as most profound definitions of mysticism and was expressed succinctly by W. R. Inge: 'Mysticism means communication with God, that is to say with a Being conceived as the supreme and ultimate reality. If what the mystics say of their experience is true, if they have really been in communion with the Holy Spirit of God, that is a fact of overwhelming importance, which must be taken into account when we attempt to understand God, the world, and ourselves.'[3]

Around this core meaning of the term is a wider subsidiary connotation, which defines mystical experience as the intuitive acquisition of knowledge that is inaccessible to rational understanding. 'The essence of Mysticism', runs one such definition, 'is the assertion of an intuition which transcends the temporal categories of the understanding, relying on speculative reason. Rationalism cannot conduct us to the essence of things; we therefore need intellectual vision. But Mysticism is not content with symbolic knowledge, and aspires to see the Absolute by pure spiritual apprehension.'[4]

Communion and Union
W. R. Inge's use of the word 'communion', rather than 'union', is significant. The concept of communion is implicit in Rufus

Jones's definition of mysticism as 'the *type of religion which puts the emphasis on immediate awareness of relation with God, on direct and intimate consciousness of the Divine Presence*'.[5] Of course such an awareness need not in any way be construed as an abnormal experience and this type of communion can be a facet of the 'ordinary' religious life of those who are far from conforming to the commonly accepted notion of what constitutes a mystic. As one writer has said, such a communion occurring in the inner life can be 'deeply sustaining without being in any sense startling'.[6]

Union, on the other hand, or the adjective unitive, is freely used in many of the classic studies of Western mysticism – notably by Evelyn Underhill, who defines the mystic's goal as union with the Absolute. The distinction between 'communion' and 'union' is an important one, although it has never been consistently observed by either the mystics themselves or their commentators. The implication of union is that there is an ontological fusion of finite human nature with the infinite nature of God; that there is, in other words, a complete negation of the human identity, of the human *being*. 'In the spark, or centre of the soul,' proclaimed Meister Eckhart, 'there occurs true union between the soul and God.' Here the presumption is that God is already within the soul, which equates with the Hindu conception of Brahman the universal deity and Atman, the eternal deity within each individual soul. The latter is our true self, as distinct from the ego of which we are principally conscious and with which we tend to identify. This is the heart of what has become known as the 'perennial philosophy', the goal of which is to discover this true self, this divine ground within, and so come to apprehend the actual lineaments of Truth.

Christian mysticism, too, asserts the existence of this divine ground and the inherent kinship with God. As the Flemish mystic John Ruysbroeck observed: 'This union is within us of our naked nature and were this nature to be separated from God it would fall into nothingness.' Yet without ever denying the presence of God in all things, Christian mysticism also holds back from pantheism – the doctrine that God is everything and everything is God. As Georgia Harkness has said, the negation of human identity in mystical experience runs counter to all the basic tenets of Christian theology:

The basic doctrines of man's creation, judgment, and redemption through Christ, man's moral imperatives and responsible freedom, centre in the unique identity of each human self. Communion with God through the presence of the Holy Spirit, with its fruits in spiritual refreshment, guidance, and strengthening – of this our faith assures us. When union is conceived in the sense of an immediate awareness of the divine Presence, this is open to us. Union as ontological or existential loss of human identity in the divine is not.[7]

The metaphysical implications of the word 'union' should therefore be borne in mind when studying mystical literature, although the mystics themselves freely used the term (and I shall do so in this book) even when the context distinctly affirms the perpetuation of an 'I–Thou' relationship in the mystical experience.

The Spark of the Soul

The spark, apex or ground of the soul, referred to in the previous section, is a fundamental concept to grasp in relation to Christian mystical theology. Terminology, emphasis and theological expression may differ, but the insight remains a constant feature of all the great Christian mystics. Ruysbroeck called it 'the inward and natural tendency of the soul towards its source . . . By this inward tendency we are like the Holy Spirit; but in the act of receiving we become one spirit and love with God.' Meister Eckhart, who never made it quite clear whether this spark was created or uncreated, wrote that:

There is in the soul something which is above the soul, Divine, simple, a pure nothing . . . It is absolute and free from all names and forms, just as God is free and absolute in Himself. It is higher than knowledge, higher than love, higher than grace. For in these there is still distinction. In this power God doth blossom and flourish with all His Godhead* and the spirit flourisheth in God.

In our own time, C. G. Jung's concept of the self comes close to the mystical idea of the spark or ground of the soul. Jung defined the self as 'the archetypal image that leads out of polarity to the union of both partial systems – through a common mid point'. The self in Jungian terms is a synthesizing mechanism, whereby

*For Eckhart's distinction between Godhead and God see p. 102.

the polarities of the phenomenal world are brought together in a perception and experience of wholeness. The terms here are psychological; but Jung did in fact write of the self in terms that directly relate to the mystical experience: 'The soul must possess some possibility of contact with God, that is something which corresponds to the divine essence; otherwise no association could possibly have taken place. This corresponding quality described in psychological terms is the archetype of the divine image.'[8] The same insight is expressed by the poet Robert Browning:

> Truth is within ourselves; it takes no rise
> From outward things, whate'er you may believe.
> There is an inmost centre in us all,
> Where truth abides in fullness; and around
> Wall upon wall, the gross flesh hems it in,
> This perfect, clear perception – which is truth.
>
> A baffling and perverting carnal mesh
> Binds it, and makes all error: and to *know*
> Rather consists in opening out a way
> Whence the imprisoned splendour may escape,
> Than in effecting entry for a light
> Supposed to be without.[9]

And in the sacred literature of Hinduism, in the *Upanishads*, the same truth is embodied: 'The Self knows all, is not born, does not die, is not the effect of any cause; is eternal, self-existent, imperishable . . . The Self is lesser than the least, greater than the greatest. He lives in all hearts.'

The Characteristics of Mystical Experience
The four principal characteristics of mystical experience were established by William James in his *Varieties of Religious Experience*, and whilst they are not absolute categories they do serve as a useful starting point in the attempt to define the mystical state.

(i) *Ineffability*. An ineffable experience is one that is incapable of verbal descriptions: it is literally unutterable.

The mystics themselves had no notion of self-deceit or self-delusion when describing their experiences. They never conceived their visions as being merely the progeny of abnormal states of consciousness, as a rare combination of processes in the brain that produced something that had no existence outside their own minds. It was not for them a psychological *condition* but a direct *experience*.

Here is a gulf that must still be bridged by anyone who wishes to understand what mysticism is: we must trust – or, if that term is too strong, suspend disbelief – in the mystical vision of Reality. It is no use objecting that the terms of reference are unscientific, unverifiable, unrepeatable under laboratory conditions, or that we have had no such visions ourselves. A genius for religious experience is like all other exceptional gifts: the ability to develop its potential to the full is, as we rightly say, God-given. We do not question the credentials of the great poet, artist or musician: we simply acknowledge their greatness. There should be no difference in our attitude towards the genuine mystic, whose authenticity can be sensed as surely as any great artist's.

And yet the mystics labour under one supreme and fundamental disadvantage: the ineffability of their experiences and the utter inadequacy of human language to communicate to others their direct apprehension of the divine. *Their* knowledge of the reality of that apprehension is to them beyond all doubt. They say to us, in W. R. Inge's words: '"Seek as we have sought, and you will see what we have seen." Such is their testimony, and it is not wise to disregard it.' Still, it remains true that the mystical experience of God's Presence is by its very nature incommunicable. As David Knowles has said: 'In this respect all the utterances of the mystics are entirely inadequate as representations of the mystical experience, but it brings absolute certainty to the mind of the recipient.' Yet although the utterances of the mystics may indeed be inadequate the *attempt* to express the inexpressible is nearly always made – as the enormous extent of mystical literature indicates.

(ii) *Noetic Quality*. Noetic (from the Greek *noetikos*) means 'of the intellect' and involves the idea of pure abstraction and of intellectual speculation motivated by feeling. James pointed to this quality by defining mystical experiences as 'states of insight into depths of truth unplumbed by the discursive intellect'. However, the use of the term 'intellectual' does not imply an act of logical, rational analysis; rather it infers that knowledge can be grasped by intuition and insight, which reflects the meaning of the Latin word *intellectus* – perception. The mystic perceives directly;

he is granted a wholeness of vision denied to logical scientific deduction or the analysis of sensory experience. More than this, his faculty for intuitively penetrating the veil of temporal reality seems to be activated by a source beyond himself. In the words of the Fourth Gospel: 'But the Counsellor, the Holy Spirit, whom the Father will send in my name, he will teach you all things.' (John 14:26)

(iii) *Transiency.* It is a mistake to suppose that the great mystics of the Church – or indeed mystics in any culture – live in a kind of ecstatic continuum. Mystical experiences rarely last long, though their significance and effects are out of all proportion to their duration. They can, however, be frequent and, by single-minded devotion to spiritual exercises, are to some degree controllable. One of the greatest of all Christian mystics, St John of the Cross, refers to the soul's ability to abandon itself whenever it wills to the 'sweet sleep of love'.

(iv) *Passivity.* The implication of this characteristic is that mystical states almost always bring with them the feeling of something *given*. At the highest level of his experience the mystic feels overwhelmed by a greater will than his own, which subsides temporarily into abeyance.

Some mystical experiences come unbidden and are akin to those sudden illuminating moments of transformation referred to earlier and which, without any specific religious connotations, can come to all of us. The resulting state is then truly passive. But most, if not all, the great mystics actively prepared themselves to receive mystical experiences: the purgative way (see p. 28) was a deliberate process of purification and spiritual preparation, and this involved both endeavour and determination to quiet the mind and insulate it from all distractions in the attempt to be conscious only of God's presence.

*   *   *

The consciousness of a Reality beyond space and time is the foundation, the raw material, of all great religions, and for most ordinary believers it appears and remains as a moral and spiritual principle, an article of faith. In mysticism this consciousness is acted upon by a deliberate attempt to bring the eternal into relationship with the temporal. At its most exalted, the authentic mystical experience confers the responsibility, indeed the overwhelming desire, to *act* on the mystic. Mysticism in its authentic form moves out from the individual experience to collective spirituality and functions as an essential vivifying current in the spiritual life of the whole Church. The life and influence of St Francis (see p. 89) is perhaps the supreme example of this creative process, emphasizing that the true Christian mystic does not withdraw from life. Christian mysticism has a definite spiritual function in the corporation of faith and does not, as Evelyn Underhill pointed out, involve 'an existence withdrawn from common duties' in some 'rapturous dreamland': 'The hard and devoted life of some of the great mystics of the Church at once contradicts this view. It is a life inspired by a vivid and definite aim; the life of a dedicated will moving steadily in one direction, towards a perfect and unbroken union with God.'[10]

W. R. Inge, the author of one of the great books on Christian mysticism, identified three fundamental propositions or articles of faith on which mysticism, as a type of religion, appears to rest.

In the first place there is the assumption of *spiritual perception*; in other words, that there are organs of sense in the soul, as there are in the body, through which we may recognize spiritual truth.

In the second place is the proposition that *we can only know what is like ourselves*. As one mystic put it: 'What we are, that we behold; and what we behold, that we are.' As we have seen, Christian mysticism affirms that man can only know God because he is already a partaker in the divine nature. The spark of the soul, as Inge described it, is 'consubstantial with the uncreated ground of the Deity ... We could not even begin to work out our own salvation if God were not already working with us.'[11] Karl Krause (1781–1832), in justifying the argument that knowledge of God was possible for man, put the matter succinctly: 'To become aware of God in knowledge we require certainly to make a freer use of our finite power of thought, but the thought of God itself is primarily and essentially an eternal operation of the eternal revelation of God to the finite mind.'

Thirdly there is the matter of *qualification*. The acquisition of mystical knowledge requires holiness: it is, as Christ taught, the pure in heart who shall see God. And in the words of St John, who emphasized both the filial relationship of man to God and our inherent identity with Him:

Beloved, now are we the sons of God, and it doth not yet appear what we shall be: but we know that, when he shall appear, we shall be like him; for we shall see him as he is.

And every man that hath this hope in him purifieth himself, even as he is pure.[12]

Besides these three propositions is a fourth factor, which indeed binds the others together – love. The love of the mystic for God was held to be wholly disinterested, with no taint of selfishness. In the words of the anonymous *Theologia Germanica*: 'So long as a man seeketh his own highest good *because* it is his, he will never find it.'

Within this framework – spiritual perception, kinship with the divine nature, holiness and love – the mystic begins his quest for God.

The *Scala Perfectionis*

Classically, the Mystic Way – the ladder of perfection or *scala perfectionis* – has been divided into three stages: The Purgative Life, the Illuminative Life and the Unitive or Contemplative Life. These are not, however, rigid categories of experience: it is an approximate classification only and it should not be assumed that all mystics undergo the same sequence of experiences. Nor does it involve automatic graduation from one stage to another: mystical literature is full of the kind of oscillations between stages described by Julian of Norwich: 'And anon after this our blessed Lord gave me again comfort and rest in the soul . . . And then the pain showed again to my feeling, and then the joy and the blessing, and now this one, and now that other, diverse times – I suppose about twenty times.'

(i) *The Purgative Life.* The Purgative Life is the process whereby the mystic detaches himself from the tyranny and distortion of the senses. Its aim is to annihilate the ego and to unbind what Browning called the 'baffling and perverting carnal mesh'. In bringing about the death of the ego a new, divine life is born within the soul. Detachment, renunciation, contrition, confession, asceticism and self-mortification – these are the main characteristics of the Purgative Life. In a series of paradoxical aphorisms, St John of the Cross describes the process of purgation and purification as follows:

In order to arrive at having pleasure in everything,
Desire to have pleasure in nothing.
In order to arrive at possessing everything,
Desire to possess nothing.
In order to arrive at being everything,
Desire to be nothing.
In order to arrive at knowing everything,
Desire to know nothing.

The philosophical roots of the Christian concept of purgation lay in Greek thought, which had devised a similar process for moving from the world of sense to the world of abiding Reality. For Plato, the ascent to Truth begins by removing the hindrances of the senses: it involves a kind of death, by which the soul, separating itself from the distracting irrelevancies of the body, is made fit for its journey back to the ground of its existence. The necessity of purification is emphasized by Plato in the *Phaedo*:

Don't you think that the person who is likely to succeed in this attempt [*sc.* the search for reality and truth] most perfectly is the one who approaches each object, as far as possible, with the unaided intellect, without taking account of any sense of sight in his thinking, or dragging any other sense into his reckoning – the man who pursues the truth by applying his pure and unadulterated thought to the pure and unadulterated object, cutting himself off as much as possible from his eyes and ears and virtually all the rest of his body, as an impediment which by its presence prevents the soul from attaining to truth and clear thinking? Is not this the person . . . who will reach the goal of reality, if anybody can?[13]

Purification, said Plato, consists 'in separating the soul as much as possible from the body, and accustoming it to withdraw from all contact with the body and concentrate itself by itself; and to have its dwelling, so far as it can, both now and in the future, alone by itself, freed from the shackles of the body'.[14]

In the Christian tradition the world of the senses is specifically identified with the dominion of the ego, whose tyranny prevents the birth of the divine life in the soul. The *Theologia Germanica* states: 'A man should stand and be so free of himself, that is from selfhood, I-hood, me, mine and the like, that in all things he should no more regard himself and his own than if he did not exist.' 'Nothing burneth in hell', the *Theologia* also proclaims, 'but self-will . . . for so long as a man is seeking his own good, he doth not seek what is best for him, and will never find it. For a man's highest good would be and truly is, that he should not seek himself nor his own things, nor be his own end in any respect, either in things spiritual or things natural, but should seek only the praise and glory of God and His holy will.'[15]

The rationale, so to call it, behind this stripping away of all sensory and selfish attributes is concisely explained by F. C. Happold:

> Reality is one single whole; but within the one reality there are different levels of significance. Man participates in all these interrelated levels. There are, however, as it were, screens separating each region of significance from the rest. What is seen at the normal level of awareness is the result of a particular combination of image-making faculties, revealing a picture, true and real within its own limitations, but, compared with the completed whole, only an appearance, what in Eastern philosophies is termed *maya*. By turning inward, away from the flux of phenomena, towards the centre of the soul, by putting aside all concepts and images, spiritual as well as bodily, in a state of stillness and passivity, it is possible to penetrate through these separating screens, and to see deeper into that which more completely *is*; perhaps, in the end, to ascend to the contemplation of God Himself.[16]

(ii) *The Illuminative Life.* Purgation results in the generation of a specific and pervading realization of the Absolute. The consciousness of the mystic is remade, focused on the divine life within him: his life is now dedicated in every respect to developing this inner life to the full, to the working out in thought and action of this unitary consciousness.

In the higher reaches of the Illuminative Life comes a perfect acceptance of what Nicolas of Cusa called *docta ignorantia* – 'learned ignorance':

> Thus, while I am borne to loftiest heights, I behold Thee as infinity. By reason of this, Thou mayest not be attained, or comprehended, or named, or multiplied, or beheld. He that approacheth Thee must needs ascend above every limit and end and finite thing. But how shall he attain unto Thee who art the End toward whom he striveth, if he must ascend above the end? He who ascendeth above the end, doth he not enter into what is undefined and confused, and thus, in regard to the intellect, into ignorance and obscurity, which pertain to intellectual confusion? It behoveth, then, the intellect to become

ignorant and to abide in darkness if it would fain see Thee. But what, O my God, is this intellectual ignorance? Is it not an instructed ignorance? Thou, God, who art infinity, canst only be approached by him whose intellect is in ignorance, to wit, by him who knows himself to be ignorant of Thee.[17]

In this stage of the mystical life the soul is content to dwell joyfully in this sublime ignorance, in this darkness. For most of us, reality presents us with an abundance of material for rational analysis: in one sense, reality is a series of problems that can be examined and eventually solved. This is the scientific view of the world. But for the mystic, as he draws nearer to the divine unity within himself, understanding is the gift of contemplation, not of rational analysis and classification. Existence, the world, everything, is a *mystery*, not a problem. To penetrate to the heart of that mystery one must enter it, become part of it, accept it. Loving contemplation of the mystery becomes a means of unlocking its secrets: it becomes a way of knowledge.

As the mystic progresses in spiritual refinement he reaches the heights of contemplation, where his knowledge is so complete that it is, paradoxically, a sublime nothingness. Here is the great German mystic Johann Tauler speaking of the fathomless abyss to which contemplation can lead:

> The great wastes to be found in this divine ground have neither image nor form nor condition, for they are neither here nor there. They are like unto a fathomless Abyss, botomless and floating in itself . . . There is no past nor present here, and no created light can reach unto or shine into this divine ground; for here only is the dwelling-place of God and His sanctuary . . . This ground is so desert and bare that no thought can ever enter there . . . It is so close and yet so far off, and so far beyond all things, that it has neither time nor place. It is a simple and unchanging condition. A man who really and truly enters, feels as though he had been here throughout eternity, and as though he were one therewith.[18]

(iii) *The Unitive Life.* This is the ultimate attainment of the Mystic Way. For the Christian mystic, the state of union is 'that perfect and self-forgetting harmony of the regenerate will with God'.[19] As Tauler expressed it:

> Now God comes, and with His finger touches the well-filled vessel of

His grace. The soul is now united to God without any intermediary, and loses itself in Him; will, love, knowledge, all overflow into God, and are lost in Him and made one with Him. The eternal God loves Himself in this Soul, all of whose works are done by Him.[20]

If illumination is the Spiritual Betrothal, to use the image of St John of the Cross, union is the Spiritual Marriage. In this stage,

the understanding of the soul is now the understanding of God; and its will is the will of God; and its memory is the memory of God; and its delight is the delight of God; and the substance of the soul, although it is not the Substance of God, for into this it cannot be changed, is nevertheless united in Him and absorbed in Him, and is thus God by participation in God, which comes to pass in this perfect state of the spiritual life . . . in this way by 'slaying, thou hast changed death into life'. And for this reason the soul may here say very truly with Saint Paul: 'I live, now not I, but Christ liveth in me.'[21]

As we have seen, Christian mysticism, in speaking of the 'deification' of the mystic in union with God, always maintains the 'otherness' of God and the uniqueness of the creature. The Unitive Life is not so much the annihilation of selfhood, as it often is in Eastern mysticism, as the transformation or transmutation of personal identity. As Henry Suso, the fourteenth-century German mystic, said: in union, 'His [the mystic's] being remains, but in another form.' And St John of the Cross, in writing of deification, maintained that 'what is divine [is] so communicated to what is human, that, without undergoing any essential change each seems to be God'. This fundamental qualification was stated explicity by Ruysbroeck: 'Though I have said before that we are one with God . . . yet now I will say that we must eternally remain other than God, and distinct from Him . . . And we must understand and feel both within us, if all is to be right with us.'

Out of the many eloquent descriptions of the Unitive Life I have chosen the following to express what indeed is inexpressible – Ruysbroeck's account of the 'Superessential' or 'God-seeing' Life:

When the inward and God-seeking man has thus attained to his Eternal Image, and in this clearness, through the Son, has entered into the bosom of the Father: then he is enlightened by Divine truth, and he receives anew, every moment, the Eternal Birth, and he goes forth according to the way of the light, in a Divine contemplation. And here begins the fourth and last point; namely, a loving meeting, in which, above all else, our highest blessedness consists . . .

Now this active meeting and this loving embrace are in their ground fruitive and wayless; for the abysmal Waylessness of God is so dark and so unconditioned that it swallows up in itself every Divine way and activity, and all the attributes of the Persons, within the rich compass of the essential Unity; and it brings about a Divine fruition in the abyss of the Ineffable. And here there is a death in fruition, and a melting and dying into the Essential Nudity, where all the Divine names, and all the conditions and all the living images which are reflected in the mirror of Divine Truth, lapse in the Onefold and Ineffable, in waylessness and without reason. For in this unfathomable abyss of the Simplicity, all things are wrapped in fruitive bliss; and the abyss itself may not be comprehended, unless by the Essential Unity. To this the Persons, and all that lives in God, must give place; for here there is nought else but an eternal rest in the fruitive embrace of an outpouring Love. And this is that wayless being which all interior spirits have chosen above all things. This is the dark silence in which all lovers lose themselves.[22]

The Knowledge of God

As one writer on mysticism has said, the entire mystic process can be termed an intellectual one: it is a yearning, a burning, a thirst for complete *knowledge*: 'The adage, "Knowledge is power", has a peculiar meaning for the mystic; and when it is said that mysticism is a philosophy of the heart, it is only true in the sense that the mystic *loves* in proportion as he *knows*.'[23] In Christian mysticism, there are two ways by which this knowledge can be achieved and expressed.

(i) *The Positive Way.* The procedure of the *via positiva* (or cataphatic way) is to arrive at a knowledge of God in affirmative terms: to see Him as the supereminence of all created perfections and actively to work towards a greater understanding of Him. Typically, by recognizing certain qualities – beauty, goodness, love, and so on – in created things, the mystic ascends to the supreme originals of those qualities contained in God. As one sixteenth-century theologian, Leonard Lessius, put it: 'By the study of the Divine Perfections, the soul rises towards God, contemplates Him, admires, fears, venerates, loves and perpetually praises and blesses Him . . . after considering the divine perfections most attentively, the soul rises to something more sublime and limitless, and infinitely more noble; to something which embraces not merely the divine perfections as the created mind conceived them, but the Divine Being itself, and in an unknown manner unites itself to Him by contemplation and love.'[24]

(ii) *The Negative Way.* The *via negativa* (or apophatic way) is predicated by the insistence that man can know nothing of God unless God *chooses* to reveal Himself.* The first great working out of the *via negativa* was the *Mystical Theology* of the Pseudo-Dionysius (see p. 75), which totally negated man's 'natural' knowledge of God. Dionysius describes God as the 'Divine Dark': He is completely transcendent and there is nothing in the human creature that can give us any idea of His nature. It is only by *negation* that man can come to 'know' God – by stripping away every aspect and attribute of the self. The *via negativa* is, indeed, the dominant path in Christian mysticism, both in the East and the West. It holds that God is unimaginably 'other' than man; language, for instance, shrinks to utter inadequacy before the unknowable but inferrable self-sufficiency of God, who is complete completeness, needing nothing from man to augment His plenitude. The *via negativa* denies to God all temporal attributes, the process leading finally to the supreme paradox – expressed by the Pseudo-Dionysius – that God is beheld 'in that superessential Darkness which is hidden by all the light that is in existing things'.

In simple terms, to follow the *via negativa* means that if, for instance, we say 'God is good', our conception of the quality of goodness must fall infinitely short of the reality of God's goodness: it is therefore futile and misleading to think of God in human terms, or even to describe Him in metaphors that derive from our experience of the temporal world. In the face of a knowledge that cannot be expressed in human terms, the mind of the mystic must submit to total negativity: it must enter, in the image of one of the most famous of all medieval mystical treatises, a cloud of unknowing.

· Although Dean Inge considered the *via negativa* to have been

*The implied distinction here is between 'acquired' and 'infused' contemplation.

'the great accident of Christian Mysticism', its concepts and methods appear time and time again, as we shall see in the following pages. For the moment, here is the Pseudo-Dionysius' prayer to the Divine Darkness:

> Supernal Triad, deity above all essence, knowledge and goodness; Guide of Christians to Divine Wisdom; direct our path to the ultimate summit of Thy mystical Lore, most incomprehensible, most luminous, and most exalted, where the pure, absolute, and immutable mysteries of theology are veiled in the dazzling obscurity of the secret Silence, outshining all brilliance with the intensity of their Darkness, and surcharging our blinded intellects with the utterly impalpable and invisible fairness of glories surpassing all beauty.
>
> Let this be my prayer; but do thou, dear Timothy, in the diligent exercise of mystical contemplation, leave behind the senses and the operations of the intellect, and all things sensible and intellectual, and all things in the world of being and non-being, that thou mayest arise, by unknowing, towards the union, as far as is attainable, with Him who transcends all being and all knowledge. For by the unceasing and absolute renunciation of thyself and of all things, thou mayest be borne on high, through pure and entire self-abnegation, into the superessential Radiance of the Divine Darkness.[25]

Christocentric and Theocentric Contemplation

The Christian mystical tradition recognizes two broad forms of contemplation – though, again, these are not rigid, mutually exclusive categories.

(i) *Christocentric Contemplation.* In this tendency, as the name implies, the ascent towards union with the Triune God is undertaken principally through the Person of the Son: Christ is, literally and figuratively, the Door through which the divine nature of the Father can be apprehended. Its roots are the Gospel narratives and the writings of St Paul and the general tenour of its approach can be seen in St Bernard of Clairvaux (see p. 81), whose great achievement, in the estimation of W. R. Inge, was 'to recall devout and loving contemplation to the image of the crucified Christ, and to found that worship of our Saviour as the "Bridegroom of the Soul", which in the next centuries inspired so much fervid devotion and lyrical sacred poetry. The romantic side of Mysticism, for good and evil, received its greatest stimulus in Bernard's Poems and in his Sermons on the Canticles.'[26]

St Bernard himself, justifying the Christocentric focus, wrote:

'Although it is true that we place our whole hope in the Man-God, we do so not because He is Man, but because He is God.' The celebrated and highly influential *Imitation of Christ (Imitatio Christi)* of St Thomas à Kempis (see p. 122) represents the full flowering of the Christocentric spirit:

> 'He who follows Me shall not walk in darkness,' said Our Lord.
>
> In these words Christ counsels us to follow His life and way if we desire true enlightenment and freedom from all blindness of heart. Let the life of Jesus Christ, then, be our first consideration.
>
> The teaching of Jesus far transcends all the teachings of the Saints, and whosoever has His spirit will discover concealed in it heavenly manna ... Whoever desires to understand and take delight in the words of Christ must strive to conform his whole life to Him.[27]

The 'way of the Cross', for St Thomas, is the way to God: 'Be assured of this, that you must live a dying life. And the more completely a man dies to self, the more he begins to live to God. No man is fit to understand heavenly things, unless he is resigned to bear hardships for Christ's sake.'

(ii) *Theocentric Contemplation.* This type of contemplation came to the Christian mystics from Greek thought via St Augustine, and at its simplest it involves drawing near to God through the contemplation of His creatures. The Platonic model can be found, for instance, in the *Timaeus*:

> The world is like, above all things, to that Living Creature of which all other living creatures, severally and in their families, are parts. For that embraces and contains within itself all the intelligible living creatures, just as this world contains ourselves and all other creatures that have been formed as things visible. For the god, wishing to make this world most nearly like that intelligible thing which is best and in every way complete, fashioned it as a single visible living creature, containing within itself all living things whose nature is of the same order ... To the end that this world may be like the complete Living Creature in respect of its uniqueness, for that reason its maker did not make two worlds nor yet an indefinite number; but this Heaven has come to be and is and shall be hereafter one and unique.[28]

Here is the co-inherence of the Creator and the created that informs Theocentric contemplation, in which the mystic ascends from God's reflection in created things to the attributes of God himself. The visible universe in all its beauty and perfection of form is the manifestation of the symmetry, order and beauty of God's mind: in Platonic terms, the beauty of the world is a reflection of its heavenly archetype. In St Paul's view: 'The invisible things of him [God] from the creation of the world are clearly seen, being understood by the things that are made, even his eternal power and Godhead.'[29] The Theocentric approach is seen at its most profound, perhaps, in St Augustine (see p. 71), in whom it encompasses a movement from a transient creation to an abiding Creator – an active growth or pilgrimage towards an eternal object of love and desire.

Such terms as these – Christocentric, Theocentric, *via negativa*, *via positiva*, purgation, illumination and union – can become obtrusive necessities in the study of mysticism and too great a use of them can obscure the vitality and spontaneity of the genuine mystical experience. It must always be remembered that Christian mysticism, though it has evolved methodologies and 'exercises', is not a rigid system: it never ceases to accommodate the concept of grace, nor does it seek to disparage the moment of sublime surprise.

Neoplatonism

The word 'mystic' has its roots in the mystery cults of ancient Greece. A mystic was someone who had passed beyond the veil of appearances into the eternal world of spirit; he was an initiate who had undergone an enactment of his own death and had received knowledge of the divine life. The word 'mystery' itself is derived from the Greek verb 'to shut' – i.e. to seal one's lips in secrecy.

In Neoplatonism, the syncretic pagan philosophy that was still flourishing during the early centuries of the Christian era and which, indeed, exerted a profound influence on the development of Christian mystical theology, the language of the Mysteries is used to express an intuitive apprehension of transcendent reality. **Plato** himself (427–347BC) was called by Justin Martyr (see p. 58) 'a Christian before Christ', whilst Clement of Alexandria (see p. 61) considered the Gospels to exhibit 'perfected Platonism'. Plato's concept of the supreme Idea – the Good – was easily assimilated into Christian thinking, which saw God as the Highest Good. Plato's description of the ascent to absolute beauty in the *Symposium*, the journey from appearance to reality, similarly contains many overtones and implications that were later developed and extended by Christian mystics:

> For he who has been taught in things of love so far, and who has learned to see the beautiful in order and succession, when he comes toward the end will suddenly perceive a world of beauty . . . not fair or foul, according to the point of view, or time, or place, but beauty absolute, apart; simple and everlasting, without increase, decrease, or any change, imparted to the ever-growing changeful beauties of all other things; he who, impelled by love, uprising thence begins to see that beauty, nears the end.
>
> The time process, of being led to things of love, is this – to use earth's beauty as the stair up which he mounts to other beauty, going from one to all fair forms, and from fair forms to actions fair, to fair ideas . . . until he comes to beauty absolute, to beauty's essence . . .
>
> Do you not see that in this communion only, beholding beauty with the mind, he will be enabled to bring forth not images of beauty, but realities? For he has hold of a reality; he brings forth and educates true virtue; to become the friend of God and be immortal, if a mortal may. Would that be an ignoble life?[30]

In the Neoplatonism of **Plotinus** (*c.* AD 205–270), union with the Absolute, or One, is the ruling goal. The speculations, insights and indeed the language of Plotinus were to have a direct, determinative influence on Christian mysticism.

The Plotinian system is based on a triad – a trinity. First comes the One, the Good or the Source, which is the fundamental principle of life and being, transcendent but also immanent, since it contains all. It is the 'fount of all that is best', the 'fountain and principle of beauty', 'good in the unique mode of being the Good above all that is good'. The One is the final goal, and we are told by **Porphyry** (*c.* 233–304) that Plotinus, under whom Porphyry studied, was 'ever tending towards the Divine which he loved with all his heart. He strove strenuously to set free his soul and to ascend above the bitter waves of this sanguinary existence. And thus by a divine illumination and by meditation and the methods described by Plato in the *Symposium*, he would lift himself up to the First and All-transcendent God.'[31]

After the One, emanating from It and distinguished ontologically, is *Nous*, usually translated as Mind or Intellect. This is the realm of eternal thought-forms or ideas. In this noumenal realm, all things coexist in an Eternal Now. In some respects, *Nous* is similar to the Christian Logos, being the principle of order and meaning permeating all things; but there is no personal identity and no historical incarnation.

The third person of the Plotinian trinity is *Psyche*, or World Soul, a motivating principle of creative energy that links the eternal world of true being with the world of time and space: it is a bridge between the perfection of pure Intellect and the imperfection of the physical universe. From the World Soul flow the souls of men, which animate the material body and link each individual with the whole. There is thus a fundamental identity (though there is also difference) between the human soul and the One, through this 'chain of becoming': human mind and human soul derive their existence from and participate in the Mind and Soul of the One. The seeker, says Plotinus, 'belongs to God and is one with him, like two concentric circles; they are one when they coincide; and two only when they are separated'.[32]

Plotinus' mystical philosophy sought to ascend through the chain of becoming back to the One: its aim was to re-unite the soul, exiled in matter, to its source. This was achieved through a process of purification: 'Virtue perfected, enlightened, and deeply rooted in the soul will reveal God to us, but without it he will be but an empty name.' The way to union with the One demands total detachment from the world of the senses, so that the soul, imbued with love for the One, recollects its identity with the Supreme Source. This is the 'flight of the alone to the Alone' and it culminates in a state of 'deification':

> He who has seen It, knows whereof I speak: that the soul has another life as it nears to God, and is now come to him, and has a share in him so that, restored, it knows that the Dispenser of true life is here present, it needs naught else; and on the other hand we must put aside everything else and abide in This alone, and become This alone – detached from all temporal things. The soul is anxious to be free, so that we may attach ourselves to It by the whole of our being; no part of it not touching God. Then it will be possible for the soul to see both God and herself divinely, and she will see herself illumined, full of intelligible light; or rather she will be light itself – pure, unfettered, agile, become a God or rather being a God, and wholly aflame.[33]

*   *   *

The earliest, and most influential, fruit of Neoplatonic thought in a Christian context were the mystical speculations of the

Pseudo-Dionysius; but with their emphasis, as we have seen, on detachment and negation, these speculations may be seen as potentially inimical to the true spirit of Christian mysticism, which has, or should have, at its heart a creative, vocational impulse.

In the Christian context, mysticism is not finally and completely an individual activity. The knowledge of God that is enjoyed by the rare company of souls we call mystics is not a passive knowledge; it can be seen more in the nature of a motivating force. It does not keep the mystic isolated from the world: in its authentic form, mysticism is concerned with *life* in the here and now as much as with the eternal verities. 'My life', said St Augustine, 'shall be a real life, being wholly full of Thee.'

The spiritual sense is latent in us all; most of us, however, have not the least impulsion to develop this capacity for knowing God into full realization. The service the mystic performs is to show us all, but particularly those within the body of the Church, that such a realization is possible. There is, in other words, a *social* function and meaning in Christian mysticism. This has been nowhere better expressed than by Evelyn Underhill:

> Their work [*sc.* the mystics'] within the religious family is to supply, and keep on supplying, the prophetic element of religion: the ever life-giving consciousness of God and His presence in and with man. We might indeed call them the eyes of the Body of Christ. They maintain that awestruck outlook towards the Infinite, and that warmly loving sense of God's indwelling grace, without which all religious institutions quickly become mechanical and cold. More than this, their vivid first-hand experience urges them to a total consecration to the service of God and of men. In them the life of prayer informs the life of action: their contemplation of Reality makes all that they do more real. Thus they show what Christian spirituality can be, and what a contribution it can make to the corporate life. By communion with them, the merely active Christian can realize the actuality of the world of spirit, and even catch something of their fire.[34]

Thus, mystical experience should not be regarded as a solipsistic, freakish activity, divorced from the moral life. To quote Evelyn Underhill again: 'The great mystics, who are geniuses in the sphere of religion, show to us the uncreated beauty of spiritual realities which we cannot find alone, and form a great body of witness to humanity's experience of God.'[35]

Christian mysticism is not typically the flight of the alone to the Alone: it is the Way of Reciprocal Love – of man for God, God for man, and man for man.

2. Mysticism In The Bible

EVEN in the earliest period of the Church's development there was no fixed type of Christianity. There were many variations, differences of emphasis and interpretation. Though Pauline Christianity (unsystematic though it was) dominated the early Church, there were other presentations of the primal events of the Christian faith, so that from the very beginning the *personal* experience of Christ within the whole fellowship of the Church became a characteristic element of that fellowship. As Harnack observed: 'Jesus sought to kindle independent religious life, and He did kindle it; yes, that is His peculiar greatness, that He led men to God so that they lived their own life with Him.'

Similarly, Rufus Jones wrote: 'It is a point of the first importance that the Gospels have given us little or no metaphysics; the language of theology is, too, quite foreign to them. They have given us instead the portrait of a Person who had a most extraordinary experience of God and of Oneness with Him.'[1]

Jesus offered a way to God, and those who followed Him could expect to be brought, like Him, to a personal consciousness of divinity. From the start, then, Christianity was an expression of man's capacity for intimate fellowship with God: it was, in other words, a fundamentally mystical religion, in which its members are able to experience what its Founder experienced.

> Christianity in the golden age was essentially a rich and vivid consciousness of God, rising to a perfect experience of union with God in mind and heart and will. It was a personal exhibition of the Divine in the human, the Eternal in the midst of time. When we get back to the head-waters of our religion we come ultimately to a Person who felt, and, in childlike simplicity, said that 'No man knows the Father save the Son' and 'I and the Father are one'.[2]

The longing to unite with whatever fulfils the individual expectations of God is common to all major religions and to the religious temperament in all cultures; but for Christians the mystical experience participates in a metaphysical event within a precise historical framework: the event we know as the Incarnation. The difference this makes to the Christian mystic cannot be exaggerated. In no other religion does God, the Being with whom the mystic yearns to be united, actually put on flesh and become manifest in time and space, not as a superhuman being but as a suffering *human* with human failings and limitations. St John's simple statement is overwhelming in its significance for the Christian mystic: 'In the beginning was the Word, and the Word was with God, and the Word was God . . . And the Word was made flesh, and dwelt among us . . .'

To the Jews this was an outrageous suggestion; but for Christian believers it offered a route to the Father. The Word, or Logos, the creative aspect of the Father, *was* God and was *with* God: it had a distinct identity but was also part of an indivisible Unity. More than this, the Word was 'made man' – was actually born of a woman and clothed in living flesh. Through the Logos, the Son, access was offered to the Father: 'He that hath seen me hath seen the Father . . . Believest thou not that I am in the Father, and the Father in me?'

For the Christian mystic, the Incarnation means that the world – the real world of men and women and everyday affairs – should not finally be denied, for 'God so loved the world that He gave His only-begotten Son'. The world is sanctified by God's love for it and by the Son's sacrifice. It therefore follows that matter is not inherently antagonistic to the mystical life: used sacramentally, it is a ladder to God. From the starting point of Christian mysticism in the New Testament we find that the life of contemplation, although the temptation for detachment and negation may be great, ultimately embraces a sense of community with others: the mystic, at least those of the first rank, is acutely sensible of his place in the corporation of faith. He approaches God not as an individual in isolation, but as an individual member of the Body of Christ.

The Old Testament
There are mystical elements in the Old Testament, although they are diffuse and undeveloped. In Genesis we find the concept –

fundamental to mystical theology in the West – that man was made in God's image; and throughout succeeding books we are shown the potential relationship that exists between man and God. In some figures this potential is realized: Abraham, for instance, to whom God appeared several times; or Jacob, whose vision of a ladder reaching down from heaven to earth symbolizes the indissoluble connection between the world of spirit and the world of matter; and Moses, to whom the Lord spoke 'face to face, as a man speaketh to his friend'.

God also spoke through the prophets, and it is in the prophetic books of the Old Testament that the conviction of a direct communion with the Lord comes through most strongly. The 'still small voice' Elijah heard in the wilderness is a component of an essentially mystical experience; a richer vision – of the Lord in glory – is to be found in Isaiah:

> I saw also the Lord sitting upon a throne, high and lifted up, and his train filled the temple.
> Above it stood the seraphims: each one had six wings; with twain he covered his face, and with twain he covered his feet, and with twain he did fly.
> And one cried unto another, and said, Holy, holy, holy, is the Lord of hosts: the whole earth is full of thy glory.[3]

In Ezekiel's vision there is an intense sense of an approach to the ultimate mystery of God's person:

> And above the firmament that was over their heads was the likeness of a throne, as the appearance of a sapphire stone: and upon the likeness of the throne was the likeness as the appearance of a man above it.
> And I saw as the colour of amber, as the appearance of fire round about within it, from the appearance of his loins even upward, and from the appearance of his loins even downward, I saw as it were the appearance of fire, and it had brightness round about.
> As the appearance of the bow that is in the cloud in the day of rain, so was the appearance of the brightness round about. This was the appearance of the likeness of the glory of the Lord. And when I saw it, I fell upon my face, and I heard a voice of one that spake.[4]

The most personal account of the prophetic sense of direct communication with God is perhaps Jeremiah's:

Then the word of the Lord came unto me, saying,

Before I formed thee in the belly I knew thee; and before thou camest forth out of the womb I sanctified thee, and I ordained thee a prophet unto the nations.

Then said I, Ah, Lord God! behold, I cannot speak: for I am a child.

But the Lord said unto me, Say not, I am a child: for thou shalt go to all that I shall send thee, and whatsoever I command thee thou shalt speak . . .

Then the Lord put forth his hand, and touched my mouth. And the Lord said unto me, Behold, I have put my words in thy mouth.[5]

Isaiah's vision of God, in particular, with its clear sense of awe and revelation, provided later mystics with an abundant source of imagery; but it lacks one important element – the overpowering consciousness of joyful intimacy that marks much Christian mysticism in later periods. God remains 'the Lord', and the prophet seems denied that feeling of tender communion that is so apparent later.

Many medieval mystics found the Song of Solomon a fertile source of inspiration – notably Bernard of Clairvaux (see p. 81). The erotic imagery of the Canticle became interpreted mystically, as well as allegorically, with Christ being seen as the Bride of the Church. For one commentator at least, W. R. Inge, this elevation of Hebrew love poetry into an allegory of individual spirituality and of the Church's relationship with its Founder was a dangerous distortion of the truth: 'A graceful romance in honour of true love was distorted into a precedent and sanction for giving way to hysterical emotions, in which sexual imagery was freely used to symbolize the relation between the soul and its Lord. Such aberrations are as alien to sane Mysticism as they are to sane exegesis.'[6]

Finally, the Psalms also coloured later mystical experience. In them the personal note is strong and expresses the kind of living certainty in God's presence, yet with a deep sense of frailty and insufficiency, that is characteristic of the great mystics of later ages:

Whither shall I go from thy spirit? or whither
shall I flee from thy presence?
    If I ascend up into heaven, thou art there: if I make my bed in hell, behold thou art there.

If I take the wings of the morning, and dwell in the uppermost parts
of the sea;
Even there shall thy hand lead me, and thy right hand shall hold
me . . .
I will praise thee: for I am fearfully and wonderfully made:
marvellous are thy works; and that my soul knoweth right well . . .
How precious also are thy thoughts unto me, O God! how great is
the sum of them!
If I should count them, they are more in number than the sand:
when I awake, I am still with thee.[7]

St Paul

Christian literature – indeed Christian mystical literature – may
be said to begin with the Pauline Epistles. The Gospels tell of
Christ's life and passion; the Epistles of Paul stand as the first
great witnesses to faith – faith in the living presence of Christ
Crucified. Paul's letters, grounded in an intense and transforming personal faith, are also rooted in the life of the Church itself,
in the community of Christ inspired and united by faith. This
intermingling of the personal and the collective was to be
distinctive of all the great Christian mystics.

St Paul, an ardent Pharisee before his conversion, was steeped
in Hebrew theology, and while there was much that was new in his
mystical apprehension his spiritual life forms a bridge between
the Old and New Testaments, across which the Christian
tradition gained full access to the heritage of Hebrew Scripture.

St Paul clearly illustrates the threefold mystical way through
the intensity of his moral struggles, the gradual illumination as the
life of prayer develops, and the final consummation of union with
Christ: 'I live, now not I; but Christ liveth in me'. His experience
on the road to Damascus is as profound as the consciousness of
the Old Testament prophets that they were being called to be the
mouthpieces of God; but the element that is wholly new in Paul's
experience is its conviction of direct person to person contact.
The voice he hears asks him: 'Why persecutest thou *me*?', to
which Paul replies, 'Who art *thou*, Lord?' (my emphasis).

Paul's union with Christ is a unity of faith and love: it is a *moral*,
not a metaphysical, union, one in which – as in all Christian
mysticism – the integrity of the human and the divine nature
remains unviolated. As Paul himself said: 'I live in the faith of the
Son of God, who loveth me and delivered himself for me.' This is
not the Neoplatonic union of the alone with the Alone: it is a

genuine mystical relationship that takes place within the very body of Christ – His Church.

In his second Epistle to the Corinthians Paul speaks – with obvious reluctance – of his own mystical experience. He describes it in the third person:

> I knew a man in Christ above fourteen years ago, (whether in the body, I cannot tell; or whether out of the body, I cannot tell: God knoweth;) such an one caught up to the third heaven.
>
> And I knew such a man ... How that he was caught up into paradise, and heard unspeakable words, which it is not lawful for a man to utter.[8]

The first significant phrase in this account is 'a man in Christ', which expresses the essential mystery of Christian mysticism – that union with the divine does not negate or subsume the personal identity of the mystic but leaves it intact to live wholly *in* the divine nature. In this ecstatic state, so sudden and intense that Paul, 'caught up', cannot recall whether his consciousness remained in his body or not, he apprehended what he now finds impossible to communicate in human language – 'unspeakable words, which it is not lawful for man to utter'.

There is a distinct ascetic element in St Paul's mysticism that was to become a feature of later Christian mystics. 'I keep under my body, and bring it into subjection,' he writes to the church at Corinth, 'lest that by any means, when I have preached to others, I myself should be a castaway.'[9] In other words, he does not chastise his body in order to *induce* mystical experiences but in order to prevent himself from falling into sin. He will not – and this is true of all the great Christian mystics – provoke ecstatic states: he will only keep himself prepared to receive them with one end in view – unity through faith and love with Christ within His Church: 'For he that cometh to God must believe that he is, and that he is a rewarder of them that diligently seek him.'[10]

The diligent seeking of God is predicated for Paul by a relationship with Christ. What the Apostle calls 'the supply of the Spirit of Jesus Christ' suffuses every phase of his spiritual life, as it is revealed through the Pauline writings, so that he can say: 'For to me to live is Christ, and to die is gain.'[11] But interpenetrating this ardent Christology is the consciousness of the ever-living Father, the Reality that encompasses all, the peace that 'passeth all understanding'. It is in this reaching out to the Father through faith in the Son that Paul's importance for the mystical tradition in the West lies.

St John

Besides the mysticism of St Paul, the New Testament also contains what Clement of Alexandria called the 'spiritual Gospel' – the Fourth Gospel of St John the Evangelist, the beloved disciple. The writings attributed to John are shot through with an elevated spirituality; above all they are a witness to the mystical power of love:

> Beloved, let us love one another: for love is of God; and every one that loveth is born of God, and knoweth God.
> He that loveth not knoweth not God; for God is love.
> In this was manifested the love of God towards us, because that God sent his only begotten Son into the world, that we might live through him . . .
> If we love one another, God dwelleth in us, and his love is perfected in us.
> Hereby know we that we dwell in him, and he in us, because he hath given us of his Spirit.[12]

The Fourth Gospel also lays great stress on the mystery of the Incarnation, which, as we have seen, is the doctrine that distinguishes Christian mysticism from all other types of mystical experience. The opening of the First Epistle General of John delineates the mystical context in which the early Church developed. It sets aside the abstraction of symbolism and offers up instead the apostolic witness to the manifestation of the eternal in the temporal:

> That which was from the beginning, which we have heard, which we have seen with our eyes, which we have looked upon, and our hands have handled, of the Word of life;
> (For the life was manifested, and we have seen it, and bear witness, and shew unto you that eternal life, which was with the Father, and was manifested unto us;)
> That which we have seen and heard declare we unto you, that ye also may have fellowship with us; and truly our fellowship is with the Father and with his Son Jesus Christ.

In the Fourth Gospel the mystical tradition of the Church

found the supreme expression of the interpenetration of matter by spirit in the revelation of the sacramental possibilities of the material world. Matter, through the incarnation of the Logos, becomes a vehicle of Spirit – supremely, in the eucharistic communion:

> I am the living bread which came down from heaven: if any man eat of this bread, he shall live for ever: and the bread that I will give is my flesh, which I will give for the life of the world . . .
> Verily, verily, I say unto you, Except ye eat the flesh of the Son of man, and drink his blood, ye have no life in you . . .
> He that eateth my flesh, and drinketh my blood, dwelleth in me, and I in him.[13]

Charity is St John's royal road to divine union, as it was for St Paul. The very essence of Christian mysticism, the authentic context in which the mystical tradition developed, is to be found in the Pauline and Johannine writings; in particular, Christ's 'new commandment', as described by St John in his account of the Last Supper, 'that ye love one another; as I have loved you', laid the obligation of true charity on all those who aspired to mystical union.

PART TWO:
THE CHURCH FATHERS
TO THE
SPANISH CARMELITES

3. The Patristic Age

THE Patristic Age – the age of the Church Fathers – usually defines a period from about the end of the first century to the end of the eighth. The Fathers were not mystics in the precise technical sense of the word. They were of necessity more concerned with the establishment of authority and permanent doctrine than with the working out of subjective experiences. Some were statesmanlike figures; others were philosophers; many combined the two roles; few described in any detail or at length the nature of their personal relationship with God.

But yet throughout patristic literature up to Augustine there are scattered insights that clearly express the inner apprehension of the Divine Presence and the elements present in union with the Absolute. Irenaeus, for example, describes the spiritual liberation brought about by the consciousness of the indwelling spirit: 'The Lord Who redeems us by His own blood gives us His Soul for our soul, His own Flesh for our flesh, and pours out the Spirit of the Father for the union and communion of God and man, imparting God to man through the Spirit, and raising man on the other hand to God.'[1] Elsewhere Irenaeus refers to 'participation in God' and says that 'The glory of God is a living man, and the life of man is the vision of God'.[2]

Tertullian evoked the natural instinct of the soul – even in pagans – to acknowledge God. In spite of all outward forms or philosophies, and even laying aside the question of whether or not the soul is divine in itself, Tertullian held that the natural reflex of the soul is to join itself to God: 'Though under the oppressive bondage of the body, though led astray by depraving customs, though enervated by lusts and passions, though in slavery to false gods; yet, whenever the soul comes to itself, as out of a surfeit, or a sleep, or a sickness, and attains something of its natural soundness, it speaks of God.'[3]

Throughout the writings of the Greek Fathers – reflecting the pervading influence of Neoplatonism – is an emphasis on the immanence, as well as the transcendence, of God. For Clement of Alexandria prayer is a means of directly communing with God and the Divine Life is formed within through faith. It is therefore imperative to arrive at a knowledge of this inner holiness – to know oneself and the Truth to which the soul is heir: 'For if one knows himself he will know God, and knowing God, he will be made like God.'[4]

The early Fathers, then, were not mystics in the all-consuming way of later figures like St Teresa or St John of the Cross – or even St Augustine. They were primarily religious philosophers, but they instinctively expressed aspects of higher religious experience that relate directly to the mystical knowledge of later ages.

Martyrdom

The connection between martyrdom and certain aspects of mystical experience is an intimate one. The first illustration of this is implied in Acts, in the account of the martyrdom of **St Stephen** – 'a man full of faith and of the Holy Ghost'. Stephen, a deacon of the Church (traditionally, the first to hold the office), was appointed by the Apostles to be amongst those who distributed alms; but he aroused the hostility of certain of the Jews and he was brought before the Sanhedrin accused of blasphemy: 'And all that sat in the council, looking stedfastly on him, saw his face as it had been the face of an angel'. After summarizing the history of Israel to show that the Temple and its laws had been established against the will of God ('the most High dwelleth not in temples made with hands; as saith the prophet'), Stephen accused the Jews in turn of having persecuted the prophets in the same way as they had persecuted and killed Jesus:

> When they heard these things, they were cut to the heart, and they gnashed on him with their teeth.
> But he, being full of the Holy Ghost, looked up stedfastly into heaven, and saw the glory of God, and Jesus standing on the right hand of God.[5]

Stephen was then taken out and stoned: 'And he kneeled down, and cried with a loud voice, Lord, lay not this sin to their charge.' Present at the execution, and consenting to it, was Saul, and more than one commentator has suggested that he was psychologically prepared for what happened to him on the road to Damascus by witnessing Stephen's martyrdom: St Augustine, for instance, wrote that 'If Stephen had not prayed, the Church would not have gained Paul.'

It is impossible to say whether or not St Stephen may be considered a true mystic: the writer of Acts merely presents us with the juxtaposition of a visionary experience and imminent death. A much fuller account of the psychology of martyrdom is to be found in the letters of **Ignatius,** Bishop of Antioch (*c.*35–*c.*107), martyred in the Colosseum during the reign of the Emperor Trajan. For Ignatius, Christ was the pattern and the perfection of the mystical life: 'There is one physician, fleshly and spiritual,' he wrote, 'begotten and unbegotten, God in man, true life in death, both of Mary and of God, first passible then impassible,* Jesus Christ our Lord.'[6] Ignatius strenuously upheld both the humanity and the reality of Christ against the Docetists, who denied both:

> Turn a deaf ear to any speaker who avoids mention of Jesus Christ who was of David's line, born of Mary, who was truly born, ate and drank; was truly persecuted under Pontius Pilate, truly crucified and died while those in heaven, on earth, and under the earth beheld it; who also was truly raised from the dead, the Father having raised him, who in like manner will raise us also who believe in him – his Father, I say, will raise us in Christ Jesus, apart from whom we have not true life.[7]

Docetism – the denial of Christ's human nature and the accounting of His sufferings as apparent rather than real – necessarily disregarded the obligation of charity, and Ignatius charges the Docetists with having 'no concern for love, none for the widow, the orphan, the afflicted, the prisoner, the hungry, the thirsty'.[8] The reality of Christ's passion becomes for Ignatius an emblem of His eternal love; it therefore followed that for the lover of Christ martyrdom was to be joyfully embraced: 'Only let it be in the name of Jesus Christ so as to share his Passion. I endure all things, since he gives me the power who is perfect man.'[9] To the Christian community in Rome he writes: 'This is the only favour I ask; that I may be poured as a libation while an altar is still ready.'[10]

*Capable and incapable of suffering.

The emphasis on the sacramental nature of mystical experience and on the mystical symbolism of Christ's blood, so typical of the later medieval mystics, is apparent in Ignatius at the outset of the Patristic Age. In an extraordinarily powerful passage Ignatius describes his longing for union with Christ through martyrdom:

> I die for Christ of my own choice . . . Let me be given to the wild beasts, for by their means I can attain to God. I am God's wheat, and I am being ground by the teeth of the beasts so that I may appear as pure bread. Rather coax the beasts, that they may become my tomb . . . May nothing, of things visible and invisible, grudge my attaining to Jesus Christ. Let all come, fire and cross and conflicts with beasts, hacking, cutting, wrenching of bones, chopping of limbs, the crushing of my body, cruel chastisements of the devil laid upon me. Only let me attain to Jesus Christ . . . I write to you while alive, yet longing for death; my desire has been crucified and there is not in me any sensuous fire, but living water bounding up in me, and saying inside me, 'Come to the Father'. I have no pleasure in food which is destined for corruption, nor in the delights of this life. I desire the bread of God, which is the flesh of Christ who was of the seed of David; and for drink I desire his blood which is incorruptible love.[11]

The Ignatian epistles were written *c.*AD 107; that is, before the New Testament existed as a single collection and less than a century after the death of Jesus. They formulate an astonishingly mature and complete theology of martyrdom, at the heart of which is a vigorous acceptance of paradox in the sacrifice of Christ. The pain and mental anguish of the martyr becomes, in the Ignatian literature, an approach to God, a means of knowing Him. 'To be in front of the wild animals', wrote Ignatius, 'is to be in front of God.'

Martyrdom, however, is as much an attainment of true human maturity as a privilege that reveals God through the pattern of Christ. As Ignatius writes of his impending martyrdom: 'When I have arrived there, then I shall have become a man.' Here, then, in the first stages of the Christian mystical tradition, is the crucial and fundamental conviction that the flesh is not something to be escaped from, but something to be perfected. The individual's experience of God, though specific and incommunicable, is not wholly private, nor does it exist inalienably over against the world of men and their affairs. The obligation on all Christians, and so on all who aspire to mystical knowledge, is to perform 'fleshly things in a spiritual way'.

Of the actual martyrdom of Ignatius, who died about the year 107, there is no reliable account. There is even some doubt that he *was* eventually martyred, although he wrote his letters in full expectation of being thrown to the beasts when he arrived in Rome from Antioch. In the fourth century his bones were supposed to rest at Antioch, which prompted Henry Bettenson to conclude that 'if this tradition is true he could scarcely have been torn to pieces by the beasts at Rome'.[12]

Gnosticism

An important implication of martyrdom for the development of Christian dogma, then, was the justification of the flesh's dignity, maintained by leading Christian apologists against the Gnostic heretics who ascribed the creation of the material world – including human flesh – to an inferior deity.

'Gnosticism' is a generic term for a bewildering variety of notions and practices and does not imply an agreed set of doctrinal concepts. The word derives from *gnosis*, the Greek word for knowledge, and the Gnostic was someone who laid claim to esoteric knowledge about God and the metaphysical structure of the universe. Gnosticism made an absolute distinction between spirit and matter, between God and the world. Its roots were in pre-Christian, oriental theosophies and its amorphous, syncretic nature could not readily accommodate the majestic simplicity of the Christian revelation. To the Gnostics, it was inconceivable that the Absolute could directly involve itself with matter; even more preposterous was the concept that Absolute Spirit could actually clothe itself in flesh and become man. Contact between man and God, between matter and Absolute Spirit, could only be achieved indirectly, through a complex chain of command, a hierarchy of graduated spiritual beings.

The Gnostics therefore distinguished between the unknowable Divine Being and the 'Demiurge' – the creator god. To the Demiurge the Gnostics ascribed the creation of the world, which was thus conceived in imperfection and antagonistic to true spirit, and between the material world and God lay 'spheres', or 'heavens' or 'angels' or 'Aeons' (the terminology and cosmology varied from sect to sect) through which the divine spark in the elect had to pass on its way back to its heavenly birthplace. The Gnostic ethic, seeing the created order of things as being wholly alien from God, could justify either asceticism, enabling the divine soul to be liberated more easily from the bonds of the flesh and from sensual appetite, or antinomianism, for if the material world is accounted as naught, what virtue could there be in resisting carnal instincts?

Amongst the most influential Gnostic theologians was **Valentinus,** a native of Egypt who lived at Rome from *c.* 136 to *c.* 165 and whose cosmology consisted of a spiritual 'pleroma' (fullness) comprising thirty 'aeons' in a succession of pairs ('syzygies'). The God of the Old Testament was identified with the Demiurge and redemption was through the aeon Christ, who united with the man Jesus to offer mankind the saving knowledge ('gnosis') of his spiritual destiny. However, this gnosis was only given to the elect, the 'pneumatics'; other Christians ('psychics') attained only to the middle realm of the Demiurge; the rest of mankind (the 'carnal') was consigned to eternal perdition.

Justinus (Justin Martyr) and Irenaeus

Born of pagan parents, **St Justin** (*c.* 100–*c.* 165) studied philosophy at Ephesus (he passed through Stoicism, Aristotelianism, Pythagoreanism and finally to Platonism) before his conversion to Christianity *c.* 130. Justin is the most famous of the so-called Apologists: in Rome some time after the year 151 he addressed his first *Apology* (*Apologia I*) for Christianity to the emperor Antoninus Pius, reissuing the work some years later with a supplement that is generally known as his *Second Apology* (*Apologia II*). Justin continued to think of himself as a philosopher and held that Christianity was the fulfilment of the philosophic quest; he identified Plato's transcendent God with the God of Scripture and made Socrates, put to death by the Athenians, a model for Christian martyrs. Socrates and Abraham were both 'Christians before Christ' and the insights achieved by Plato and the other Greek philosophers were fulfilled and completed by the moral perfection of Christ.

Justin's great contribution to Christian thought was his notion of the 'Spermatic Logos'. With his liberal attitude towards the pagan philosophers, Justin argued that portions of the truth were arrived at by the wise in ages past because Divine Reason (the Logos) was 'seeded' throughout creation. Justin met his death *c.* 165, in the reign of Marcus Aurelius, when he and some of his disciples, having refused to sacrifice, were scourged and beheaded.

St Irenaeus (*c.* 130–*c.* 200) was Bishop of Lyons from *c.* 178 and is the first great Catholic theologian. He threw his full force against gnostic heresies and in his *Adversus Haereses* refuted 'false gnosis' and exposed the baseless fabric of Gnosticism. His main concern was to establish the apostolic tradition and affirm the scriptural revelation: he emphasized the traditional Faith of the Church and for the first time the New Testament was appealed to as Scripture. He developed a doctrine of 'recapitulation', which referred to the redemptive work of Christ. By this work 'the end' was joined to 'the beginning': Christ is the second Adam who enables man to reach the perfection that existed as a potential in the first Adam. Irenaeus had this to say concerning the knowledge of God:

> We cannot know God in his greatness, for the Father cannot be measured. But by his love (for this it is which leads us to God through the agency of his Word) we ever learn, in obeying him, that this great God exists, and that he himself by his own will and act disposed, ordained, and governs all things.[13]

God comes within the grasp of man's knowledge through his love and infinite kindness: in that belief is concentrated the central motivation of the entire Christian mystical tradition.

Tertullian

Quintus Septimius Florens Tertullianus (*c.* 160–*c.* 225), known as Tertullian, was with Irenaeus the other great anti-gnostic Father, though he was a man of a very different stamp to the Bishop of Lyons. He was the son of a pagan centurion and studied for the law. He was becoming well established in his legal career when, in 193, he was converted to Christianity after witnessing for himself the courage and fortitude of Christians under persecution. In time he joined the Montanists, an apocalyptic sect who expected an imminent descent of the Holy Spirit (the Paraclete) on the Church. Montanus himself began preaching in Phrygia and the movement spread to Africa, where Tertullian (a Carthaginian) passionately embraced the ascetic aspects of the movement.

Tertullian sternly resisted all attempts to combine the teachings of the Church with academic philosophy, which he saw as the parent of error. Like Irenaeus he anchored the Church's teaching in the Scriptures, interpreted by the Church in the light of the apostolic tradition. In refutation of Gnosticism, he upheld the humanity of Christ and the reality of his sufferings in the bold and famous paradox: 'The Son of God died; it must needs be believed because it is absurd. He was buried and rose again; it is certain because it is impossible.'[14]

One heretic against whom Tertullian exerted his considerable powers of argument was Marcion (died *c.*160), who was excommunicated in 144. Unlike the Gnostics, with whom he is sometimes classed, Marcion was not interested in abstruse cosmological conceptions but in ethics and the interpretation of Scripture. He held that the Christian Gospel was wholly a Gospel of Love, to the total exclusion of Law. As a consequence he rejected the Old Testament and proposed the existence of two Gods: the God of the Old Testament, an inferior God of Law who created the world (cf. the Gnostic Demiurge); and the God of the New Testament, the God of Love revealed by Jesus. But like many of the Gnostics, the Docetists in particular, Marcion denied the humanity of Christ and held that the divine spark in man could only be freed from imprisoning matter by ascetic discipline.

Tertullian also wrote against the Monarchian heresy. Monarchianism, which flourished in the second and third centuries, reverted to a monotheistic theology, upholding the unity ('monarchy') of the Godhead by denying the independent subsistence of the Son. One branch of the heresy, the 'Adoptionist' or 'Dynamic' Monarchians, held that Jesus was but a man on whom the power of the Godhead, through Spirit, had descended; another branch, the 'Modalist' Monarchians, denied the permanence of the three Persons in the Trinity, seeing Christ and the Spirit (the Holy Ghost) merely as transitory distinctions in the Godhead. Although Tertullian wrote a treatise on the Trinity against Praxeas, a Modalist, he did not uphold the concept of the Son's eternal co-existence, unlike Irenaeus. He defended distinction without division: 'The Son is not other than the Father by separation from him but by difference of function, nor by division but by distinction: for the Father and the Son are not identical but distinct in degree. For the Father is the whole substance, while the son is derivative and a portion of the whole . . . At first, when the Son was not yet manifest, God said, "Let there be light, and light came into being". And the Word himself was straightway the "true light which lights every man coming into this world", and through him the light of the world came to be.'[15]

Although he ended his days outside the fold of orthodoxy, Tertullian exerted a strong influence on the development of Western theology, and thus on the doctrinal background of mysticism: for instance, his treatise against Praxeas provided a basic terminology for later doctrines of the Trinity. Though he recognized the flawed nature of man, he believed that the image of God, though obscured, was yet intact and that men had an intuitive knowledge of divine truth. As a Montanist he vigorously proclaimed the power of the Paraclete, the Holy Spirit, to inspire, and in his tract *Adversus Marcionem (Against Marcion)* he describes, perhaps from personal experience, the ecstatic visions that can result. He maintained that 'a state of ecstasy, of being "out of one's mind"' accompanies 'the operation of grace': 'For a man who is "in the spirit", especially when he beholds the glory of God and when God speaks through him, must inevitably lose consciousness, overshadowed as he is by the Divine Power.'[16]

Clement of Alexandria

The mystical element in early Christianity divides into two main streams, the first deriving from the New Testament mysticism of St Paul and St John, the second nourished on Hellenic thought, producing a tradition of Christianized Neoplatonism under the particular influence of Plotinus, the near contemporary of Clement of Alexandria (*c.*150–*c.*215). Evelyn Underhill denies the title of mystic to St Clement, but his influence on the development of mystical theology was nonetheless considerable.

Clement, of whose life little is known, was not born at Alexandria but was attracted there by its reputation as the intellectual centre of the Greek world. The Septuagint (the most important of the Greek versions of the Old Testament) was produced there and **Philo** (*c.*20 BC–*c.*AD 50) had worked there to produce his synthesis of Greek philosophy and Judaistic theology. There was also at Alexandria the famous Catechetical School, which existed to propagate Christianity amongst the cultured classes. The first known head of the school was a Sicilian called Pantaenus. Clement succeeded him and his teaching, some of it highly unorthodox, is contained in three main works: the *Protrepticus* (Exhortation to the Greeks), the *Paedagogus* (Tutor) and the *Stromateis* (Miscellanies).

The *Stromateis* is an unsystematic, deliberately allusive and imprecise defence of what may be called 'true' Gnosticism. Christian Gnosticism, as described by Clement, is the complete esoteric knowledge of God and in the *Stromateis* Clement comes close to the concept of the mystical life as we have come to understand it. His starting point is the inexpressible infinity of God the Father:

> One could not rightly describe him as the Whole, for the whole is a term applied to spatial extension, and he is the *Father* of the whole universe. Nor can one speak of him as having parts; for the One is indivisible, and therefore infinite, not in the sense of being inexhaustible to thought, but of being without dimension or limit. Thus the deity is without form and nameless. Though we ascribe names, they are not to be taken in their strict meaning; when we call him One, Good, Mind, Existence, Father, God, Creator, Lord, we are not conferring a name on him. Being unable to do more, we use these appellations of honour, in order that our thought may have something to rest on and not wander at random.[17]

Such appellations do not express the being of God. Descriptions rely on known relationships and qualities; but God 'cannot be comprehended by knowledge, which is based on previously known truths, whereas nothing can precede what is self-existent'. And yet Clement asserts the mystical belief that God, the Unknown, *can* be apprehended – by 'divine grace and the Word proceeding from him . . .'.

At the heart of Clement's theology is the synthesis of knowledge (gnosis) and faith. Faith is the foundation on which the ladder of knowledge is reared; through knowledge the soul ascends to the contemplation of God and the final recovery of the divine likeness in man. Clement clearly signifies here the notion of a moral and spiritual ascent through a threefold way: purification (the action of faith), illumination (the action of knowledge) and union (achieved through loving contemplation). In the following passage Clement sets out the pattern of true gnosis, the fusion of knowledge and faith:

> We must *believe* truly in the Son; that he is the Son, that he came, and how he came, and why; and about his suffering. But we must also have *knowledge* of the person of the Son. But, to begin with, there is no faith without knowledge, nor knowledge without faith. Nor does the Father

exist without the Son, for 'Father' immediately implies 'Father of a Son'; and the Son is the true teacher about the Father. And in order that a man may believe in the Son, he must know the Father in relation to whom the Son exists. Again in order that we may come to know the Father, we must believe in the Son, because the Son of God is our teacher; for the Father brings us from faith to knowledge by means of the Son, and knowledge of the Son and the Father which follows the Gnostic rule – the rule of the genuine 'Gnostic' – is an intuition and apprehension of truth through 'the Truth'.[18]

Mystical knowledge, according to Clement, is certainly not achieved without effort; it is not, to use later terminology, 'infused'. But yet it cannot be achieved without God's help: the ability finally to perfect the 'gnostic soul' is God's alone.

On the face of Moses there settled a kind of bloom of glory, because of his righteous acts and his continual converse with God, who spoke to him. So on the righteous soul there steals a kind of divine power of goodness, through the divine visitation, revelation, and directing activity. This power, as it were of an intellectual radiance, like the sun's warm beam, stamps on the soul a kind of visible seal of righteousness, light that is united to the soul through unfailing love, which bears God and is borne by God. Thence the growing likeness to God the Father arises in the 'Gnostic', as far as human nature admits, since he becomes 'perfect as the Father in heaven' . . . .[19]

Origen

Origen (Origenes Adamantius, *c.*185–254) was born in Alexandria of Christian parents; indeed, he is the first of the Church Fathers known to have come from a Christian background. In 203, when Clement fled from Alexandria at the outbreak of the persecution of Severus (in which Origen's father died), Origen succeeded him as head of the Catechetical School. Origen himself was eager to embrace martyrdom, but his mother prevented him from doing so by hiding his clothes, 'rightly judging that modesty would get the better of zeal'.[20]

Origen studied Scripture (learning Hebrew so that he could read the Old Testament in the original tongue) with intense application and, to his later regret, underwent castration, taking literally the statement in Matthew 19:12 that there are 'eunuchs who have made themselves eunuchs for the kingdom of heaven'. He was also thoroughly familiar with Greek philosophy and attended the lectures of Ammonius Saccas, the Neoplatonist who later taught Plotinus himself. In 215 Origen was forced to leave Alexandria by the massacre of Christians known as the 'Fury of Caracalla'. He went to Caesarea in Palestine, where he eventually established a school. During the persecution of Decius in 250 he was imprisoned and tortured. He died a few years later.

Origen was a great teacher and became one of the greatest exponents of the allegorical interpretation of Scripture. A patient, humble search of Scripture was his starting point for a knowledge of 'the secret and hidden things of God'. His mystical doctrine is based on the fact of the soul's beauty being created in the image of God – a fundamental concept in much patristic theology:

> The fact that after God has said, 'Let us make man in our image and likeness', the narrator goes on to say, 'In the image of God he made him' and is silent about the likeness, indicates just this: that in his first creation man received the dignity of the image of God, for the fulfilment of the likeness is reserved to the final consummation; that is, that he himself should appropriate it by the eagerness of his own efforts, through the imitation of God having the possibility of perfection given to him at the beginning by the dignity of the image, and then in the end, through the fulfilment of his works, should bring to perfect consummation the likeness of God.[21]

'There is a kinship', he writes more explicitly, 'between the human mind and God; for the mind is itself an image of God, and therefore can have some conception of the divine nature, especially the more it is purified and removed from matter.'[22]

Another important concept expressed by Origen and taken up by later writers is the supreme necessity of self-knowledge, by which the soul completely understands its natural relationship with God and through which the soul contemplates the beauty it received when it was created in God's image and judges how the image may be renewed and restored. Origen's faith in the power of the sacraments, especially baptism, to bring about renewal is extremely strong. Baptism, for him, truly washed body and soul clean and was an essential precondition of the spiritual ascent. The threefold way is apparent in Origen's thinking – from baptism through purgation to illumination and the final knowledge of God, the perfection of both the mystical life and of martyrdom.

Love is central to Origen's mystical insights. His pupil Gregory

Thaumaturgus wrote of him: 'He kindled in our hearts the love of the divine Logos, the supreme object of love, who by his unspeakable loveliness draws all irresistibly to himself.' He spoke as though from personal knowledge of what happens when someone who has reached 'the peak of perfection' is possessed by the Word of God and receives the 'wound of Love': 'If there is anyone who has at some time burned with this faithful love of the Word of God . . . so that he yearns and longs for him day and night, can speak of nought but him . . . can think of nothing else, and is disposed to no desire nor longing nor yet hope except for him alone . . .' – then he has received the wound of love.

We began this chapter by considering martyrdom. For Origen, martyrdom indicated the love of the whole soul for God. The martyr was, literally, a witness and 'he who bears witness to someone, especially in a time of persecution and trial of faith, unites and joins himself to him to whom he bears witness'. To two friends imprisoned during the persecution of Maximinus Thrax (235) Origen wrote that the compensations of martyrdom far outweighed the sufferings, which indeed could be seen as supplementing Christ's own sacrifice: 'As those who attended on the altar of sacrifice according to the law of Moses seemed to minister remission of sins by means of the blood of bulls and goats, so the souls of these who have been executed for the witness of Jesus, if their attendance on the heavenly altars be not in vain, minister remission of sins to those who pray . . . Perhaps also as we are bought "by the precious blood of Jesus" . . . so by the precious blood of the martyrs certain have been bought.'[23]

Asceticism
If Gnosticism and movements like Montanism, with its feverish emphasis on ecstatic phenomena amongst the elect, encouraged spurious mysticality, the growth of asceticism (the practice of rigorous self-discipline) and monasticism added significant and creative elements to Christian mysticism.

The craving for solitude, in which the anchorite travels towards God through solitary self-mortification, usually in some wild and unpopulated place, is not exclusive to Christianity: Buddha, for instance, spent six years in virtual solitude before his enlightenment beneath the sacred bo-tree at Gaya. The spiritual potential of desert solitude is apparent in the Old Testament; and the elder Pliny describes the lifestyle of the Essenes, a Jewish ascetic sect that originated some two centuries before Christ and with which John the Baptist may have been associated. Pliny wrote that: 'The Essenes have established themselves to the west of the Dead Sea, far enough from the shore to avoid discomfort. They lead a solitary life, different from that of all other men. They have no wives, having renounced the love of women. The palm trees are their sole companions.'[24] In the remote cells of Qumran, as one writer has said, can be found 'evidence of that lofty and spiritual life which was to animate the Christian cloisters, both those of the desert and of the Middle Ages: a rigorous rule, asceticism, divine election to the perfect life, meditation and contemplation, the confident expectation of the final judgement'.[25]

Those who turned to the desert had the example of Christ before them, who 'by the Spirit' had been led into the wilderness for forty days, where he had been tempted by the devil. St Benedict later described how those who followed Christ's example went out into the wilderness 'to fight against the devil . . . in the single-handed combat of the desert, without the support of others, by the strength of their own arm, God helping them, against the vices of the flesh and their evil thoughts'.[26]

Before them, too, were the examples of Old Testament figures, who had been forced into the desert by persecution, where they 'wandered about in sheepskins and goatskins; being destitute, afflicted, tormented' (Hebrews 11:37). The Christian persecutions of Nero, Domitian, Trajan, Marcus Aurelius, Maximinus Thrax and particularly Decius had the same effect. After Decius ordered that all his subjects must sacrifice to the State gods on pain of death, the wilderness became a refuge for thousands of Christian ascetics: 'The quest of solitude was forced upon them': 'Their favourite place of voluntary exile was Egypt, where the climate was warm and almost rainless. The deserts were not too far removed from the narrow stretch of cultivable land beside the Nile; and the mountains were riddled with caves for shelter.'[27] As well as escaping from persecution, many of the desert exiles believed in the imminent Second Coming of Christ, the *Parousia* – a belief encouraged by the growing corruption and degeneracy of the Roman world.

The solitaries provided the Christian mystical tradition with the idea that self-denial was a means to spiritual development. The idea had been expressed before in the writings of the early Fathers, but now it became a full rule of life and, in Evelyn

Underhill's words, 'The heroic denunciations of the early Fathers of the Desert deeply impressed the general Christian consciousness.' There were certainly excesses and much self-deception; but the ascetic life did much to enrich the spiritual life of the Church: 'The spontaneous enthusiasm, the loving ardours of primitive Christian spirituality here submitted to a drastic – even a ferocious – education: the idea of deliberate purification and discipline, implicit in the Greek mysteries, entered the Christian scheme, and mysticism became allied for good or evil with asceticism.'[28]

Our knowledge of the early Christian hermits comes principally from **John Cassian** (see below) and **Palladius** (*c.*365–425). Both men spent several years collecting first-hand information about the monastic communities and solitary hermits living in the Egyptian desert. Cassian's works are known as the *Institutes* (which sets out the ordinary rules for monastic life as well as discussing the hindrances to perfection) and the *Conferences* (which contains a record of Cassian's conversations with the Egyptian monks); Palladius, who became Bishop of Helenopolis in 400, presented his account of monastic life in his *Historia Lausiaca* (Lausiac History), which takes its name from the dedication to Lausus, the founder of Constantinople University in 425. Other historians of Egyptian monastic life included **St Jerome, St Melania** and **Rufinus**.

Probably the most famous and influential of all early Christian solitaries was **St Antony** (*c.*251–356), whose life by St Athanasius (written in Greek and translated by Evagrius of Antioch into Latin) did much to disseminate the idea of eremitical monasticism through the Christian world. The *Vita S. Antonii* drew the eloquent contempt of Gibbon, who wrote: 'There is perhaps no phase in the moral history of mankind of a deeper or more painful interest than this ascetic discipline. A hideous, distorted and emaciated maniac, without knowledge, without patriotism, without natural affection, spending his life in a long routine of useless and atrocious self-torture, and quailing before the ghastly phantoms of his delerious brain, had become the ideal of nations which had known the writings of Plato and Cicero and the lives of Socrates and Cato.' But the 'temptations' of St Antony exerted a lasting influence on the Western imagination, inspiring painters and writers (for example, Flaubert) as well as generations of those who embraced the 'mysticism of the cloister'.

The early Christian solitaries were not exclusively men. Devout women faced the perils of the trackless deserts in large numbers to consult with such ascetics as Macarius, who was 'said to be in a continual ecstasy, and to spend far longer with God than with things sublunary'. **St Pachomius** (*c.*290–346), the great organizing spirit of eremetical monasticism, was responsible for eleven desert monasteries, two of which were for women. At Oxyrhynchus – a monastic 'city' of some 30,000 inhabitants – two-thirds of the population were nuns intent on finding God through ascetic disciplines and worship, whilst in Antinoë the women religious were housed in twelve convents.

The male hermits, however, outdid their female counterparts in bizarre ascetical methods. The Shepherd solitaries, for instance, ate no food except freshly-cut grass. Even more extreme were the pillar-hermits, the *stylites*. St Simeon the Elder built a nine-foot high pillar, gradually increased to sixty feet, surmounted by a platform three feet in diameter. Here he stayed, completely shelterless, for thirty-six years until his death in 459. St Daniel Stylites remained thirty-three years on his pillar; St Alypius spent a staggering fifty-three years on a column in Asia Minor. A Syrian solitary mentioned by Theodoret of Antioch (*c.*393–458) passed ten years in a tub suspended from poles.

Cassian

John Cassian (*c.*360–435) was a pupil of **St John Chrysostom** (meaning 'golden-mouthed'). He entered a monastery in Bethlehem before leaving to study monasticism in Egypt. The way to God, for Cassian, was a perpetual spiritual combat, a struggle to divest the soul of all transient, personal and material interests; hence the ultimate experience of God cannot be considered possible for married people or even for celibates living in ordinary communities. Cassian even considers it difficult for those in desert monasteries: it is the desert solitary alone who is best placed to reach the heights of contemplation, for he alone undergoes, in complete isolation, a continual act of renunciation that brings the soul into uninterrupted communion with God. 'The end of all our perfection', he writes, 'is thus so to act that the soul, stripping itself daily of all earthly and carnal inclinations, lifts itself up without ceasing more and more towards spiritual things; so that all its works and thoughts, and all the movements of the heart, may become nothing else but a continuous act of prayer.'

This rigorous commitment to a single end could encompass no distractions – even acts of charity, when the higher stage of the contemplative life was reached, were to be so considered. The natural tendency of the mind to wander, even during the celebration of the Eucharist, is accounted by Cassian as a sin; to deviate for one moment from the goal of the contemplative life is 'to be drawn unwillingly, even without knowing it, to the law of sin and death; to be turned away from the vision of God . . . even by good and just, nevertheless earthly works, is a good reason why the saints should sigh constantly to God and proclaim themselves sinners'.

This exaggerated stance was not taken up by the main stream of the mystical tradition; but the monastic ideal remained a powerful attraction for generations of contemplatives. The ideal of virginity, a necessary goal for the true ascetic, was actively preached in *The Symposium* of **Methodius** (d. *c.*311), who held that virgins are true martyrs 'because they had the courage all their lives not to shrink from the truly Olympic contest of chastity'. Virginity, in fact, is held by Methodius to be the very foundation of the mystical life. These ideas generated explicit images of betrothal and espousal: Christ becomes the Bridegroom of the soul within a mystical marriage. **St Athanasius** (*c.*296–373) was another influential advocate of virginity. Through fasting, obedience, virginity and mortification, the mind is purified and the 'inner eye' becomes capable once more of seeing God – echoing the Beatitude 'Blessed are the pure in heart: for they shall see God'.

Gregory of Nyssa
Gregory of Nyssa (*c.*330–*c.*395) is, with his brother **Basil** ('the Great') of Caesarea (*c.*330–379) and **Gregory of Nazianzus** (320–389), one of the so-called Cappadocian Fathers. St Basil was born into a wealthy and well-connected family, but he abandoned everything to take up a life of ascetic solitude near Neocaesarea, where he was later joined by companions, making his hermitage a cenobium (a community of monks in separate dwellings who observed the rule of silence). One of those companions was Gregory of Nazianzus. Basil's brother Gregory also spent some time at the cenobium and in 371 was appointed bishop of Nyssa.

Gregory of Nyssa was a highly original thinker and theologian, the first systematic theologian in fact since Origen, whom Gregory greatly admired. In his mystical doctrine, Gregory describes the spiritual life as an ascent (he is perhaps the first Christian author to do so); he is also one of the great representatives of the 'mysticism of darkness'. The ascent to God is not a simple journey from darkness to light. Christianity illumines a man's life; from this point, however, the soul intent on ascending further moves into another kind of darkness. The more one 'knows' of God, the greater is the realization of His mystery. As the mind progresses towards the contemplation of the divine 'the more clearly does it see the invisibility of the divine nature. For having left behind all that appears, not only what the senses perceive, but also what the intelligence believes it sees, it penetrates into the invisible and incomprehensible, and there sees God. For in this consists the true knowledge of him . . . that he cannot be seen, because he transcends all knowledge.' The 'true enjoyment' of the soul consists in 'always to progress in seeking and never to cease ascending': 'When the veil of despair has thus been taken away, and she [the soul] sees the beauty of the beloved defying all hope and all description . . . she is seized with an even more vehement desire, because she has received the chosen arrow of God in herself, and her heart has been wounded by the barb of faith, she has been mortally wounded by the arrow of love.'

Through faith alone can man grasp God. Faith and love arouse in the contemplative a never-ending desire – inflict a wound that, paradoxically, never heals, but which yet has the power to heal. Every stage of the mystic's knowledge of God is but a beginning; the journey never ends: 'As God continues to reveal himself, man continues to wonder, and he never exhausts his desire to see more, since what he is waiting for is always more magnificent, more divine, than all he has already seen.'

Gregory maintained that there was already existing in each soul a divine element – an 'eye' that was capable of glimpsing the transcendent God – though man has no capacity to communicate what this 'eye' 'sees'. A key element in Gregory's mystical thought is the concept of 'the kindred Deity', which proposes a relationship between part of man's nature and God's. God's love for man 'drags that which belongs to Him [i.e. the soul] from the ruins of the irrational and material, just as after an earthquake bodies are drawn from mounds of rubbish – so God draws that which is His own to Himself'.[29]

St Augustine

The ascetic ideals of the Desert Fathers played a decisive part in the life of St Augustine of Hippo (354–450), the greatest of all the Latin Fathers. He was born in North Africa to a pagan father and a Christian mother (St Monica). He went to Carthage to study and there abandoned what little Christianity he had and took a mistress, by whom he had a son (Adeodatus) and to whom he remained faithful for fifteen years. He studied philosophy and rhetoric and eventually adopted Manichaeism, a dualistic belief that saw existence as a perpetual conflict between the powers of light and darkness. Gradually, Augustine moved back towards Christianity and was baptized in 387. He returned to Africa in 388 and established a monastery at Tagaste.

Combining the militant dogmatist and the passionate contemplative, the figure of Augustine refutes the idea that mysticism is a reaction against ecclesiasticism and institutional religion. He reconciles an intensely personal relationship with God and a deeply conservative attitude towards the authority of the Church. As a mystic, he combines great intellectual strength with powerful intuition; and though he knew the joys of inner solitude, he lived to the full a life in the world.

As a theologian, there are again two distinct facets to Augustine. On the one hand, he held relentlessly to the conviction that man was inherently sinful (the inherited guilt of Adam) and that Saving Grace, predicated by the 'prevenient grace'* of God, God, could only be attained through the sanction of the Church – which was the City of God on earth and the only means of entering its heavenly counterpart. On the other hand, he knew from his own experience that every human soul has a direct pathway to God at hand; that even in the most depraved soul there is a need for, and hence an impulse towards, God. The *Confessions*, one of the greatest spiritual autobiographies ever written, begins by establishing this intuitive movement Godwards: 'Thou hast made us for Thyself, and our heart is restless until it rests in Thee.'

Whilst the theologian of the Church in Augustine regards man as a worm of the dust, his mystical instinct and experiences testify to an inborn relationship with the Absolute. Speaking of himself

---

*The technical term 'prevenient grace' was coined by Augustine. It means the grace that is antecedent to conversion, as opposed to 'co-operant' or 'subsequent' grace.

before his conversion he wrote: 'By inward goads Thou didst rouse me, that I should be ill at ease until Thou wert manifested to my inward sight.' The *difficulty* of knowing God is never underestimated: the two-way pull on the soul – upwards towards God and downwards to materiality – is always acknowledged: 'I tremble and I burn, I tremble, feeling that I am unlike Him; I burn, feeling that I am like Him.' The whole work of a man's life, for Augustine, is 'to heal the eye of the heart by which we see God'.

Though he formulated the doctrine of election, Augustine also proposed the will – 'the momentous will' – as a way to God: 'Thither one journeyeth not in ships, nor in chariots, nor on foot; for to journey thither, nay, even to arrive there, is nothing else but to will to go'. The momentous will is one key to the mystical knowledge of God: 'To will God entirely is to have Him'. Augustine, as a close student of Plato, also upholds the ability of the mind (or rather the higher faculty of the mind) to directly apprehend God. God, indeed, is the Reality that is already within us: 'Thy God is unto thee, O my soul, even the Life of thy life.' Augustine always recognized the Real – the 'Self-same' – beyond the mere appearance of reality: again, this is a legacy of Platonism. The soul searches for God through visible creation, looking for imperishable and unchanging Truth. It is impelled by an intense longing, but progress towards the desired goal is impossible without discipline: there can be no real mystical experience without asceticism, without rigorous spiritual training – 'When,' asks Augustine, 'art thou to desire the Fountain of Wisdom, whilst thou art yet labouring in the venom of iniquity? Destroy in thyself whatever is contrary to the truth. . . .'[30]

Augustine's mystical doctrine is nowhere presented in a systematic fashion but is scattered throughout his writings, notably throughout the *Confessions*, where deep mystical insights mingle with the autobiographical narrative. In an early part of the *Confessions*, for instance, he describes his experience of the 'Light Unchangeable':

> And being thence admonished to return to myself, I entered even into my inward self, Thou being my Guide: and able I was, for Thou wert become my Helper. And I entered and beheld with the eye of my soul (such as it was), above the same eye of my soul, above my mind, the Light Unchangeable. Not this ordinary light, which all flesh may look upon, nor as it were a greater of the same kind, as though the

brightness of this should be manifold brighter, and with its greatness take up all space. Not such was this light, but other, yea, far other from all these. Nor was it above my soul, because It made me; and I below it, because I was made by It. He that knows the Truth, knows that that Light is; and he that knows It, knows eternity. Love knoweth it. O Truth Who art Eternity! and Love Who art Truth! and Eternity Who art Love! Thou art my God, to Thee do I sigh night and day . . . And Thou didst beat back the weakness of my sight, streaming forth Thy beams of light upon me most strongly, and I trembled with love and awe.[31]

Though the presence of a massive intellect is always evident in Augustine's writings, the language of first-hand experience, expressing insights beyond the reach of the intellect, is everywhere apparent:

Step by step was I led upwards, from bodies to the soul which perceives by means of the bodily senses; and thence to the soul's inward faculty to which the bodily senses report external things, which is the limit of the intelligence of animals; and thence again to the reasoning faculty, to whose judgement is referred the knowledge received by the bodily senses. And when this power also within me found itself changeable, it lifted itself up to its own intelligence, and withdrew its thoughts from experience, abstracting itself from the contradictory throne of sense images, that it might find what that light was wherein it was bathed when it cried out that beyond all doubt the unchangeable is to be preferred to the changeable . . . And thus, with the flash of one hurried glance, it attained to the vision of THAT WHICH IS. And then at last I saw Thy invisible things understood by means of the things that are made, but I could not sustain my gaze; my weakness was dashed back, and I was relegated to my ordinary experience.
. . . ,[32]

There is little trace in Augustine of the Christocentric mysticism of St Paul. For Augustine, the spiritual life is a perpetual movement towards the eternal object of love – towards the unchanging, all-loving Absolute: 'What then do I love, when I love Thee? . . . I love a certain light, and a certain voice, a certain fragrance, a certain food, a certain embrace when I love my God: a light, voice, fragrance, food, embrace of the inner man. Where that shines upon my soul which space cannot contain, that sounds which time cannot sweep away, that is fragrant which is scattered not by the breeze, that tastes sweet which when fed upon is not diminished, that clings close which no satiety disparts. This it is that I love, when I love my God!'[33]

The most moving description of mystical experience in the *Confessions* occurs in Book IX and was shared with his mother shortly before her death at the port of Ostia:

> And when our discourse was brought to that point, that the very highest delight of the earthly senses, in the very purest material light, was, in respect of the sweetness of that life, not only not worthy of comparison, but not even of mention; we raising up ourselves with a more glowing affection towards the 'Self-same' did by degrees pass through all things bodily, even the very heaven, whence sun and moon and stars shine upon the earth; yea, we were soaring higher yet, by inward musing, and discourse, and admiring of Thy works; and we came to our own minds, and went beyond them, that we might arrive at that region of never-failing plenty, where Thou feedest Israel for ever with the food of truth ... We were saying then: If to any the tumult of the flesh were hushed, hushed the images of earth, and waters, and air, hushed also the poles of heaven, yea the very soul be hushed to herself, and by not thinking on self surmount self, hushed all dreams and imaginary revelations, every tongue and every sign, and whatsoever exists only in transition, since if any could hear, all these say, We made not ourselves, but He made us that abideth forever – If then having uttered this, they too should be hushed, having roused only our ears to Him who made them, and He alone speak, not by them, but by Himself, that we may hear His Word, not through any tongue of flesh, nor angel's voice, nor sound of thunder, nor in the dark riddle of a similitude, but, might hear Whom in these things we love, might hear His Very Self without these (as we two now strained ourselves, and in swift thought touched on that Eternal Wisdom, which abideth over all;) – could this be continued on ... so that life might be forever like that one moment of understanding which now we sighed after; were not this, *Enter into thy Master's joy*?[34]

All the fundamental elements of true mystical experience can be found in this passage: the gradual transcendence of sense experience, the journey within, the enfolding hush of contemplation, the certainty of God's presence and its accompanying, incommunicable joy. Incommunicable – and yet Augustine is a master of the language of paradox, by which, unlike the followers of the *via negativa*, he succeeds in making human utterance a fit tool for describing the completeness of mystical experience:

Most highest, most good, most potent, most omnipotent; most merciful, yet most just; most hidden, yet most present; most beautiful, yet most strong; stable, yet incomprehensible; unchangeable, yet all-changing; never new, never old; all renewing . . . ever working, ever at rest; still gathering, yet nothing lacking; supporting, filling, and over-spreading; creating, nourishing, and maturing; seeking, yet having all things . . . And what have I now said, my God, my life, my holy joy? or what saith any man when he speaks of Thee? Yet woe to him that speaketh not, since mute are even the most eloquent.[35]

Dionysius the Areopagite

Besides Augustine, there was another figure who fused Christian and Greek thought in the expression of mystical doctrine and who by so doing acted as a seminal influence on later Christian mystics. Dionysius the Areopagite (more properly, the pseudo-Areopagite) flourished c.500. The conversion by St Paul at Athens of a man called Dionysius the Areopagite and a woman named Damaris is recounted in Acts (17:34); but the mystical theologian we know as Dionysius has no connection with this converted Athenian, nor with St Dionysius (St Denys) of Paris. The Dionysian writings were written around the year 500 in Greek and probably originated in Syria. They comprise: the *Celestial Hierarchy*, the *Ecclesiastical Hierarchy*, the *Divine Names* and *Mystical Theology*. The influence of these writings on the mystical tradition of the West can hardly be exaggerated. The supposed connection with the Dionysius of Acts gave them a spurious but widespread authority in both the Eastern and the Western Church and they entered the main stream of medieval religious thought through the influential Latin version of John Scotus Erigena (see p. 80), made during the reign of Charles the Bald (843–876).

For Dionysius, as for all 'orthodox' mystics, the Godhead is a Unity: He is the 'Hidden Dark', the Cause beyond all causes, the Origin of all origins. The particular emphasis of Dionysius' doctrine is on the unknowableness of God, who is above thought because thought can only deal with relationships and differences. Yet though God cannot be *known*, he can be *experienced*; he can be *reached*. Dionysius does not dismiss the affirmative way to God, which involves a partial knowledge of Him through various manifestations, through Church doctrine and through faith. The Godhead overflows into creation: 'He goes forth in an unlessened stream into all things that are, though in things divided. He remains undivided.'[36] But this is knowledge only of the shadow, as it were, of God: it communicates but the echo, or the reflection, of the Ultimate Reality.

> God is neither sonship nor fatherhood nor anything else known to us or to any other beings, either of the things that are or of the things that are not; nor does anything that is, know Him as He is, nor does He know anything that is as it is; He has neither word nor name nor knowledge; He is neither darkness nor light nor truth nor error; He can neither be affirmed nor denied; nay, though we may affirm or deny the things that are beneath Him, we can neither affirm nor deny Him; for the perfect and sole cause of all is above all affirmation, and that which transcends all is above all subtraction, absolutely separate, and beyond all that is.[37]

Affirmation brings only a relative knowledge of God: the highest mystical experience, on the other hand, brings union with the unknowable God through negation. Dionysius exhorts those who devote themselves to mystical contemplation to leave the senses behind and insulate themselves from the operations of the intellect that they may 'arise, by Unknowing towards the union, as far as is attainable, with Him Who transcends all being and all knowledge. For by the unceasing and absolute renunciation of thyself and of all things, thou mayest be borne on high, through pure and entire self-abnegation, into the superessential Radiance of the Divine Darkness.' Dionysius illustrates the methodology of the negative way through the analogy of a sculptor. Those who create lifelike statues, he says, 'chip off all the encumbrances, cut away all superfluous material, and bring to light the Beauty hidden within. So we negate everything in order that without veils we may know that Unknown which is concealed by all the light in existing things.'[38] God, says Dionysius in a tyically powerful phrase, must be sought out with 'the eyeless mind'. The final ecstasy is a union above all thought, consciousness and knowledge: 'By the inactivity of all knowledge one is united, in his better part, to the altogether Unknown, and by knowing nothing, knows above mind.'[39]

The atmosphere of the Dionysian writings is headily Neoplatonic. We do not read of God the Father and we are far from any Christological approach to mystical experience. The Father is the Absolute One of Neoplatonic metaphysics, and the mystical path is a solitary one, a Christianized version of the flight of the alone to the Alone, to the hidden centre. But yet Dionysian mysticism established itself as one of the great fountainheads of the religious life in the West – in particular of the cloister:

> The goal is beatific gazing, absorption in the Godhead. The world, with its tasks and calls, is left behind and forgotten. Salvation is thoroughly individualistic. We hear enough of 'love', but it is no longer the love which fills the primitive message. The 'love' of this monk is not a word which means self-sharing and self-giving. It is rather an emotional, sensuous thrill, an exhilaration, intoxication even, which the person experiences from Divine contact – and it descends easily to unwholesome dreams and pathological states.[40]

And yet these anonymous writings, for all their lofty abstractions and unhealthy implications, inspired a passion for God on a wide scale. To quote Rufus Jones again:

> He iterated and reiterated that God Himself is the ground of the soul, and that there is an inward way to Him open to all men. He insisted on personal experience as the primary thing in religion, and so became the father of a great family of devout and saintly mystics, who advanced true religion in spite of errors of conception. And he did well in maintaining that there is an experience of Reality which transcends mere head-knowledge – a finding of God in which the whole being, heart, will, and mind, are expanded and satisfied, even though language cannot formulate what is being experienced.[41]

The Eastern Church
The Eastern Church, in the words of Vladimir Lossky, 'has never made a sharp distinction between mysticism and theology; between personal experience of the divine mysteries and the dogma affirmed by the Church'; and he quotes the Metropolitan Philaret of Moscow (*Sermons and Addresses*, 1844): 'None of the mysteries of the most secret wisdom of God ought to appear alien or altogether transcendent to us, but in all humility we must apply our spirit to the contemplation of divine things.'[42] Dogma, in other words, should be experienced mystically. Lossky therefore concludes: 'There is ... no Christian mysticism without theology; but, above all, there is no theology without mysticism.'[43]

The spiritual literature of the Christian East has few autobiographical texts, few equivalents of the personal accounts left by such as Julian of Norwich, St Teresa, or even Suso.

Mystical experience is not described in terms of private revelation, but is the means of invigorating and deepening theological understanding. The whole theological temper of the Eastern Church is apophatic (see p. 34) and finds authoritative expression in the *Mystical Theology* of the pseudo-Dionysius, a text that has had as seminal an influence on the spiritual tradition of Eastern Christianity as it has on that of the Western Church. Examples of this pervasive apophaticism abound; for instance, St Gregory Palamas in the fourteenth century writes:

> The super-essential nature of God is not a subject for speech or thought or even contemplation, for it is far removed from all that exists and more than unknowable, being founded upon the uncircumscribed might of the celestial spirits – incomprehensible and ineffable to all for ever. There is no name whereby it can be named, neither in this age nor in the age to come, nor word found in the soul and uttered by the tongue, nor contact whether sensible or intellectual, nor yet any image which may afford any knowledge of its subject, if this be not that perfect incomprehensibility which one acknowledges in denying all that can be named. None can properly name its essence or nature if he be truly seeking the truth that is above all truth.[44]

We have already encountered some leading Eastern mystical theologians, including the pseudo-Dionysius, Gregory of Nyssa and Gregory of Nazianzus. Other notable figures include St Maximus, Macarius of Egypt, Evagrius and **John Climacus** (*c.*570–649), who was an enthusiastic and influential apologist of the monastic life as it was practised in the Near East. He himself entered the monastery on Mount Sinai when he was sixteen and subsequently became its abbot, though he spent the last portion of his life in total seclusion. His most famous work is the *Ladder of Paradise*, consisting of thirty chapters (corresponding to Christ's age at his baptism) that set out the stages of the mystical ascent. For John Climacus, the solitary life demanded total spiritual dedication and could not be embraced out of either misanthropy or vanity. The anchorite must be an angel on earth, enjoying intimacy with God through purity and strength of soul.

Brief mention must be made of one other figure, **Simeon the New Theologian** (949–1022). He exercised a formative influence on the development of Hesychasm, the tradition of mystical prayer associated in particular with the monks of Mount

Athos and which attached especial importance to the constant repetition of the Jesus Prayer. The aim was to unite the mind and the heart, the prayer thus becoming the 'prayer of the heart', leading through grace to a vision of the Divine Light, described thus by St Simeon:

> We do not speak of things of which we are ignorant, but we bear witness to that which we know. For the light already shines in the darkness, in the night and in the day, in our hearts and minds. This light without change, without decline and never extinguished enlightens us; it speaks, it acts, it lives and gives life, it transforms into light those whom it illumines. God is Light, and those whom He makes worthy to see Him, see Him as Light; those who receive Him, receive Him as Light. For the light of His glory goes before His face, and it is impossible that He should appear otherwise than as light. Those who have not seen this light, have not seen God: for God is Light. Those who have not received this light, have not yet received grace, for in receiving grace, one receives the divine light, and God Himself.[45]

4. Early Medieval Mysticism

THE potent mystical speculations of Dionysius the Areopagite were fed into the great stream of medieval theology by **John Scotus Erigena** (*c.*810–*c.*877), an Irishman by birth who became head of the palace school at Laon and whose own writings (notably the *De Divisione Naturae*) attempted to reconcile Neoplatonic and Christian metaphysics.

Man, in Erigena's mystical scheme, has in the depths of his consciousness an ultimate ground of truth, a point at which the eternal and the temporal meet. If a man *completely* understands his mind he understands everything, because God is that ground of truth in the soul. In contemplation, the soul becomes that which it beholds: 'Whoever rises to pure understanding becomes that which he understands. We, while we discuss together, in turn become one another. For, if I understand what you understand, I become your understanding, and in a certain unspeakable way I am made into you. And also when you entirely understand what I clearly understand you become my understanding, and from two understandings there arises one.' The soul can find God because at its centre the soul *is* God: the soul, that is to say, reveals God, and so Erigena can proclaim that 'There are as many unveilings of God [Theophanies] as there are saintly souls.'[1] The pantheistical possibilities in this doctrine are clear and they were to be taken up and developed into extreme positions some three centuries later.

Medieval mysticism really begins in the eleventh century, with such monastic reformers as **St Peter Damian** (1007–1072), part of whose impulsion was the desire to create an environment in which the mystical life could be developed to its full. The *Meditations* of **St Anselm** (*c.*1033–1109), Archbishop of Canterbury from 1093, display a deep strain of mystical devotion. Anselm was also one of the first great scholastic theologians of the

Middle Ages and was responsible for elaborating the so-called Ontological Argument for the existence of God – that is to say, the *a priori* argument that the existence of the idea of God necessarily implies the objective existence of God and that the non-existence of God is inconceivable.

St Bernard

The dominant figure of the twelfth century, and indeed one of the great mystics of the Christian tradition, was St Bernard of Clairvaux (1090–1153), the compiler of the Rule of the Order of Knights Templar. All of Bernard's writings were anchored in a profoundly mystical faith, in which devotion to Christ and the Virgin Mary played a central role.

Bernard was born into a noble French family. After the death of his parents, in 1112, he entered the small and ailing monastery of Cîteaux, near Dijon. Three years later he founded a new monastery at Clairvaux, where he remained as abbot for the rest of his life. As well as his work at Clairvaux, which in time generated some sixty-eight associated houses, Bernard was at the centre of the religious and political life of his time: he helped secure the victory of Innocent II in the disputed papal election of 1130, he championed orthodoxy against the teachings of Peter Abelard, and in his last year preached the Second Crusade.

But in spite of these temporal involvements Bernard lived an intense inner life. Many of his mystical pronouncements are to be found in a collection of eighty-six sermons on the Canticle (The Song of Songs), which reveal Bernard's primary focus on the person – especially the childhood and suffering – of Christ. The mystical contemplation of the wounds of Christ crucified, one of the great themes of medieval mysticism, begins to be fully articulated in St Bernard: 'The nail calls, the wound calls that truly God has reconciled the world to himself in Christ. The iron has penetrated his soul and approached his heart, that he may thoroughly know to have compassion on my infirmities. The secret of the heart is revealed through the openings of the body; there is made manifest the great mystery of His mercy.'

St Bernard was an example of what Evelyn Underhill called a 'creative mystic' – he translated his mystical experiences into concrete pastoral acts: activity for him was the necessary complement to the contemplative life. 'The embrace of divine contemplation', he wrote, 'must often be interrupted in order to give nourishment to the little ones, and none may live for himself alone, but for all.'[2]

For Bernard, taking over the imagery of the Canticle, Christ is the Bridegroom. Commenting on the opening words of the Canticle ('Let him kiss me with the kisses of his mouth') he describes the threefold Mystical Way as the kiss of the Feet of Christ (the Illuminative Way), the kiss of the Mouth of Christ (the Purgative Way), and the kiss of the Hand of Christ (the Unitive Way). Christ is seen not only as the Bridegroom of the Church: he is also the Bridegroom of the soul, though Bernard is careful to caution against a too literal and earthly interpretation of his imagery: 'Take heed that you bring chaste ears to this discourse of love; and when you think of these two lovers, remember always that not a man and a woman are to be thought of, but the Word of God and a soul. And if I shall speak of Christ and the Church, the sense is the same, except that under the name of the Church is specified not one soul only, but the united souls of many, or rather their unanimity.'[3] The final, unitive 'kiss' is the reception of the infused Holy Spirit, a special revelation of the Spirit that 'enlightens unto knowledge' and 'inflames unto love'. This most intimate union is not, however, a unity of substance – there are no pantheistic overtones in St Bernard's expressions; it is rather a 'communion of wills and an agreement in charity' – charity, of course, in its original sense.

Towards the end of his life Bernard, with deep and unaffected modesty, attempted to describe how he himself experienced the coming of the Word – the Bridegroom – to the soul. It is such an immensely moving and significant passage that it needs to be quoted in full:

> But now let me try to tell you of my own experience, as I set out to do. I speak as a fool; and yet I must admit that the Word has come even to me, and that many times. But never, when He has thus entered into me, have I perceived the actual moment of his coming. I have felt that He was present; I remember afterwards that He was then with me; and sometimes I have sensed His coming in advance. But never have I been aware of the particular moment when He came or went. Whence He came from into my soul, or whither He goes on leaving me, or by what road he enters or departs, I know not even now. Certainly it was not by my eyes, that He entered, for He has no colour; nor was it by my ears, for He made not a sound. Neither was it my nostrils that discerned His presence, for His sweetness mingles with the mind,

not with the air. The sense of taste did not detect Him either, for He is nothing that one eats or drinks; and touch was likewise powerless to apprehend Him, for he is utterly intangible. How, then, did He come in? Or did He *not* come in, perhaps, because He never was outside? For He is not one of the things that exist exteriorly to us. And yet how can I say that He comes from within me, when I know that in me there is nothing that is good? I have ascended to the highest in myself, and lo! the Word was towering far above it. My curiosity has led me to explore my lowest depths as well, only to find that He went deeper yet. If I looked out from myself, I saw Him stretching farther than the farthest I could see; and if I looked within, He was more inward still. So I recognized the truth of the apostle's words, 'In Him we live and move and are'.

You ask, then, how I knew that He was present, since His ways are past finding out? Because the Word is living and effective, and as soon as ever He entered into me, He has aroused my sleeping soul, and stirred and softened and pricked my heart, that hitherto was sick and hard as stone. He has begun to pluck up and destroy, to build and to plant, to water the dry places and shed light upon the dark, to open what was shut, to warm the chill, to make the crooked straight and the rough places plain; so that my soul has blessed the Lord and all that is within me praised His Holy Name. Thus has the Bridegroom entered into me; my senses told me nothing of His coming; I knew that He was present only by the movement of my heart; I perceived His power, because it put my sins to flight and exercised a strong control on all my impulses. I have been moved to wonder at His wisdom too, uncovering my secret faults and teaching me to see their sinfulness; and I have experienced His gentleness and kindness in such small measure of amendment as I have achieved; and, in the renewal and remaking of the spirit of my mind – that is, my inmost being – I have beheld to some degree the beauty of His glory and have been filled with awe as I gazed at His manifold greatness.[4]

This was the characteristic note of St Bernard's mysticism, representing less an experience of the transcendent eternal Father than the deepest communion with the Son, the one true source of moral and spiritual strength. Yet he also expressed a further stage of mystical apprehension. The Christocentric devotion to the humanity of Jesus, the very centre of the Christian life for Bernard, is but a stage on a far greater journey. The love of God, he said, divided into four stages: the 'Fourth Degree of Love' is utter self-forgetfulness, in which the soul seems merged with God – 'suddenly, and for the space of hardly a moment': 'In a certain manner to lose yourself as though you were not, and to be utterly unconscious of yourself and to be emptied of yourself and, as it were, brought to nothing, this pertains to heavenly intercourse, not to human affection.' Then, Bernard goes on to say, the soul is transported out of itself and is granted 'a clearer vision of the Divine Majesty, yet only for a moment and with the swiftness of a lightning flash'.

This is the highest and rarest of all mystical experiences. More within reach of those dedicated souls who seek authentic mystical insights are those moments when the human will achieves union with the will of God:

> Just as a little drop of water mixed with a lot of wine seems entirely to lose its own identity, while it takes on the taste of wine and its colour; just as iron, heated and glowing, looks very much like fire, having divested itself of its original and characteristic appearance; and just as air flooded with the light of the sun is transformed into the same splendour of light so that it apears not so much lighted up as to be light itself; so it will inevitably happen that in saints every human affection will then, in some ineffable manner melt away from self and be entirely transfused into the will of God.[5]

The gentle Christocentric spirituality of St Bernard was constantly drawn on by succeeding mystics in the Middle Ages and his authority was regularly appealed to. 'It is scarcely excessive', considered Evelyn Underhill, 'to say that his teaching coloured the whole spiritual life of the medieval church.'[6]

William of Saint-Thierry (c.1085–1148), theologian and mystical writer, was a close friend of St Bernard and in 1119/20 was elected abbot of the Benedictine abbey of Saint-Thierry near Rheims. He was well versed in patristic theology (especially Origen) and was the author of two commentaries on the Song of Songs, a treatise on contemplation and the famous *Epistola ad Fratres de Monte Dei de Vita Solitaria*, the so-called 'Golden Letter' (sometimes attributed to St Bernard). Though William stresses the humanity of Christ it is not for him the primary focus of the contemplative life, as it was for St Bernard, and he does not dwell on the mystical significance of the wounds and blood of Christ. More emphasis is placed on the role of the Holy Spirit, which renews the divine image in man and leads him towards a knowledge of God. The mystical experience for William fuses intellectual illumination and love: the intellect is 'enlightened' and elevated far beyond normal human understanding, whilst the

Holy Spirit activates the soul's apprehension of God through love.

St Hildegard and Mechthild of Magdeburg

A near contemporary of St Bernard and William of St-Thierry was the German abbess **Hildegard of Bingen** (1098–1179), the 'Sibyl of the Rhine', so called because of her vivid apocalyptic visions and prophecies of disaster (about which the abbess consulted St Bernard). Hildegard's psychic constitution was certainly unstable and this, as is so often the case, was combined with poor physical health. In spite of this, she was a woman of determination and indomitable energy, founding two convents, involving herself in ecclesiastical politics, travelling long distances in the pursuit of her duties, and writing hymns, a herbal and the curious *Scivias* (probably an abbreviation of 'Sciens vias', 'Know the ways'), a dictated account of twenty-six of her visions.

Some of Hildegard's visions and the 'revelatory' messages they carried were undoubtedly the result of psychological mechanisms, which produced spontaneous effects that could easily be misinterpreted. This was to be a particular danger for many devout women, who did not have the benefit of the kind of intensive theological and scholastic training enjoyed by their male counterparts. It must be said, however, that psychological abnormality, hysteria and misapprehension were by no means solely characteristic of women: from the extraordinary penetential disciplines of the first desert solitaries onwards, the dangers and pitfalls of the religious life are as tragically apparent in men as in women. Yet in Hildegard's case, in spite of what one might call psychological distortions, there does seem to be a core of authentic mystical insight.

Hildegard had been a spiritually precocious child and her mystical experiences continued until the end of her life; for her, God was the Living Light:

> From my infancy until now, in the 70th year of my age, the soul has always beheld this Light; and in it my soul soars to the summit of the firmament and into a different air . . . The brightness which I see is not limited by space and is more brilliant than the radiance round the sun . . . Its name, which has been given me, is 'Shade of the Living Light' . . . Within that brightness I sometimes see another light, for which the name *Lux Vivens* has been given me. When and how I see *this*, I cannot tell; but sometimes when I see it all sadness and pain is

lifted from me, and I seem a simple girl again, and an old woman no more![7]

Hildegard states that she did not see these things with her bodily eyes or hear them with the outward ear: 'I beheld them according to God's will, openly and fully awake, considering them in the full light of the mind, eyes and ears of the inner mind. How is this? It is hard for carnal man to understand . . . When fully penetrated by my light I said many things strange to those who heard them.'[8]

Her eccentricities apart, Hildegard expressed several classic attributes of the mystical way as a result of her experiences – for instance, she speaks eloquently of what the Greek Fathers called *akedia*, the listlessness that besets even the most dedicated contemplative: 'A great sorrow comes over me, so that I perform no work in high sanctity nor in the fullness of good will, but feel nothing within myself but the unrest of doubt and despair . . . all happiness, all good both in man and God becomes wearisome and distasteful to me.'

In the next century the Cistercian convent of Helfta in Thuringia sheltered three more women visionaries: **Mechthild of Magdeburg** (*c.* 1210–1280), **St Gertrude the Great** (1256–*c.* 1302) and **Mechthild of Hackeborn** (1240–1298).

St Mechthild of Magdeburg came from a noble Saxon family and had her first spiritual experience when she was twelve. In 1233 she left her family and became a Beguine* at Magdeburg. Like Hildegard of Bingen, Mechthild claimed to have had revelatory visions inspired directly by God and the unorthodox nature of some of these divinely infused teachings caused her to be excommunicated for a time.

The book in which Mechthild describes her experiences is called *The Flowing Light of the Godhead* (Das Fliessende Licht der Gottheit), which clearly shows the highly wrought spiritual and psychological state in which Mechthild and those like her lived. The visions they experienced were vividly pictorial in character; in Mechthild's case they were influenced by the language and

---

*The Beguines were semi-religious sisterhoods founded in the Netherlands in the twelfth century. Both they and their male counterparts the Beghards were accused of heresy. The name comes from the founder of the movement, a priest from Liège called Lambert le Begue (Lambert the Stammerer).

imagery of the liturgy and religious art and also by the secular poetry of courtly love, which occasionally coats her ecstasies with a kind of elevated eroticism: she speaks, for instance, of being taken into the divine arms of Christ, and being kissed by Him, and of enduring His absence. She in turn is complemented: she is God's desire, a cooling presence to His breast, a caress to His mouth. These images reflect a radical development in the language of mystical experience, which now absorbs and feeds on a new sensuous realization of Christ's humanity and sufferings. These, in turn, become a means of turning away from the world. In Mechthild, the mysticism of the Sacred Heart, which was to become so prominent in later devotional literature, is fully articulated. The abbess of Helfta, **St Gertrude the Great**, also had visions of the Heart of Christ, the beating of which filled her with overpowering joy. The Heart becomes for her a treasure house, a lyre whose strings are moved by the Holy Spirit: it is her final and abiding home, to which her divine lover calls her: 'Come, my love, to me, enter, my love, into me.'

As with Hildegard of Bingen, Mechthild of Magdeburg displayed clear signs of psychological disturbance; she was besides a difficult person to get on with and reacted violently to criticism. But occasionally her fecund and poetic imagination seems eclipsed by a greater experience, in which she felt herself to have been 'engulfed', 'immersed like a fish in the sea', in the Triune God.

The Victorines
In 1113 William of Champeaux, a friend of St Bernard, founded the Augustinian monastery of St Victor near Paris. Throughout the twelfth century the Victorines included a number of prominent scholars, poets and mystics, among them Adam of St Victor, Hugh of St Victor, Richard of St Victor and Walter of St Victor.

The Victorines' leading theologian was **Hugh of St Victor** (d.1142), amongst whose many writings was a commentary on the *Celestial Hierarchy* of Dionysius the Areopagite. There is a pronounced mystical tendency in Hugh's writing; but the great mystic amongst the Victorines was **Richard of St Victor** (d.1173), who became prior in 1162 and held the office until his death. A Scot by birth, Richard first studied philosophy before dedicating himself to the mystical possibilities of the spiritual life. His doctrine is developed in *Benjamin Minor, or the Preparation of the Soul, Benjamin Major, or Contemplation*, and in the tract *Four Degrees of Burning Love*. Dante refers to Richard in the *Paradiso* (X,132), describing him as being 'In speculation not a man, but more.'*

Richard of St Victor is the first medieval mystic to apply a systematic psychology to mystical experience. The mind of the mystic, in his view, ascended in an orderly fashion from the contemplation of visible things, through the contemplation of invisible things to the final transforming union. In his systematic way, Richard enumerates three activities of mind: thinking, meditation and contemplation. The first is a largely undisciplined process; meditation requires sustained mental effort to keep the mind on its object; contemplation takes the mind and the soul beyond the reach of reason (the sphere of meditation), to a state of ecstatic 'alienation'.

The spiritual life begins with contrition and a sense of sin. Then the soul begins to be visited by a sense of God's presence and meditation, aided by the imagination, starts to nourish the mystic's aspirations. The 'second degree of love' is the 'wedding' of the human with the divine spirit, expressed through the 'prayer of quiet'; the 'third degree' is a state of utter self-surrender: 'The soul no longer thirsts *for* God, but *into* God'. This is a state of ecstasy – caused by intense devotion, wonder and joy; but there is a 'fourth degree of love', when the soul, having tasted the sublimest fruit of contemplation, withdraws to creative, compassionate work in the world, in imitation of Christ who 'emptied himself' in the Incarnation. 'In the third degree,' wrote Richard, 'the soul is so to speak put to death; in the fourth it is raised in Christ.' Elsewhere he speaks of this fourth degree, which all the great mystics that followed him considered to be the pinnacle of the mystical life, as a state in which 'the soul brings forth its children'. 'In this doctrine,' wrote Evelyn Underhill, 'Richard gives us a key to the lives of the great mystics, and demolishes any

*Dorothy Sayers' translation. Evelyn Underhill, in *Mystics of the Church*, p. 81, renders this line 'in contemplation more than man'; but Barbara Reynolds observes that 'Dante does not use the verb "contemplare" in connection with Richard, but, instead, the verb "considerare". We have not yet reached the heaven of the contemplatives, and it would seem from this choice of word that Dante did not include Richard among them.' (*The Divine Comedy: 3. Paradise*, Penguin, 1962, pp. 146–7.)

conception of mysticism centred on the soul's mere enjoyment of God. All the great figures of Christian sanctity – Paul, Augustine, Bernard, Francis, Teresa – are in their last and life-giving stages triumphant examples of Richard's "divine fecundity".[9]

St Francis

St Francis of Assisi (1181/2–1226) gave an entirely new impetus to the mystical life of the Church, indeed to its spiritual life in general; and yet the simplicity and freshness of his vision was, paradoxically, a remaking of the apostolic model and drew its inspiration from a return to the very fountain of Christianity – the Galilean circle of Christ. The simple monk of Assisi had nothing of the theologian about him: man for him was not a philosophical or metaphysical abstraction to be speculated upon but a child of God, to be loved as Christ had loved. 'O Lord my Saviour,' he prayed, 'I ask two favours before I die. Let me feel in my soul, in my body even, all the bitter pains which Thou hast felt. And in my heart let me feel that immeasurable love which made Thee, Son of God, endure such sufferings for us, poor sinners.'*

This penitential and Christ-like figure generated a new spiritual consciousness in the West, making Francis one of the truly creative personalities of the Middle Ages. He craved ceaselessly to know the uncreated Father. A famous story describes how one night he 'rose up from his bed and set himself to pray, lifting up his hands and eyes unto heaven, and with exceeding great devotion and fervour said, "My God, my God!" and thus saying and sorely weeping, he abode till morning, always repeating, "My God, my God" and naught beside.'

Francis Bernadone was born in 1181 or 1182, the son of a cloth merchant of Assisi. As a young man he had plenty of money and lived an easy, carefree social life, though he was always generous, and, in the words of one chronicler, 'given unto jests and songs, going around the city of Assisi day and night in company with his like, most free-handed in spending. Even in his clothes he was beyond measure sumptuous.' During hostilities between Assisi and neighbouring Perugia, Francis was imprisoned for a year and not long after his release he became seriously ill. This left him

---

*This quotation is from the *Little Flowers of St Francis*, a collection of legends about Francis and his companions. It is a vernacular version of earlier Latin material and dates from c.1375.

restless and oppressed by the emptiness of his life. He continued in this state until one day, whilst praying in the Church of St Damian near Assisi, he felt that the figure of Christ on the altar crucifix was coming alive and was asking him to dedicate himself to a new way of life.

Francis now gradually began to cut himself off from his family (his father disowned him), impelled by an uprush of tremendous spiritual power that never left him. In 1208, hearing in church one day the words of Christ to his disciples to leave all they had and devote themselves to the salvation of 'the lost sheep of Israel' (Matthew, 10:7–19), Francis took the gospel text with passionate literalness and devoted himself to 'Lady Poverty'.* He went about preaching 'in words like fire, penetrating the heart'. It seemed, said St Bonaventura, the Franciscan theologian, as though the Spirit of God spoke through Francis' mouth. There was no fanaticism; the external poverty was merely a way of lifting all hindrances from his soul 'so that she may be free to unite herself to the Eternal God'. The essence of the Franciscan ideal, which is far removed from the self-torturing asceticism of the desert hermits, was distilled into a lyric by Jacopone da Todi (*c.*1230–1306), the Franciscan poet: 'Poverty is naught to have, and nothing to desire; and all things to possess in the spirit of liberty.'[10]

In time there developed around the charismatic figure of Francis a small band of followers and Francis began to evolve his Rule of the Order of Poor Little Brothers, which was authorized by Pope Innocent III in 1210 and had its headquarters in the Porziuncola Chapel at Santa Maria degli Angeli near Assisi. In 1212 a second Order, the Poor Clares, was founded by Francis and the daughter of a prominent citizen of Assisi, in whom a mystical love for Christ had been kindled by hearing Francis preach. The Franciscan chroniclers added a supernatural element to the only occasion Francis and the Lady Clare ate together:

> When came the day ordained by him, and the hour of breaking bread being come, they sat down together. St Francis and St Clara ... and all the other companions took each his place at the table with all humility. And at the first dish St Francis began to speak of God so

*There is a painting by Sassetta (1395–1450) in the Musée Condé, Chantilly, that depicts Francis' betrothal to Lady Poverty.

sweetly, so sublimely, and so wondrously, that the fullness of Divine grace came down on them, and they were all rapt in God. And as they were thus rapt, with eyes and hands uplift to heaven, the folk of Assisi and the country round about saw that St Mary of the Angels, and all the house, and the wood that was hard by the house, were burning brightly, and it seemed as it were a great fire that filled the church, and the house and the whole wood together. For which cause the people of Assisi ran thither in great haste to quench the flames – but coming close up to the house and finding no fire at all, they entered within and found St Francis and St Clara and all their company in contemplation rapt in God . . . Whereby of a truth they understood that this had been a heavenly flame, and no earthly one at all, which God had let appear miraculously, for to show and to signify the fire of love divine with which the souls of those holy brothers and holy nuns were all aflame. . . .[11]

There was also a third Franciscan Order, the Tertiaries or Brethren of Penitence, formed for people who wished to lead a dedicated devotional life in their own homes. The formation of this order was in keeping with Francis' mission to awaken in every ordinary Christian a desire to strive after holiness and perfection in Christ.

St Francis left so few authentic writings that it is impossible to illustrate the precise nature of his mystical life by direct quotation; but his importance in any survey of the Christian mystical tradition is unequivocal. He is the supreme example of how the mystical life expresses itself completely through a spontaneous and effective love for God's creation, and in the whole history of Western mysticism there is no greater illustration of the creative interplay of the human and the divine will than Francis' consuming consciousness of God's presence and purpose. 'Thou wishest to know', asked Francis of one Brother Masseo, 'why it is I whom men follow? Thou wishest to know? It is because the eyes of the Most High that continually watch the good and the wicked have not found among sinners any smaller man, nor any more insufficient and more sinful, therefore He has chosen me to accomplish his marvellous work. He chose me because He could find no one more worthless, and He wished by me to confound the nobility and grandeur, the strength and beauty and the learning of the world.'[12]

In 1224 Francis, worn out with work and with the physical effects of the many deprivations he had joyfully embraced, retired to the hermitage of La Verna in the Appennines. For weeks he had been fasting and contemplating Christ's Passion and one entire night was spent in prayer. As the sun rose he had a vision:

> A seraph with outspread wings flew towards him from the edge of the horizon, and bathed his soul in raptures unutterable. In the centre of the vision appeared a cross, and the seraph was nailed upon it. When the vision disappeared, he felt sharp sufferings mingled with ecstasy in the first moments. Stirred to the very depths of his being, he was anxiously asking the meaning of it all, when he perceived upon his body the Stigmata of the Crucified.[13]

The episode of the Stigmata – the appearance on Francis' body of the five wounds of Christ – made a profound impression on the medieval mind. Whatever one's view of the La Verna episode, it shows beyond any doubt the intensity of Francis' inner life; though this physical manifestation of inward longings is in no sense the most significant episode of Francis' life, it is certainly one of the most dramatic. It did, however, capture the imagination of many later mystics and gave the Franciscan movement 'the passionate enthusiasm for suffering on the one hand, the rapturous and almost lyrical joy in surrender on the other'.[14]

*　　　　*　　　　*

The spiritual legacy of St Francis was not transmitted through a coherent organization. The 'Poverello' himself was a creative mystic of the highest order; but he was no builder of systems. The movement that developed after his death was incapable of perpetuating his ideals, even though it was, and remained, a potent force in the spiritual life of the West. Francis had been for many the perfect imitator of Christ (Jacopone da Todi announced boldly 'Christ hath shown Himself in thee!'). His sense of God's sanctifying presence in every created thing – from Brother Sun to Sister Bodily Death – brought the challenge of the mystical life to countless Christians.

The Spiritual Franciscans

Even before Francis' death his followers had been divided by dissension and controversy. On one side were those (the *Conventuali*, headed by Brother Elias of Cortona) who felt that the original Franciscan ideal was beyond the reach of most people and that a less rigorous observance of Francis' Rule was necessary. On the other side were the *Spirituali*, led initially by Brother Leo, who maintained that Francis, divinely inspired, had revealed a new spiritual epoch and that his Rule therefore had the authority of Gospel. At first the 'Spiritual' Franciscans triumphed. The Minister General of the Order from 1247 to 1257 was John of Parma, who was devoted to restoring a strict observance of the original Rule; but after 1257 the Spirituals became an ever more ineffectual and persecuted opposition party.

The great poet of Franciscan spirituality, **Jacopone da Todi**, has already been mentioned. He had been a lawyer and was converted in middle age after the death of his young wife. His lyrics are influenced on the one hand by the spiritual ideals of St Francis and on the other by the Platonically coloured mysticism of St Augustine and Dionysius the Areopagite. Jacopone's younger contemporary **Angela of Foligno** (*c.*1248–1309), a Franciscan Tertiary, is another example of the highest type of Franciscan piety and was, in the opinion of Evelyn Underhill, 'in many respects the most remarkable of the great Franciscan mystics'. Her visions are described in the *Liber Visionum et Instructionum*. Like Jacopone, and like Francis himself, she had led a comfortable life before her conversion. She had been married and had lived – and enjoyed – a thoroughly worldly existence. Angela described herself as being 'full of greediness, gluttony and drunkenness' even when she was a nominal Franciscan Tertiary: 'I diligently made an outward show of being poor, but caused many sheets and coverings to be put where I lay down to sleep, and to be taken up in the morning so that none might see them . . . I was given over to pride and the devil, but I feigned to have God in my soul and His consolation in my chamber, whereas I had the devil alike in my soul and my chamber.'

There then followed a long series of 'spiritual steps' lasting some years. Gradually she embraced an ever more ascetic lifestyle, a slow and painful alignment to the Franciscan ideal. She was helped in this process by the deaths of her husband, her children and her mother – 'a great hindrance to me,' she said, 'in following the way of God'. When at last she embarked fully on a life of genuine poverty she began to feel 'the sweetness and consolation of God' in her heart. Her most famous spiritual experience occurred on a pilgrimage from Foligno to Assisi, as she came to a chapel dedicated to the Holy Trinity. She had previously heard a voice during prayer promising that the whole Trinity would descend on her; now she felt flooded by God's Presence and heard His voice. Her visions were dictated to her uncle Arnaldo, a Franciscan friar. Unlike those of the Helfta nuns, they are truly mystical in spirit, being self-critical as well as ecstatic and showing no concern for manifestations or prophetic utterances: all that is desired is to know the 'Love Uncreate' and its image within the soul. 'Oh, my beloved sons!', she cried, 'every vision, every revelation, all sweetness and emotion, all knowledge, all contemplation, availeth nothing if a man know not God and himself!'

The foremost Franciscan theologian, who laid particular emphasis on mystical illumination, was Giovanni di Fidanza (*c.* 1217–1274), better known as **St Bonaventura** or 'Doctor Seraphicus'. Bonaventura was elected Minister General of the order in 1257, succeeding John of Parma; he was created a cardinal in 1273 and took part in the Council of Lyons, the main achievement of which was to bring about union with the Greek Church, in 1274, the year of his death. Bonaventura was the author of a life of St Francis and in writings such as *On the Threefold Way, The Mind's Journey to God* and *The Mystical Vine* described the soul's mystical ascent to God within the setting of Franciscan spirituality. Union with God is predicated by the usual Franciscan emphasis on self-denial and the awareness of sin: St Bonaventura advises that natural desires should be suppressed by meditation on imminent death, the blood of the Cross (conceived as having been recently shed) and the face of the soul's Judge. There is also a fundamental Christocentric emphasis on and devotion to the Sacred Heart: 'Behold, I have one heart with Jesus.' In the highest state of spiritual ecstasy, when the mystic has been thoroughly purified and has passed towards the Father by means of the crucified Son, the incarnate Word, the mind transcends itself in a state of complete, unassailable tranquillity.

Though there were many specifically Franciscan touches to his theology, St Bonaventura expressed the constitution of the mystical life in classic terms: his is essentially a mysticism of darkness (influenced by Gregory of Nyssa and Dionysius the Areopagite) achieved through the threefold way of purgation, illumination and union. But the thirteenth century also saw the development of some extremely unorthodox – indeed, as far as the Church was concerned, heretical – mystical doctrines. One group within the Franciscan Spirituals was responsible for the creation of 'The Eternal Gospel', proclaimed in 1254 in a book written by Gerard de Borgo San Domingo, although the true originator was a Calabrian monk, **Joachim of Floris** (or Fiore), a strange prophet who had died back in 1202 and who had calculated that a new era would begin in 1260, when an order of men, inspired by a mystical consciousness of God, would found a new religion of direct revelation called the 'Spiritual Gospel of Christ'. 'I saw the angel of God,' wrote Joachim in a commentary on the Apocalypse, 'who flew into the middle of heaven, having the eternal Gospel. This gospel is called eternal by John because that which Christ and the apostles have given us is temporal and transitory so far as concerns the form of the Sacraments, but eternal in respect to the truths which these signify.'[15]

A number of pious followers supplemented Joachim's prophetical writings with books of their own, which, however, purported to have been written by their master. The 'Joachim writings' went on to inspire the creation of a prophetical movement within the Spiritual Franciscans that culminated in the 'Eternal Gospel' book of Gerard of San Domingo, which was denounced as heretical by a papal commission in 1255 and ordered to be burned.

Pantheistic Mysticism
John Scotus Erigena, as we have seen, rendered the mystics of the Church an inestimable service by translating the Greek writings of Dionysius the Areopagite into Latin; he also translated a selection from the writings of the mystic Maximus the Confessor (580–662), a monk and martyr and a disciple of both Dionysius and Gregory of Nyssa.

For some three centuries after his death John Scotus was all but forgotten (he was not the sort of figure the orthodox theologians of the medieval Church could readily take to their hearts); but then towards the end of the twelfth century his influence suddenly fuelled a new popular mystical movement centred on a certain **Amaury** (or Amalric) of Bene (died *c.*1207), a master at the

University of Paris who taught that God is the one essence that underlies creation and that those who live in the love of God cannot sin: 'Every man ought to believe, as an article of his faith without which there is no salvation, that each one of us is a member of the Christ.' Amaury's teaching was condemned by the University authorities in 1204 and by Pope Innocent III the following year; Amaury died soon afterwards but his ideas gave rise to a sect that believed the reign of the Holy Spirit had begun. According to **Jean Gerson** (1363–1429), Chancellor of the University of Paris and a man of mystical temper himself, Amaury's followers held that 'the soul, when it has risen to God by means of love, sloughs off its own particular nature, and finds in God its eternal and immutable essence. Such a soul loses its own being, and receives the being of God, so that it is no longer a "creature", it no longer sees and loves God as a foreign object, but it becomes God Himself, the object of all contemplation and love.'

In 1209 the leaders of this pantheistical movement, whose beliefs were open to immoral practical applications, in theory if not always in practice, were arrested and those who remained unrepentant were burned. The bones of Amaury de Bene were dug up and thrown on to unconsecrated ground (or burned, according to another account). The influence of John Scotus Erigena and Amaury de Bene appeared amongst the Albigensian heretics of southern France and in the pantheistical mysticism of the group known as the **Brethren of the Free Spirit**, which sprang up in Strasbourg a few years after Amaury's death.

The mystical outlook of this latter sect (which, like all similar movements, distinguished between the 'perfect' and the ignorant) took an extreme view of the doctrine of Divine Immanence and held that every man is of the same substance as God. Union with God, therefore, is possible for every soul in which the will to realize its divine nature is activated. Sin was impossible for those who had become 'perfected': 'Sin is the will to offend God, and he whose will has become God's will cannot offend God. His will is God's will, and God's will is his will. A man may become so completely Divine that his very body is sanctified, and then what it does is a Divine act. In this state the instincts and impulses of the body take on a holy significance.'[16]

Such pseudo-mystical concepts were preached by numerous groups in Europe throughout the thirteenth century. Groups such as the Beghards and the related sisterhoods of Beguines (see p. 86n) translated the abstract speculations of Dionysius, Erigena and Amaury into a practical mysticism that had great popular appeal: in so doing they ignited a flame of heresy that the authorities everywhere were determined to stamp out. The persecution of pantheistical heresies continued into the four-teenth century and was carried on with the full power of the Inquisition. As with the Montanists of the primitive Christian era, the 'Free Spirit' mystic, believing that the perfect soul is incapable of sin and having, like Dionysius, a negative understanding of God's nature, tended either to asceticism or antinomianism: the absence of absolute moral imperatives grounded in a positive conception of God gave rise to a spurious and tragic vision of spiritual liberty.

St Thomas Aquinas

Before leaving the thirteenth century brief mention must be made of both the Dominican Order and one of its principal theologians, St Thomas Aquinas (*c.*1225–1274), 'Doctor Angelicus'.

The Mendicant Order of Dominicans, for which St Dominic (1170–1221) obtained formal sanction from Rome in 1216, was devoted specifically to preaching and theological study, including what is generally known as speculative mysticism. It was also closely associated with the work of the Holy Office, better known as the Inquisition. Thomas Aquinas was of noble birth and was educated at the Benedictine abbey of Monte Cassino. In 1244, though opposed by his family, he joined the Dominicans and studied under St Albertus Magnus (see p. 100) in Paris. The extent of Aquinas' writings is immense, his two major works being the *Summa Contra Gentiles* and the *Summa Theologica*, which, although unfinished at his death, is one of the greatest and most influential works of medieval systematic theology.

It is felt by many people that the influence of Thomism has had a detrimental – indeed, a deadening – effect on the development of genuine mystical realization in Christianity. The truth is otherwise. Aquinas's systematic theology has at its heart a living apprehension of mystical knowledge – of true *gnosis*, or *sapienta*, rather than rational knowledge. The reason is that although Aquinas is now thought of principally as a scholastic theologian and philosopher, he was also a mystic (one eyewitness account describes him levitating during ecstatic prayer) and his positive influence can be traced in several of the greatest Christian mystics, including Ruysbroeck, Eckhart, Francis de Sales and, in the modern period, Thomas Merton. When, at the end of his life, he was urged to resume writing the *Summa* he replied that everything he had written seemed like straw in comparison with what contemplation had revealed to him.

Though he seems fully to have apprehended the highest possibilities of the spiritual life, Aquinas is at one with all the great Christian mystics in laying stress on combining the fruits of the contemplative life with action in the world of men: 'The greater and the more exalted the contemplative life is as compared with the active life, the more seems to be done for God by a man who suffers detriment to his beloved contemplation in order to devote himself to the salvation of his neighbour for the sake of God. This ... seems to belong to a higher perfection of love than if a man were so attached to the sweetness of contemplation that he would not give it up in any circumstances, even when the salvation of others is at stake.'[17]

5. The Later Middle Ages

LEAVING the genesis of the Franciscan movement in Italy our focus is now Germany, the German mystical tradition and its dominating figure, Meister Eckhart.

All the German mystics of the fourteenth century, principally Eckhart, Tauler and Suso, developed their teachings amidst extensive popular interest in mysticism. This upsurge of interest in the transcendental took place against a chaotic and violent background – political conflict, wars and a host of natural disasters, from famine to pestilence. It is not surprising that the deep-seated insecurities of such a troubled age should encourage apocalyptic tempers of the most lurid kind; but they also played some part at least in focusing interest on the timelessness of mystical experience. Dogmatism, weakness and corruption in the Church also, perhaps, produced a reflex in the spiritually minded, a turning away from the temporal.

It seems likely that the increase in the number of nunneries, housing many well-born ladies, bore a relationship to the widespread loss of life amongst the knights. The Dominican friars, in Germany as elsewhere, were obliged to supervise the spiritual instruction in the nunneries. This meant that men well versed in the subtleties of the Schools had to translate (literally) the technical terminology of scholastic theology into language appropriate to the nuns in their charge, and this interchange stimulated the mystical sense amongst the conventuals so that a great number of important statements of mystical doctrine can be found in vernacular sermons delivered by the Dominican fathers. The change from Latin to German also had an effect on the preachers: 'The learned tone becomes popular and homely. The enthusiasms which are restrained in the Latin treatises burst forth freely.'[1]

Meister Eckhart

The Dominicans typified German mysticism in the fourteenth century, though the Franciscans (for example, David von Augsburg and Marquart von Lindau) also made significant contributions. Towering above them all is the figure of Meister Eckhart (*c.* 1260–1327/8). He was born at Hocheim in Thuringia, of noble parents, and like many youths of rank and ability he was attracted to the Dominican Order, becoming a novice at Erfurt. After his preliminary training he went to the famous *studium generale* at Cologne, whose reputation had been established by Albertus Magnus (1193–1280) and Thomas Aquinas. **Albertus** himself wrote of the mystical life in the terms of the Negative Way and his teaching had a direct influence on Eckhart. The treatise *De Adhaerendo Dei*, generally attributed to Albertus, for instance, begins by describing how the mind must be emptied and made dark in order to approach the divine mystery: this, as we shall see, was a characteristically Eckhartian doctrine:

> When St John says that God is a Spirit, and that He must be worshipped in spirit, he means that the mind must be cleared of all images. When thou prayest, shut thy door – that is, the doors of thy senses. Keep them barred and bolted against all phantasms and images. Nothing pleases God more than a mind free from all occupations and distractions. Such a mind is in a manner transformed into God, for it can think of nothing, and love nothing, except God . . . He who penetrates into himself, and so transcends himself, ascends truly to God. He whom I love and desire is above all that is sensible, and all that is intelligible; sense and imagination cannot bring us to Him, but only the desire of a pure heart. This brings us unto the darkness of the mind, whereby we can ascend to the contemplation even of the mystery of the Trinity.[2]

In 1300 or thereabouts Eckhart was studying at the *studium generale* of St Jacques in Paris, where he gained the degree of Master of Theology in 1302. He was henceforth known as Meister Eckhart, a title that served to distinguish him from others of the same name. He quickly climbed to a position of eminence in the Dominican hierarchy. In 1303 he was elected first Provincial of the Dominican province of Saxony; and in 1307 he became Vicar-General of Bohemia, his main task being to restore order and orthodoxy to the convents of that area in which discipline had become lax and heretical tendencies were beginning to show themselves.

By 1314 Eckhart was in Strasbourg, which was at this time the foremost religious centre of Germany and accommodated a spectrum of opinion from the severely orthodox to sects with heretical overtones such as the Beghards and Beguines and the Brethren of the Free Spirit. Eckhart was to become associated with such sects in the eyes of the official Church, but there seems little doubt that he never consciously embraced the teachings of these 'Inner Light' sects. However, it is equally clear that his lofty, subtle teachings, delivered in German to crowded congregations of the religiously-minded laity and to the inmates of religious communities, were extremely susceptible to distortion and misapprehension. The result was that the authorities suspected Eckhart of encouraging speculation in dangerous areas, even though Eckhart clearly distinguished between the false notion of liberty propounded by the Quaker-like Free Spirit sects and the true liberty that arises from a total conformation to God's will.

In about 1322, possibly earlier, Eckhart took the place of Albertus at the *studium* in Cologne. The Archbishop of that city was a formidable Franciscan, Heinrich von Virneburg, who was bitterly opposed to mystical speculation, which he associated with the heretical sects he had been assiduously suppressing for some years. In 1326 the archbishop began proceedings against Eckhart, accusing him of spreading dangerous doctrines amongst the common people. Though Eckhart, as a high-ranking Dominican, was technically answerable only to the University of Paris or to the Pope, he nonetheless agreed to appear before the three inquisitors (two of whom were Franciscans) appointed to deal with the case. The inquisitors deliberated on a number of articles and propositions taken from Eckhart's writings, including fifteen from the *Book of Divine Comfort*, written about 1308 for the widowed Queen Agnes of Hungary. The enquiry dragged on for some time, until Eckhart finally appealed to the Pope. In February 1327 he declared that he was not a heretic, though he conceded that many of his teachings had been distorted or misunderstood. He died before a final judgment was made. About a year after his death, in March 1329, Pope John XXII issued the bull *In agro dominico*, which listed twenty-six articles from Eckhart's Latin works and two from his German sermons. Fifteen of the former were declared heretical and the remainder were termed 'dangerous and suspect of heresy'. The two vernacular articles were also condemned.

Eckhart's principal preoccupation was the nature of God: he was, to use his own phrase, 'God-intoxicated'. The distinction he drew between *God* and the *Godhead* is fundamental to an understanding of his thought. Eckhart taught that there is a final and central mystery eternally beyond what we can conceive of as knowledge. 'God', the God of religious experience, is a manifestation of the divine nature, a revelation in the form of a Person; but if there is a revelation there must be a revealer – a 'Ground'. This is the Godhead, unrevealed and unrevealable; an abiding potentiality, undifferentiated, above all distinction – 'that eternal Unity which was mine before all time, when I was what I would, and would what I was . . . a state above all addition or diminution . . . the Immobility whereby all is moved'. The Godhead is completely depersonalized in Eckhart's scheme: 'It' has no anthropomorphic attributes and can be neither an object of worship nor of knowledge. One can say nothing of the Godhead that is not untrue, so totally does It transcend knowledge and human understanding. 'Be still,' one of Eckhart's sermons counsels, 'and prate not of God [*sc.* the Godhead], for whatever you prate in words about Him is a lie and is sinful.' If one says that God, as Godhead, is good, it is not true: 'for what is good can grow better; what can grow better can grow best'. None of these concepts can be applied to the Godhead, which is above all attributes and characteristics. The Godhead is 'the Nameless Nothing', the 'Still Wilderness'; it is 'naked'. In the summation of Rufus Jones: 'The unoriginated Being, the Ground of all that is, is the central mystery, and he who would fathom this mystery must transcend knowledge, must have recourse to some other form of experience than that which defines and differentiates as the knowing process does.'[3]

In a passage full of subtle and startling paradoxes Eckhart attempts to explain the distinction between God and Godhead in relation to his own being:

> When I dwelt in the ground, in the bottom, in the stream and source of the Godhead, no-one asked me where I was going or what I was doing. There was no-one who could have asked me. When I flowed

out, all creatures said 'God'. If one were to ask me: 'Friar Eckhart, when did you leave your home?' I was still in it! All creatures speak of God in this way. And why do they not speak of the Godhead? Everything that is in the Godhead is one, and it is not to be spoken of. God works, the Godhead does not work. It has not to work; there is no work in it. It never considered any work. God and the Godhead are distinguished by working and not working. When I return to God I do not remain in him [i.e. in the triune God]. Then my break-through [the mystic union] is much nobler than my outpouring [the Creation] ... When I enter the ground, the bottom, the stream and the source of the Godhead, no-one asks me where I came from or where I have been. No-one missed me there, for there even God disappears.[4]

'God' is the 'natured Nature', as distinguished from the 'unnatured Nature' of the Godhead. The Godhead is Wordless; God is the uttered Word. God is the Trinity, which flows out from the unity of the Godhead. The Godhead, in an Eternal Now, beholds Himself: becoming an object of consciousness to Himself, He is revealed to Himself, a process Eckhart calls 'the begetting of the Son' and which takes place eternally. The three Persons of the Trinity are not simply modes of the Godhead: they are inherent in the Godhead. God, says Eckhart, is 'ever working in one Eternal Now, and His working is a giving birth to His Son. He bears Him at every instant.' The Father is the manifestation of the Godhead; the Son is 'the image and countenance of the Father'; the Holy Ghost is 'the light of his countenance and the love of them both; all they have have they gotten eternally from their own selves'.

The Son represents 'the first outpouring of the Divine nature' and is thus properly called the image of the Father. The Holy Spirit cannot be so called: 'The Holy Spirit alone is the out-blossoming of the Father and the Son, and yet He has one nature with them both.' God eternally begets the Son and the procession of the Holy Spirit is likewise an eternal activity: 'When the Father begets the Son, He gives Him everything that He has essentially and by nature. In the act of giving, the Holy Spirit springs forth.'

To know God, said Eckhart, is to be known by Him; to see God is to be seen by Him. Just as a man cannot be wise without wisdom, 'so he cannot be a man without the filial nature of God's Son, without having the same being of God that the Son has'. Though Eckhart nowhere denied the historical Incarnation, he interprets it mystically. Human nature being universal and not the unique possession of each individual, Christ became Man, not *a man*. It therefore follows that the process can be reversed: Man can become Christ – and hence become God. To engender Christ, the Eternal Word, in the soul it is necessary to cultivate complete detachment and self-abandonment: 'The Eternal Word never put on a person. Therefore leave whatever is personal in you and whatever *you* are, and take just your bare *human nature*, then you will be to the Eternal Word just what His human nature is to Him. For your human nature and His are *not different*: it is one nature, for what is in Christ, that is in you.'[5]

The mystic achieves union with God through that indestructible faculty of the soul that Eckhart calls the spark, the *seelenfünklein*. (Eckhart sometimes uses the Greek term *synteresis* for this faculty – as did Thomas Aquinas, who also referred to it as the *scintilla animae*). The *fünklein*, which has an ethical aspect, being the seat of the conscience, and a metaphysical aspect, being the source of religious consciousness, is the Apex, the Centre, the Ground: it partakes of the very nature of God. The spark of the soul is immaterial. In it 'God glows and burns unceasingly and in all His glory, with all His sweetness and with all His joy'. Elsewhere Eckhart calls this spark the 'citadel in the soul' and the 'light' of the soul; but he also described it, typically, as 'neither this nor that':

> It is 'that which eternally is', higher above this or that than the heavens are above the earth. Therefore I now call it by a nobler name than ever before, but it repudiates this nobility and this mode and is far above them. It is free from all names, and altogether unimpeded, untrammelled and free from all modes, as God is free and untrammelled in Himself. This same power of which I have spoken, in which God is blossoming and budding in all his Divinity, and the spirit in God, in this same power the Father begets his only-begotten Son as truly as in Himself, for He truly lives in this power; and the spirit begets with the Father the same only-begotten Son and Himself as the same Son, and the spirit is this same Son in this light.[6]

The 'citadel' of the soul, says Eckhart, is so truly unique, so completely 'onefold', that God Himself, in so far as He acts according to the modes and characteristics of the Divine Persons, cannot look into it: only the undifferentiated Godhead can do that:

If God should look therein, it would cost Him all His Divine names and His personal characteristics: He must abandon these, if He is ever to look therein. But in so far as He is neither Father nor Son nor Holy Ghost in this sense, but 'that which eternally is', which is neither this nor that; look! just in so far as He is one and simple, He can enter what I call the 'citadel in the soul'. He does not enter it in any other way, but in this way He enters and dwells therein. In this part the soul is like God and not otherwise.[7]

In order for the soul to be united with God it must be purified: 'God sends His only-begotten Son into the pure soul and begets Him there and Himself. He does this if the soul is pure. It becomes pure by not loving anything that is created. For everything created is, by reason of its nothingness, ugly and divided from God, as night is from day, nothing from being.' Eckhart elsewhere symbolizes the mystic union by the speaking of the Word in the soul, where it can only be heard and understood when there is absolute silence.

Eckhart is frequently described as a 'speculative' mystic. This does not mean that he arrived at his teachings solely through the activities of the intellect: it means that his intellectual processes were refined and illuminated by his mystical experience: what he had *experienced*, what he truly knew he had 'seen', he tried to express in the utterly inadequate language of the intellect. It was through trying to give expression to the ineffable that Eckhart came into conflict with Church orthodoxy, though it is clear that he never intended to undermine the belief system to which he gave his total allegiance. Let us leave Eckhart with one eloquent and characteristic passage, describing the way the virtuous soul draws near to the eternally creative 'secret Word':

Mark now the fruit and use of this mysterious Word and of this darkness. In this gloom which is his own the heavenly Father's Son is not born alone: thou too art born there a child of the same heavenly Father and no other, and to thee also He gives power. Observe how great the use. No truth learned by a master by his own intellect and understanding, or ever to be learned this side the day of judgement, has ever been interpreted at all according to this knowledge, in this ground. Call it, if thou wilt, an ignorance, an unknowing, yet there is in it more than in all knowing and understanding without it, for this outward ignorance lures and attracts thee from all understood things and from thyself.[8]

The Friends of God

Meister Eckhart predominantly but also St Hildegard, Elizabeth of Schönau and Mechthild of Magdeburg were the seminal influences behind a widespread spiritual and mystical movement whose members were known as the Friends of God (*Gottesfreunde*). It was in no sense an organized sect or society; rather, it was a loosely constituted informal brotherhood, with a large lay membership, bound together by the emphasis the Friends placed on mystical, visionary and prophetic experience. They were formed into small groups, each with a spiritual leader; the movement also produced itinerant prophets as well as a considerable body of mystical literature. In many respects the *Gottesfreunde* were similar to the Beghards and Beguines: they differed fundamentally, however, by being opposed to the antinomian potentialities of the latter – indeed they vigorously embraced ascetic practices and self-renunciation.

Amongst the leaders of the Friends of God was the shadowy and mysterious **Rulman Merswin** of Strasbourg, with whom is associated the anonymous and still unidentified 'Friend of God from the Oberland'. Merswin was born in Strasbourg about the year 1310. He became a wealthy banker but at the age of forty gave up his business activities and devoted himself, in the manner of a Franciscan Tertiary, to cultivating the spiritual life. His money he kept 'to use for God', and though he was married he resolved to live a celibate life henceforth. He underwent extraordinary psychic and spiritual experiences, intensified no doubt by the fierce asceticism he practised to subdue his 'hated body': at last he received what the Friends called 'the light of grace' and passed into 'the joy and peace of the Holy Spirit'.

The Friends of God were all loyal Catholics, in spite of the startling nature of some of their claims and the way the movement exalted lay experience. The mediation of the Church was upheld by them, although they also held that it could be circumvented by the operation of grace upon the soul. They vigorously denounced temporal abuses: one of their number, Christina Ebner, even castigated the actions of the Pope towards the clergy, which made 'groans and cries rise to heaven'. The Friends saw themselves as an inner Church directly guided by the Holy Spirit and their teaching was based on the Eckhartian concept of a divine spark latent in every soul. When this spark becomes uncovered, as it were, a regenerative process begins: through the destruction of selfhood the Inner Light shines forth and the teaching of the Holy Spirit is directly imparted.

With their moral zest went a susceptibility to abnormal experiences. The Friends shared the superstitious fancies of their age – the belief in the efficacy of relics, for example.

> In the earlier stages of what they called their 'commencement', the Friends of God subjected themselves to terrible bodily tortures, self-inflicted, often of the most ingenious sort, and they generally emerged from this aberration with enfeebled constitutions and wrecked nervous systems. Certain typical 'experiences' were expected, and sooner or later they generally occurred. The stress and strain of the troublous epoch produced a mental type of person easily affected by suggestion, and thus the ideas and experiences of the leaders spread in this responsive material.[9]

Ecstasies, prophecies and visions were frequently claimed by the members and behind the many writings of the movement is the implication – and often the direct assertion – that the words the members speak come directly from God. Though never renouncing the authority of Scripture they also spoke of a higher stage of truth – the truth of immediate revelation:

> If two men gave thee a description of the city of Rome, one by mere hearsay, and the other by experience after he had been there, thou wouldst give thy attention mainly to the second. So also, if a man who has been touched inwardly by divine grace hears the preaching of a doctor who still loves himself, he feels that the preaching of such a doctor does not come from pure and unadulterated love of God. The soul that is filled with divine love is not touched by such a sermon. Such a preacher is speaking only by hearsay of the heavenly Rome, and of the roads which lead to it. He knows only what he has learned from Scripture. But if the same man hears the preaching of a master who knows both from the Scripture and through his own spiritual experience, a master who has renounced all self-love and self-advantage, who knows the heavenly Rome, not only by hearsay, but because he has travelled the road to it, and because he has seen the form of its buildings, he rejoices to hear his message, because it proceeds from the Divine Love itself.[10]

Here is the central idea of the Friends of God: the superiority of actual mystical experience over mere head-knowledge. The idea is worked out at length in the *Book of the Master of Holy*

Scripture, in which 'a great doctor, a master of Holy Scripture' is instructed by a layman – the 'Friend of God from the Oberland' – to distinguish between the knowledge of the intellect and the illumination that comes from first-hand spiritual experience. The ideal Friend of God is drawn in the apocalyptic *Book of the Nine Rocks.* In this the writer describes how a man who beholds the Divine Origin 'loses his own name and no longer bears an earthly name. He has now become God by grace, as God is God by nature!' The author himself is granted a vision of the Divine Origin, after which he hears a voice speaking to him: 'Thou hast been in the upper school where the Holy Spirit teaches directly within the man himself. This august Master of the school has taken thy soul and filled it with such an overflowing love that it has flooded even thy body and transfigured it.'

What is the modern reader to make of mystical experience on the scale described in the Friends of God literature? Is it not the result of extreme morbidity, a classic instance of self-delusion on a grand and tragic scale? Take the case of Ellina of Crevelsheim, described by Rufus Jones. Ellina, in an ecstasy of God's love, remained seven years without uttering a word:

> At the end of this period God touched her with His hand, so that she fell into an ecstasy which lasted five days, and in this ecstasy the pure truth was revealed to her, and she was given the privilege of entering the holy interior of the Father's heart. She was raised to an experience of God and the Supreme Unity; she was bound with the chains of love; enveloped in light; filled with peace and joy; her soul carried above all earthly sufferings; and she attained a complete submission to the will of Christ, whatever it might be.[11]

But against the violent, calamitous and superstitious age in which they lived, the Friends of God stand out less as misdirected psychotics than representatives of the ancient Christian tradition of unconscious holiness – the humble seeking out of God through the forgetfulness of self. They had their share of those for whom the unhealthy side effects of renunciation became predominant; but there were many others who acquired genuine saintliness. The great preacher Johann Tauler described one such: 'One day the Lord offered to kiss a Friend of God with a kiss of divine love. The Friend replied: "I do not want to have it, for the joy would flood my heart so that I should lose consciousness, and then I could no longer serve thee!"'[12]

The *Theologia Germanica*

The spiritual teaching of the Friends of God movement is crystallized in the small anonymous book known as the *Theologia Germanica*, written during the latter half of the fourteenth century. It has become one of the classic books of Western mystical literature: W. R. Inge even considered it in some ways superior to the *Imitation of Christ* by Thomas à Kempis (see page 122).

The *Theologia* has a preface containing a few details about the anonymous author:

> This little book hath the Almighty and Eternal God spoken by the mouth of a wise, understanding, faithful, righteous man, His Friend, who aforetime was of the Teutonic Order* . . . in Frankfort; and it giveth much precious insight into divine truth, and especially teaching how and whereby we may discern the true and upright Friends of God from those unrighteous and false free-thinkers, who are most hurtful to the holy Church.[13]

The influence of Meister Eckhart is apparent throughout the *Theologia*, which also reflects the fundamental spirit outlook of the *Gottesfreunde*. At its heart is the central conception that differentiated temporality – the world and characteristics of the creature – must be transcended in order for the soul to know Divine Reality: this process can be reduced to the absolute negation of the selfhood. So long as a man takes account of anything that is 'this or that'; so long as he frames a purpose for his own likings, desires, opinions or ends he will fail to come 'unto the life of Christ'.

> So long as a man seeketh his own will and his own highest good, because it is his and for his own sake, he will never find it. For so long as he doeth this, he is seeking himself and dreameth that he is himself the highest Good. But whoever seeketh, loveth, and pursueth Goodness (*i.e.* the Good *per se*), and for the sake of Goodness, and maketh *that* his end, for nothing but the love of Goodness: not for the love of I, me, mine, self, and the like, he will find the highest Good, for he seeketh it aright.

*The Teutonic Order was made up of knights, priests and lay brothers. It was originally founded as a nursing community in 1190, but in 1198 it was converted into a military order following the Rule of the Templars. It received its own Rule in 1245.

The motivating force that allows the soul to escape from the chains of selfhood is a combination of will and desire: 'He who is made a partaker of the Divine Nature neither willeth, desireth nor seeketh anything save Goodness as Goodness for the sake of Goodness . . . where this Light is, the man's end and aim is not this or that, Me or Thee, or the like, but only the One, Who is neither I nor Thou, this nor that, but is above all I and Thou, this and that; and in Him all goodness is loved as one Good.'[14] Self-will is the prime evil, the drive that prevents the soul's journey towards God: 'If there were no self-will there would be no devil and no hell; and by self-will we mean willing otherwise than as the One and Eternal Will of God willeth.'

Like all the Friends of God, the author of the *Theologia* lays stress on the primacy of first-hand experience. He says:

> Although it be good and profitable that we should ask and learn and know what good and holy men have wrought and suffered, and how God hath dealt with them, and what He hath done in and through them, yet it is a thousand times better that we should in ourselves learn and perceive and understand who we are, how and what our life is, what God is and is doing in us, what He will have from us, and to what ends He will or will not use us.

The *Theologia* can be criticized for advocating a negative quietism, which follows on from the author's conception of the Perfect One as a Being without attributes or distinctions: 'To God, as Godhead, appertains neither will, nor knowledge, nor manifestation, nor anything that we can name, or say, or conceive.' And yet the author goes on to affirm the necessity of the creature operating in a world of differentiated phenomena:

> But to God as God (that is as a person) it belongeth to express Himself, and know and love Himself, and to reveal Himself to Himself; and all this without any creature. And all this resteth in God as a substance but not as a working, so long as there is no creature. And out of this expressing and revealing of Himself unto Himself, ariseth the distinction of Persons. But when God as God is made man, or where God dwelleth in a godly man, or one who is 'made a partaker of the divine nature', in such a man somewhat appertaineth unto God which is His own, and belongeth to Him only and not to the creature. And without the creature, this would lie in His own Self as a Substance or well-spring, but would not be manifested or wrought out into deeds. Now God will have it to be exercised and clothed in a

form, for it is there only to be wrought out and executed. What else is it for? Shall it lie idle? What then would it profit? As good were it that it had never been; nay better, for what is of no use existeth in vain, and that is abhorred by God and Nature. However, God will have it wrought out, and this cannot come to pass (which it ought to do) without the creature. Nay, if there ought not to be, and were not this and that – works, and a world full of real things, and the like – what were God Himself, and what had He to do, and whose God would He be?[15]

Johann Tauler

Tauler (*c.*1300–1361) was commonly regarded as the greatest figure in the Friends of God movement and was certainly its most inspiring preacher. He was born in Strasbourg and as a young man entered the Dominican Order. By the time he was ordained priest he had come under the influence of Meister Eckhart and was also deeply read in the writings of the Christian mystical tradition.

Tauler continually urged the encouragement of spiritual religion and proclaimed the superiority of inward experience over the mere knowledge of externals: 'Great doctors of Paris read ponderous books and turn over many pages,' he said. 'The Friends of God read the living Book where everything is life.' He also naturally insisted on the existence of the Inner Light, the inward, divine knowledge that illuminates the Friend of God and raises him into union with God. When God illuminates His true Friends in this way they are suffused with such power, purity and truth that they become 'divine and supernatural persons'. They are given 'all truth [*alle warheit*] – a wonderful discernment, more perfect than can be gained in any other manner here below'. In one short hour, he says, 'you can learn more from the inward voice than you could learn from a man in a thousand years'.

Though Tauler generally speaks of the spiritual gifts of the illumined few, he does, like Eckhart, refer to the 'uncreated ground of the soul' in all men – the particle of God that lodges in us all: 'As a sculptor is said to have exclaimed on seeing a rude block of marble, "What a godlike beauty thou hidest!" so God looks upon man in whom His image is hidden.' The 'outward man' must be converted into the 'inward' man in order to make the 'Divine soul centre' operative: the two are gathered up into the very centre of the mystic's being, 'where the image of God dwelleth – and thus he [the mystic] flings himself into the Divine

Abyss in which he dwelt eternally before he was created; then when God finds the man thus solidly grounded and turned towards Him, the Godhead bends and nakedly descends into the depths of the pure, waiting soul, drawing it up into the uncreated essence, so that the spirit becomes one with Him.'[16]

The terms here are pure Eckhart; and Tauler follows his mystical and philosophical master in describing God in negative terms:

> God is a pure Being, a waste of calm seclusion – as Isaiah says, He is a hidden God – He is much nearer than anything is to itself in the depth of the heart, but He is hidden from all our senses. He is far above every outward thing and every thought, and is found only where thou hidest thyself in the secret place of thy heart, in the quiet solitude where no word is spoken, where is neither creature nor image nor fancy. This is the quiet Desert of the Godhead, the Divine Darkness – dark from His own surpassing brightness, as the shining of the sun is darkness to weak eyes, for in the presence of its brightness our eyes are like the eyes of the swallow in the bright sunlight – this Abyss is our salvation![17]

And yet, as this passage shows, Tauler's use of lofty abstractions co-existed with a homely, pastoral sensibility – 'our eyes are like the eyes of the swallow in the bright sunlight'. Throughout his sermons the imagery encompasses the ordinary experiences of everyday life and the most profound metaphysical metaphors.

For those who were able, Tauler put forward a severe regime of self-renunciation as a way of confronting the divine ground within. This required that the mind should be emptied of and untroubled by all things: the true Friend of God was marked by a 'consuming thirst' for suffering: 'That a man should have a life of quiet or rest in God is good; that a man should lead a painful life in patience is better; but that a man should have rest in a painful life is best of all!'[18]

The way to God for Tauler – very much a *via negativa* – is a threefold way of self-dying. The first stage is practised by those who act in fear of hell and who hope for a place in heaven through mortification. The second stage involves those who endure with patience, humility and fortitude all spiritual and physical deprivations with no thought of self. The third stage is complete harmonization of the human will with God's – the supreme joy of having the will overwhelmed so that the soul can will nothing on its own account.

The Friend of God must rid himself of everything that pertains to the creature: his motivation must be solely directed towards the eternal origin of what he truly is. 'We shall never find God anywhere so perfectly, so fruitfully, and so truly', says Tauler, reiterating the impulsion felt by the Desert Fathers, 'as in retirement and in the wilderness.' Using Eckhart's image of the temple, he describes how all 'traders' must be driven out of the soul – all self-enhancing pleasures, imaginings and needs: everything, that is, that keeps God from dwelling in His house.

And yet Tauler balances this process of negation by a strong affirmative spirituality and he maintained that works of love were more acceptable to God than contemplation. 'Spiritual enjoyments are the food of the soul, but they are to be taken only for nourishment and support to help us in our active work.' This emphasis on translating experience into action gives life to Tauler's scholastic speculations and makes him one of the more approachable of the *Gottesfreunde* mystics. 'One man can spin,' he says in a famous passage that expresses the humility of the authentic mystic, 'another can make shoes, and all these are gifts of the Holy Ghost. I tell you, if I were not a priest, I should esteem it a great gift that I was able to make shoes, and I would try to make them so well as to be a pattern to all.'

Henry Suso

Heinrich or Henry Suso (*c.*1295–1366), like Tauler, was another member of the *Gottesfreunde* who fell deeply under the influence of Meister Eckhart and like Eckhart he acted as spiritual director in several women's convents. He was born into a noble Swabian family, of a thoroughly worldly father who cared little for spiritual matters and a devout mother. One of Suso's earliest psychic experiences occurred when his mother died: she appeared to him and told him to love God; she then kissed him, blessed him, and vanished. When Suso was thirteen he entered a Dominican house at Constance and five years later he underwent a spiritual awakening: the 'hidden drawing of God', he says, 'turned him away from creatures and called him to the inward hidden life'.

The period that followed was one of intense inner loneliness and spiritual sorrow punctuated by visions and the occasional 'sweet taste of heaven'. In the *Life of the Blessed Henry Suso*, written by himself, he describes one of these ecstatic visions:

He was alone after his midday meal, undergoing a severe suffering. Of a sudden he saw and heard what no tongue can express. What he saw was without definite form or shape, and yet had in itself the beauty of all forms and all shapes. It was at once the climax of his desires and the realisation of his hopes, in a forgetfulness of everything and of self in a blessed state. He felt the sweetness of eternal life in calm and silence. This experience lasted an hour or less, and when he came to himself again he felt that he had come back from another world, and he was still full of divine joy, and felt himself as if he were soaring in the air.[19]

About the year 1320 Suso went to Cologne and completed his studies under the tutelage of Meister Eckhart, whose speculations form the basis of Suso's *Book of Eternal Wisdom*. Like Eckhart, Suso identified ultimate reality as 'the eternal, uncreated truth', in which all things have their source and eternal beginning. Indeed Suso even goes beyond Eckhart in the way he describes ultimate divine and human oneness – a state in which 'something and nothing are the same'.

Like a being which loses itself in an indescribable intoxication, the spirit ceases to be itself, divests itself of itself, passes into God, and becomes wholly one with Him, as a drop of water mingled with a cask of wine. As the drop of water loses its identity, and takes on the taste and colour of wine, so it is with those who are in full possession of bliss; human desires influence them no longer; divested of self they are absorbed in the Divine Will, mingle with the Divine Nature, and become one with it.

The image of the water drop and the wine is taken from St Bernard of Clairvaux (see p. 84), and in spite of the denial of individuality implicit in Suso's extreme concept of mystical absorption in the Godhead he never went so far as to say that the personal 'I' was ever destroyed in what he called the theopathic state: there is simply no personal consciousness of it.

At the same time as Suso indulged in chilly and barren speculations – which represent the negative influence of Eckhart – he constantly expressed a passionate, sensual and poetic view of mystical experience. He speaks of Eternal Wisdom, for example, as 'a gentle loving Mistress' and addresses God in this aspect almost in the language of courtly love:

Thus it grew into a habit with him, whenever he heard songs of praise, or the sweet music of stringed instruments, or lays, or discourse about earthly love, immediately to turn his heart and mind inwards, and gaze abstractedly upon his loveliest Love, whence all love flows. It were impossible to tell how often with weeping eyes, from out the unfathomable depth of his outspread heart, he embraced this lovely form, and pressed it tenderly to his heart. And thus it fared with him as with a sucking child, which lies encircled by its mother's arms upon her breast. As the child with its head and the movement of its body lifts itself up against its tender mother, and by these loving gestures testifies its heart's delight, even so his heart many a time leapt up within his body towards the delightful presence of the Eternal Wisdom, and melted away in sensible affections.[20]

In this, as Evelyn Underhill recognized, one senses Suso's 'starved human affections seeking an outlet'.[21] He also practised the most extraordinary austerities: in the extremity of his self-mortification, indeed, he stands almost in a class by himself. His quite appalling asceticism was undertaken in imitation of Christ's suffering and because, as he said, he wished to conquer his 'lively nature'. He strove with unbelievable ferocity and determination to subdue and mortify his 'comfort-seeking body'. The following passage is from his autobiography, which is written throughout in the third person:

He wore for a long time a hair shirt and an iron chain, until the blood ran from him, so that he was obliged to leave them off. He secretly caused an under-garment to be made for him, and in the under-garment he had strips of leather fixed, into which a hundred and fifty brass nails, pointed and filed sharp, were driven, and the points of the nails were always turned towards the flesh. He had this garment made very tight, and so arranged to go round him and fasten in front, in order that it might fit closer to his body, and the pointed nails be driven into his flesh; and it was high enough to reach upwards to his navel. In this he used to sleep at night.

Now in summer, when it was hot, and he was very tired and ill from his journeyings . . . he would sometimes, as he lay thus in bonds, and oppressed with toil, and tormented also by noxious insects, cry aloud and give way to fretfulness, and twist round and round in agony, as a worm does when run through with a pointed needle . . . The nights in winter were never so long, nor was the summer so hot, as to make him leave off this exercise. On the contrary, he devised something further – two leathern hoops into which he put his hands, and fastened one on each side of this throat . . . This he continued until his hands and arms had become almost tremulous with the strain, and then he devised something else: two leather gloves, and he caused a brazier to fit them all over with sharp-pointed brass tacks, and he used to put them on at night, in order that if he should try while asleep to throw off the hair under-garment, or relieve himself from the gnawings of the vile insects, the tacks might then stick into his body. And so it came to pass. If ever he sought to help himself with his hands in his sleep, he drove the sharp tacks into his breast, and tore himself, so that his flesh festered. When, after many weeks, the wounds had healed, he tore himself again and made fresh wounds.[22]

These self-inflicted torments continued for an incredible sixteen years, until, one Whit Sunday, a 'messenger from heaven' told Suso that God required such acts of mortification from him no longer. But, driven to imitate the sufferings of the crucified Christ, Suso then made himself a cross out of which protruded thirty iron nails and needles, which he bore on his back both day and night: 'It made his back, where the bones are, bloody and seared. Whenever he sat down or stood up, it was if a hedgehog skin were on him. If anyone touched him unawares, or pushed against his clothes, it tore him.' The Servitor of Eternal Wisdom, as Suso called himself, also scoured himself mercilessly.

In winter he suffered very much from the frost. If he stretched out his feet they lay bare on the floor and froze; if he gathered them up the blood became all on fire in his legs, and this was great pain. His feet were full of sores, his legs dropsical, his knees bloody and seared, his loins covered with scars from the horsehair, his body wasted, his mouth parched with intense thirst, and his hands tremulous from weakness. Amid these torments he spent his nights and days; and he endured them all out of the greatness of the love which he bore in his heart to the Divine and Eternal Wisdom, our Lord Jesus Christ, whose agonizing sufferings he ought to imitate.

The visions Suso experienced included the Virgin Mary, the celestial landscape, his own soul 'lying entranced and drowned in the arms of the God he loved' or spiritually espoused to Eternal Wisdom, his heavenly bride; on one occasion he was given the Holy Child to hold by the Virgin: 'He contemplated its beautiful little eyes, he kissed its tender little mouth, and gazed again and again at the infant members of the heavenly treasure.'
After some twenty years of savage asceticism Suso abandoned these practices, having come to the realization that they were

'nothing more than a good beginning' and that he was still far from 'the highest knowledge'. There followed a long period of spiritual desolation, during which he suffered from the fear of being damned and from the obloquy of friends and enemies alike. Eventually, after some years, he received the call to 'go forth to his neighbour'.

One of those to whom he now gave spiritual instruction and comfort was a Swiss nun, Elizabeth Stäglin, to whom Suso wrote that 'True bliss lies not in beautiful words but good works': 'Seek not', he counselled, 'to imitate the severe exercises of thy spiritual father . . . God has many kinds of crosses with which He chastens his friends.' And in answer to Elizabeth's plea to be told more of what God is, Suso discards all abstract concepts, puts behind him the long years of bloody torment and replies to his pupil's wishes with one of the most passionate and beautiful paeans in all Christian mystical literature:

Ah, gentle God, if Thou art so lovely in Thy creatures, how exceedingly beautiful and ravishing Thou must be in Thyself! But look again, I pray thee, and behold the four elements – earth, water, air, and fire, with all the wondrous things which they contain in manifold variety . . . and mark how they all cry aloud together. Praise and honour be to the unfathomable immensity that is in Thee! Who is it, Lord, that sustains all this? Who feeds it all? It is Thou who providest for all, each in its own way; for great and small, for rich and poor. It is Thou, O God, who doest this. Thou, O God, art God indeed!

Come, daughter, thou hast now found thy God, whom thy heart has so long sought after. Look upwards, then, with sparkling eyes and radiant face and bounding heart, and behold Him and embrace Him with the infinite outstretched arms of thy soul and thy affection, and give thanks and praise to Him, the noble Prince of all creatures. See how, by gazing on this mirror, there springs up speedily, in a soul susceptible of such impressions, an intense inward jubilee; for by jubilee is meant a joy which no tongue can tell, but which pours itself with might through heart and soul.[23]

John Ruysbroeck

The Blessed John Ruysbroeck (1293–1381) was an intimate friend of both Tauler and Suso. He was born in Brabant in the Low Countries, the son, it would seem, of simple village folk. He was not, apparently, university trained but took priest's orders when he was twenty-four. For nearly twenty-five years he was attached to the collegiate church of St Gudule in Brussels, but in 1343 he retired to Groenendael in the forest of Soignes with two companions. In 1349 the group became a community of Augustinian canons and it was at Groenendael that Ruysbroeck wrote his principal mystical works.

Some of Ruysbroeck's admirers were to exaggerate his lack of a formal education and he was often portrayed as a 'simple and unlettered man'. Denis the Carthusian said of him: 'He had no teacher but the Holy Ghost. He was ignorant and illiterate. Peter and John were the same. His authority I believe to be that of a man to whom the Holy Ghost has revealed secrets.' Though Ruysbroeck himself maintained that everything he wrote had been directly impelled by the Holy Ghost, he was certainly no illiterate rustic. He knew the masters of Latin mystical theology, including St Augustine, the Pseudo-Dionysius and Aquinas, and indeed needed Latin to become a priest. He was soaked, also, in vernacular mystical literature – for example the letters of Hadewijch of Antwerp and the writings of Gerard Appleman.

Ruysbroeck, in fact, was a man of great intellectual energy and subtlety and was perfectly at home in the didactic presentation of mystical speculation. He was also a firm Churchman, denouncing false doctrine and developing his personal relationship with God within the sacramental corporation of the Catholic Church, to whose ordinances he urged constant fidelity. He saw the spiritual life in terms of a graduated procession, in the context of orthodoxy, towards 'that wayless being which all interior spirits have chosen above all other things'. One of his great themes is 'deification', which stands in distinct contrast to the false illuminism of many of the Free Spirit heretics, one of whose number – a woman caled Bloemardinne – Ruysbroeck preached against. In every soul, he taught, the eternal image of God dwells as its root and essence. 'Flying from brightness to brightness,' he writes, 'the spirit aspires with outstretched arms to reach this immortal pattern according to which it was created.' The source of Ruysbroeck's mystical doctrine is the fact – for so it is to the Christian understanding – that God made man in His own image:

> Holy Scripture teaches that God, the heavenly Father, created all men in His image and in His likeness. His image is His Son, His own eternal Wisdom, and St John says that in this all things have life. And the life is nothing else than the image of God, in which God has

everlastingly begotten things, and which is the cause of all creatures. And so this image, which is the Son of God, is eternal, before all creation; and we are all made in this eternal image, for in the noblest part of our souls, that is, in the properties of our highest powers, we are made as a living, eternal mirror of God, in which God has impressed His eternal image, and into which no other image can ever enter.[24]

Ruysbroeck clearly distinguished between unity with God through love and the false notions of unity in nature professed by some Free Spirit heretics. He counselled aloofness from the empty ignorance of those who were 'so deceived that crassly and foolishly they believe that out of their own natures they have found within themselves the indwelling of God, and who wish to be one with God without His grace and without the exercise of virtue'. God's being, he resolutely insisted, is uncreated; our being is created: 'God and the creature are immeasurably unlike; and therefore, though they may be united, they cannot become one.' In the *Book of the Sparkling Stone* he defines 'the nobility of our nature now and everlastingly, that is impossible for us to become God and lose our created essence'; and yet we can be so overwhelmed in the love of God that we are united with Him.

The image of the Trinity permeates Ruysbroeck's mystical thought. In God Himself there is a trinity beyond the Persons: there is the divine essence, the Godhead, which is 'simple' and 'without manner' ('simple' in this sense conveys the idea of completeness, a total synthesis); then there is the divine nature and then the Persons. Man, too, has a threefold nature: he is the 'created trinity' consisting of the 'in-forming' *anima* or spirit; the *animus*, reason; and the essential nature of the soul. There are three stages to the spiritual ladder by which the created spirit ascends to the uncreated God. The first stage is the active life, which involves rectitude, self-denial, service to others and duty to the Church.

The second stage is the inward life, when good works are carried out from sheer love – when, that is, the heart conforms precisely to God's loving purposes: 'The pure soul', says Ruysbroeck, 'feels a constant fire of love, which desires above all things to be one with God, and the more the soul obeys the attraction of God the more it feels it, and more it feels it the more it desires to be one with God.'[25] The inward life is characterized by selflessness and spontaneity, 'when Christ the Eternal Son rises in our hearts and sends His Light and fire into our wills, and draws the heart from the multitude of "things', and creates unity and close fellowship, and makes the heart grow and become green through inward love, and bear flowing of loving devotion.'[26]

The third and final stage is the contemplative life, attained by only a few, and even for them the experience is momentary. For the briefest of instants they fully *know* God by *seeing* Him: 'It is as when you stand in the dazzling radiance of the sun, and turning away your eyes from all colour, from attending to distinguishing all the various "things" which the sun illuminates, you simply follow with your eyes the brightness of the rays, and so are led up into the sun's very essence.'[27] In seeing God, the soul becomes God: 'What we are, that we behold; and what we behold, that we are; for in this pure vision we are one life and one spirit with God.'[28] As noted in Chapter 1, Ruysbroeck never taught the annihilation of the self even at this level of mystical experience: the soul's identity is never lost, and God remains God. This obviates all charges of pantheism and quietism in Ruysbroeck's teaching, for it means that the creature man will always stand in need of grace; that he can never be fully like God in this life; for even at the highest levels of the spiritual life the soul still thirsts for God, a sensation described by Ruysbroeck as

> an impatient hunger, ever striving for what it lacks, ever swimming against the stream. One cannot leave it, one cannot have it: one cannot lack it, one cannot gain it: one cannot tell it, one cannot conceal it, for it is above reason and understanding . . . but if we look deep within ourselves, there we shall feel God's Spirit driving and urging us on in the impatience of love; and if we look high above ourselves, there we shall feel God's Spirit drawing us out of ourselves and bringing us to nothing in the essence of God, that is, in the essential love in which we are one with Him, the love which we possess deeper and wider than every other thing.[29]

In Ruysbroeck the language and speculations of Meister Eckhart, and before him the Pseudo-Dionysius, are bonded to an affirmative, active vision of love. The pinnacle of the mystical life is not, in Evelyn Underhill's words, 'an achieved condition of still beatitude, a blank absorption in the Absolute': it is, in total contrast, a life of *caritas*, rich in action, yet drawing strength from profound inward repose. 'There are we emptied of ourselves and of every creature,' says Ruysbroeck of the 'superessential life', 'and made one with God in love. But between us and God this unity for ever ceaselessly renews itself; for the Spirit of God, outflowing and indrawing, touches and stirs our spirit, urging us to live according to the beloved will of God, and love Him as he deserveth . . . as God sendeth us forth, with all His gifts, to live according to His beloved will, so His Spirit draweth us within, to love Him as He deserveth.'

Gerard Groote

Gerard, or Geert de, Groote (1340–1384) was Ruysbroeck's most famous disciple and founder of the Brethren of the Common Life, an association devoted to the cultivation of the spiritual life but which demanded no vows of its members – though after Groote's death a group amongst the Brethren adopted a rule and organized themselves as Augustinian Canons.

Groote was born in Deventer, the son of wealthy parents. He received a Master's degree from the University of Paris at the age of eighteen, became a professor at Cologne and began to carve out a distinguished Church career for himself, dabbling between times in magic and astrology. Then, so tradition has it, this brilliant but worldly figure was approached one day while he was watching a public game in Cologne by a stranger, apparently a Friend of God, who asked him: 'Why standest thou here? Thou oughtest to become another man.' These words sowed a seed in Groote's mind that was nurtured by his Carthusian friend Henry de Kalkar. Eventually Groote felt the full power of spiritual awakening: 'Oh the power and grace of the ineffable Spirit, who can so easily change the heart of a man whom he inwardly visits and illumines! This is the mighty power of God alone. He has turned the lion into a lamb, predestinating him who was before in the world to be incorporated into Himself.'

After a preparatory period, during which he drew deeply on the influence of Ruysbroeck, he embarked, in 1379, on an evangelizing mission and was granted a permit to preach in the diocese of Utrecht. Like St Francis his power and fire as a preacher came from his simplicity and the directness of his message, which derived from a deep personal knowledge and experience and not from abstract speculation. An epitaph, recorded by Thomas à Kempis, described Groote thus: 'He did what he said, and what he taught *that* he also lived.'

He preached with zeal against the decadence of the Church, the ruin of which, he said, had been a long time threatened; he openly castigated 'the cupidity and luxury of the ecclesiastics' and prayed 'that a veritable Eliakim would descend upon the earth to establish peace, if only he be not of this race of vipers'.[30] It was not surprising that his preaching permit was revoked; but though Groote gave up peripatetic evangelizing he continued to exert a powerful influence on the spirtual life of his times through the formation of a new brotherhood – the Brethren of the Common Life, or, as its members called the movement, the 'New Devotion'.

It was Groote's friend Florentius Radewyn who suggested that the members should live in common and the first community was set up at Deventer, led by Florentius. Soon brother- and sister-houses were set up throughout Holland and Germany: 'The members took no permanent vows, they mingled freely in the world for purposes of service, and lived from their manual labour without any resort to begging. They wore a simple grey garb, and followed a very simple manner of life – it was an effort to make daily life spiritual.'[31]

Groote's emphasis was on the experience of religion, on living out as completely as possible the implications of the spiritual life. 'The Holy Spirit', he said, 'inwardly visits, illumines, and changes the heart of a man'; and with that change of heart must come a change of life, in which the experience of Christ is relived at every moment. Groote died of the plague with the plans for another brotherhood, to be composed of those who wished to devote themselves completely to the service of God, unrealized. His friend Florentius, however, who was Groote's legitimate spiritual successor, continued the master's work and the new order of Augustinian Canons Regular was founded at Windesheim. There was another monastery at Mount St Agnes, which is forever associated with the order's greatest member – Thomas à Kempis.

Thomas à Kempis

Thomas Haemerken (1380–1471) was born at Kempen near Düsseldorf of humble parents. At the age of thirteen, after being educated at Kempen Grammar School, Thomas went to Deventer, where his elder brother John was a member of the Brethren of the Common Life. At Deventer Thomas was guided by Florentius Radewyn and in 1399 entered the monastery of

Mount St Agnes (Agnetenburg), where his brother John was now Prior. He became a priest in 1413, at the age of thirty-five.

Much of his time was spent copying scriptural and devotional texts, and Thomas was also a prolific author in his own right. His books included *Prayers and Meditations on the Life of Christ, The Elevation of the Mind, The Soliloquy of the Soul, On Solitude and Silence, On the Discipline of the Cloister*, and of course the *Imitation of Christ*. In addition he wrote biographies of both Florentius Radewyn and Gerard Groote. In 1425 he became Sub-Prior of Mount St Agnes and was Master of Novices and Chronicler. His successor in the last named post, John Busch, wrote of him after his death at the age of ninety-two: 'He copied out our Bible and various other books . . . Further, for the instruction of the young, he wrote various little treatises in a plain and simple style, which in reality were great and important works, both in doctrine and efficacy for good. He had an especial devotion to the Passion of Our Lord, and understood admirably how to comfort those afflicted by interior trials and temptations. Finally, having reached a ripe old age, he was afflicted with dropsy of the limbs, slept in the Lord in the year 1471, and was buried in the east side of the cloister*. . . .'[32]

The community at Mount St Agnes was composed of a small group of men 'who thought only of Christ and strove to imitate Him; whose sins were minute fallings away from their ideal of the Man of Nazareth – sins wept over and watched; whose hope lay on the other side of the grave that offered them no terror; whose faith came so near to the faith of the first Christians that the days of Christ seemed to have returned':

> The rule of the Community inculcated the fundamental law of love towards God and man; the lessons of humility as taught by Christ; the preparation of body and soul for orderly prayer, by proper and simple attention to both body and mind. Nothing in excess was the ideal of the Community. The body was to be made absolutely efficient for the purposes of the soul, and the duty of man to his neighbour was to shadow forth the duty of man to his God. Perfect simplicity in dress and manners, food and drink, work and play, was the ideal for the body; perfect charity to all men, to the young, to the sick, to the sinful, was the ideal for the mind; and the love of God which passeth all understanding was the ideal for the soul.[33]

---

*The monastery of Mount St Agnes was destroyed in 1573. The remains of St Thomas were discovered a century later and reburied in the Church of St Michael in Zwolle.

It was in this atmosphere that Thomas wrote one of the greatest and most enduring classics of Christian devotional literature – the *Imitatio Christi*: the *Imitation of Christ*. One of the most eloquent testimonies to its inspirational power is to be found in a most unlikely context – George Eliot's *The Mill on the Floss*:

> This small, old-fashioned book, for which you need pay only sixpence at a bookstall, works miracles to this day, turning bitter waters into sweetness; while expensive sermons and treatises, newly issued, leave all things as they were before. It was written down by a hand that waited for the heart's prompting; it is the chronicle of a solitary, hidden anguish, struggle, trust and triumph – not written on velvet cushions to teach endurance to those who are treading with bleeding feet on the stones. And so it remains to all time a lasting record of human needs and human consolations; the voice of a brother who, ages ago, felt, suffered and renounced . . . with a fashion of speech different from ours, but under the same silent, far-off heavens, the same strivings, the same failures, the same weariness.[34]

There has been much scholarly dispute as to the authorship of the *Imitation of Christ*: Jean Gerson and Walter Hilton have been put forward as possible authors, though the arguments in favour of Thomas à Kempis are really unanswerable.* But as Leo Sherley-Price rightly remarks: 'The importance and value of this golden book in no way depend on its authorship, but on its contents, since no other book of Christian devotion has ever exercised such unbroken and world-wide influence for good as the *Imitation*.'[35] The importance of the *Imitation* is that, in the words of Rufus Jones, 'it took men away from creeds and systems to the eternal idea of Christianity'.

The *Imitation* is in four books: Counsels on the Spiritual Life; On the Inner Life; On Inward Consolation; and On the Blessed Sacrament. The aim throughout is to show the divine Logos – Jesus, the Incarnate Word – as the source of all truth: Christ is both the pattern and inspiration of the spiritual life, which is illuminated by the Light of Truth and the Life of Grace: 'Following in the footsteps of Christ, heeding His words, living in intimate union with Him, loving Him with a love that counts no sacrifice too great, trampling underfoot all things displeasing to

*Other putative authors include St Bernard of Clairvaux, St Bonaventura, Landolph of Saxony and Gerard Groote.

Him, bearing one's burden cheerfully for His sake – such is the life of the soul as revealed in this wonderful book.'[36]

But the singlemindedness required for such a life carries with it the ever-present danger of extreme negativity. Throughout the *Imitation* the world of finite things is undervalued, sometimes to the point of complete negation:

> Who is more perfectly at rest than the man of single purpose? Who more free than he who desires nothing upon earth? Rapt in spirit, a man must rise above all created things, and perfectly forsaking himself, see clearly that nothing in creation can compare with the Creator. But unless a man is freed from dependence on creatures, he cannot turn freely to the things of God. This is the reason why there are so few contemplatives, for there are few who can free themselves entirely from transitory things.[37]

A soul, Thomas continues, needs grace to be carried beyond itself.

> Yet, unless a man's soul is raised, set free from all attachment to earthly things, and wholly united to God, neither his knowledge nor his possessions are of any value. So long as he esteems as precious anything outside the One, Infinite, and Eternal Good, he will remain mean and earthbound in spirit. For whatever is not God is nothing, and is to be accounted nothing. There is a great difference between the wisdom of a devout man enlightened by God, and the knowledge of a learned and studious scholar. More noble by far is the learning infused from above by divine grace, than that painfully acquired by the industry of man.[38]

There is, then, in the *Imitation* a dualistic tendency that insists on a total contrast between the things of this world and the life of the spirit in God; that negates every aspect of earthly experience; that views the finite as worthless. This dualism 'turns the gaze away from the very stuff out of which moral and spiritual fibre is to be woven. It is an attempt to climb up by first destroying the ladder which has been given to us.'[39] From one point of view, forcefully expressed by Thackeray, the scheme presented by the *Imitation*, if carried out, 'would make the world the most wretched, useless, dreary, doting place of sojourn. There would be no manhood, no love, no tender ties of mother and child, no use of intellect, no trade of science – a set of selfish beings, crawling about, avoiding one another, and howling a perpetual Misere!'

And yet the *Imitation* is not in its cumulative effect a work of negative mysticism: it is suffused with the positive affirmation of spiritual reality and love. It is a matter of finding the soul's true centre. As Thomas has Christ say in regard to the Saints: 'All are one in the bond of charity; their thoughts and aspirations are one, and all love each other as one.'

> But this is higher still, that they love Me more than themselves and their own merits. Caught up out of themselves, and carried beyond love of self, they are wholly engaged in loving me, in whom they rest in peace and joy. Nothing can distract or dismay them, for they are full of the eternal Truth, and burn with the fire of unquenchable charity.[40]

It is more than a change of mind, it is a change of heart and self that is required in order to become inwardly united with God through Christ. To tread this path is to assume total humility:

> CHRIST. My son, whoever strives to withdraw from obedience, withdraws from grace ... There is no enemy more wicked or troublesome to the soul than yourself, when you are not in harmony with the Spirit ... Is it so hard for you, who are dust and nothingness, to subject yourself to man for God's sake, when I, the Almighty and most high, who created all things from nothing, humbly subjected Myself to man for your sake? I became the humblest and least of all men, that you might overcome your pride through My humility. Learn to obey, you who are but dust; learn to humble yourself, earth and clay, and to bow yourself beneath the feet of all. Learn to curb your desires, and yield yourself to complete obedience.[41]

Catherine of Siena

In Thomas à Kempis medieval mysticism shakes off the potentially deadening burden of scholastic speculation. There is in Thomas a fundamental awareness of social responsibility, no matter if this may be overlaid with an occasional tendency to quietism. Though Thomas' is still a mysticism of the cloister it is motivated by a consciousness of spiritual community; gone are the abstractions of the Pseudo-Dionysius and his heirs: 'He does well', said Thomas, 'who serves the community before his own interests.' Through the imitation of Christ, Thomas à Kempis and those like him were seeking to revitalize the spiritual life of the Church by reaffirming the principles of primitive Christianity, the spirituality of which stood in stark contrast to the degeneracy and corruption of the medieval Church.

St Catherine of Siena (1347–1380), who died in the year à Kempis was born, was also part of this movement. She had been born, in Evelyn Underhill's words, 'at a time of almost unequalled ecclesiastical degredation'. Catherine was the youngest of the twenty-five children of Jacopo Benincasa, a prosperous house-holder of Siena. At the age of six she longed to imitate the austerities of the Desert Fathers; she took a vow of virginity when she was seven; and at the age of fourteen she became a Dominican Tertiary and dedicated her life to God. Even at this age she experienced visions, ecstasies and struggles with 'evil spirits'; but she quickly moved through these subjective experiences towards an affirmative, altruistic spirituality.

The culmination of these early experiences was her 'Mystical Marriage with Christ' in 1366, which had the effect of helping to make her see the need to go out into the world and serve her neighbour, not for her own profit but from pure love. In her own famous words, when she spoke of God's love for man: 'For nails would not have held the God-man fast to the cross had not love held Him there.' She devoted herself to the sick and the poor of Siena, following in every detail of her life her maxim that 'there is no perfect virtue – none that bears fruit – unless it is exercised by means of our neighbour'.

Catherine exhibited astonishing spiritual and intellectual maturity and became for her followers, though still a young girl, 'our Holy Mother'; and she was, evidently, as charming as her personality was compelling. She remained cheerful in spite of frequent illness – the result of the austerities she had practised – and her visions continued. In 1370 she fell into a mystical trance lasting four hours, during which time she was supposed dead by her companions. She maintained that her soul did indeed leave her body but that it was called upon to return from eternal life in order to minister to the souls of others:

Because my soul shrank with horror from this return, the Lord said to me, 'The salvation of many souls demands thy return, and thou shalt no more live as thou hast lived hitherto, nor have henceforth thy cell for habitation, but shalt go out from thine own city for the good of souls. I shall be ever with thee, and shall guide thee and bring thee back. Thou shalt bear the honour of My name and witness to spiritual things before small and great, layfolk, clergy and religious; and I shall give thee words and wisdom none shall be able to withstand.[42]

This experience, at the age of twenty-three, was the start of Catherine's public ministry, which was to continue for only ten years more, until her death in 1380. Before her always was the idea of the Church – the kingdom of God on earth. Sustained constantly by this spiritual vision, she also learned to address herself to political realities, so that she was able to write in the following terms to the Papal Legate:

When I told you that you should toil for Holy Church I was not thinking only of the labours you should assume about temporal things, but chiefly that you and the Holy Father ought to toil and do what you can to get rid of the wolfish shepherds who care for nothing but eating and fine palaces and big horses. Oh me, that which Christ won upon the wood of the Cross is spent with harlots! I beg that if you were to die for it, you tell the Holy Father to put an end to such iniquities. And when the time comes to make priests or cardinals, let them not be chosen through flatteries or moneys or simony; but beg him, as far as you can, that he notice well if virtue and a good and holy fame are found in the men.[43]

Nor did Catherine shrink from writing in forthright terms to the Pope (Gregory XI) himself: 'I hope by the goodness of God, venerable father mine, that you will quench this perverse and perilous self-love in yourself, and will not love yourself for yourself, nor your neighbour for yourself, nor God; but will love Him because He is highest and Eternal Goodness, and worthy of being loved. . . .' Her dearest hope was that the Church should return 'to her first condition, poor, humble, and meek, as she was in that holy time when men took note of nothing but the honour of God and the salvation of souls, caring for spiritual things, not for temporal.'

Like St Francis, Catherine's public ministry derived its strength and authority from the profundity of her personal spiritual experiences; and like St Francis, the psychological intensity of her experiences produced the physical imprinting of the five wounds of Christ – the stigmata:

I saw the crucified Lord coming down to me in a great light . . . Then from the marks of His most sacred wounds I saw five blood-red rays coming down upon me, which were directed towards the hands and feet and heart of my body. Wherefore, perceiving the mystery, I straightaway exclaimed, 'Ah! Lord, my God, I beseech Thee, let not the marks appear outwardly on the body.' Then, while I was speaking, before the rays reached me, they changed their blood-red colour to splendour, and in the semblance of pure light they came to the five places of my body, that is, to the hands, the feet, and the heart. So great is the pain that I endure sensibly in all those five places, but especially within my heart, that unless the Lord works a new miracle, it seems not possible to me that the life of my body can stay with such agony.[44]

Though the modern mind sees here the formidable power of auto-suggestion, the psychological effects of such a life as Catherine's are something other than the authentic note of mystical insight and knowledge that is to be found elsewhere in her writings. In her work the *Divine Dialogue*, for instance, she writes movingly of her experience of God: 'The more I enter, the more I find, and the more I find the more I seek of Thee. Thou art the Food that never satiates, for when the soul is satiated in Thine abyss it is not satiated, but ever continues to hunger and thirst for Thee.'

St Catherine of Genoa

Caterina Adorna was born in 1447 and died in 1510. Unlike her namesake, Catherine of Siena, she was an aristocrat and she did not come to mystical experience until the age of twenty-six, after her naturally melancholic temperament had been intensified by an unhappy marriage. In 1474 religious indifference was suddenly thrust aside:

Her heart was pierced by so sudden and immense a love of God, accompanied by so deep a sight of her miseries and sins and of His Goodness, that she was near falling to the ground; and in a transport of pure and all-purifying love she was drawn away from the miseries of the world.

From this point her life was transformed. Her former fastidiousness was put to the test by voluntary work amongst the sick and the poor, and she balanced a tendency towards intellectual abstraction by a rigid adherence to penitential discipline and active philanthropy. This phase of her life, which included the constant mortification of her will, severe physical austerities and much prayer, lasted until 1477, when she founded the first hospital in Genoa. Around her sprang up a devoted band of followers, in conversation with whom, between 1499 and 1507, she described her mystical experiences.

Though Catherine always displayed an intense devotion to the Eucharist, her mysticism is distinctly theocentric in character. The focus of her life was the Infinite God, not the Person of Christ, and she was at home with the soaring abstractions of Plato and the Pseudo-Dionysius. At the height of her mystical experiences her personality, she said, underwent a transmutation in which she was unable to distinguish her selfhood from God: 'My being is God,' she claimed, 'not by simple participation but by a true transformation of my being.' Her most powerful image for this absorption in the totality of God is the Ocean of His Reality: 'I am so placed and submerged in His immense love, that I seem as though immersed in the sea, and nowhere able to touch, see or feel aught but water.'

(ii) THE ENGLISH MYSTICS

In England, as on the Continent, the Christian mystical tradition produced a notable company of contemplatives – the four principal figures being Richard Rolle, the anonymous and still unknown author of *The Cloud of Unknowing*, Walter Hilton and Julian of Norwich. Perhaps it will be useful at this point to remind ourselves what contemplation meant to medieval Catholics. In its fullest sense, the term signified the highest union with God that was possible for the earthbound soul: it was transcendent prayer, culminating in the direct knowledge of God. It is beyond natural human power to achieve such a union, which is indeed, in comparison with the Beatific Vision enjoyed by the soul after death, only a partial experience: the aspiring contemplative requires the action of grace to bring him into direct contact with the Godhead. The attainment of this state of contemplation was the motive for the writings of all the major English mystics, for whom the parable of Martha and Mary (a favourite with mystical writers) provided full justification of the detachment necessary for the complete realization of the contemplative life:

> Housewifery is Martha's part. Mary's is quietness and exemption from all the disturbances of the world, so that nothing may prevent her from hearing God's voice . . . Martha has her own work; leave her alone, and sit with Mary in perfect quiet at God's feet, and listen only to Him.[45]

This quotation is from the *Ancrene Riwle* (The Anchoresses' Rule),* a treatise dating from the early thirteenth century and written by an unknown author for three well-born ladies embarking on the spiritual life. The emphasis in the *Ancrene Riwle* is predominantly on mortification, the avoidance of sin and the pursuit of virtue; but a few passages indicate that the author expected the three ladies to achieve some degree of contemplative apprehension; for instance, he says: 'After the kiss of peace in the Mass, when the priest communicates, forget the world, be completely out of the body, and with burning love embrace your Beloved who has come down from heaven to your heart's bower, and hold Him fast until he has granted you all that you ask.' Elsewhere the author, following St Augustine, maintains that the soul is God's own image and the highest thing under God: 'Dear sisters,' he counsels, 'for love of Him whom the soul resembles, treat it with honour, and do not allow the ignoble flesh to have too much sway. The soul on earth is set in a foreign country and in prison, shut in a torture-chamber. Its dignity, its high nature, is obscured. It is not seen as it will be seen in its own country . . . an anchoress . . . should be altogether spiritual, if she wants to fly well, like a bird with little flesh and many feathers.'[46]

Richard Rolle

Rolle (*c.*1300–1349) is the earliest of the great English fourteenth-century mystics. His work was widely known, but the facts of his life are rather uncertain. He was a prolific author, writing in both English and Latin (commentaries, Scriptural

---

*An anchoress, the female equivalent of an anchorite, was a religious recluse or hermit. The title *Ancren Riwle* was given to the work in 1853; this was later changed to *Ancrene Riwle* (Ancrene being the correct genitive plural), which is now the accepted title. The English MS at Corpus Christi College, Cambridge, is titled *Ancrene Wisse* (The Anchoresses' Guide).

translations, letters and lyrics), and his celebrity is attested to by the ascription to him of several Latin and English works, amongst them the genuine writings of St Anselm, St Bonaventura and St Edmund of Canterbury. He enjoyed a great reputation for sanctity and there is a liturgical office of Richard the Hermit, which was prepared for his canonization – though this never took place.*

Rolle was born at Thornton Dale, near Pickering in Yorkshire. He studied at Oxford but does not seem to have taken his Master's degree. He adopted a hermit's dress and way of life when he was about nineteen and finally settled at Hampole near Doncaster, where he became the spiritual director of Margaret de Kirkby, a nun of Hampole.

Though he left Oxford without a degree, Rolle was widely read and was at home with scholastic terminology and technicalities. He was also an accomplished poet and has an important place in the history of English prose. The distinctive feature of all his writings is their accessibility: he did not confine his words to a cloistered and learned élite but addressed himself to all who had ears to hear. The following extract from one of his English lyrics, for instance, shows the passionate simplicity of his style:

> Jesu, my saviour,
> Jesu, my comfortoure,
> Of all my fairness flowre,
> My helpe in my socoure,
> When may I see thy towre?
> When will thou me call?
> Me langes to thy hall,
> To se thee than all . . .
> Jesu, Jesu, Jesu,
> When war I to thee ledde?
> Full wele I wate
> Thou sees my state:
> In luve my thoght es stedde.[47]

> towre = tower of Heaven
> Me langes to = I long to go to
> se = see; than = then
> wate = know
> stedde = firmly fixed

*The lessons composed in anticipation of Rolle's canonization are printed as Appendix V to *The York Breviary* (Surtees Society, 75, ii, 1882) and translated by Comper in *The Fire of Love* (see Bibliography). Rolle is sometimes, erroneously, referred to in MSS as St Richard.

Rolle, however, was in every sense a solitary figure, interpreting his experiences in such a way as to convince some of his contemporaries that he was mad. His experiences were, in truth, unusual enough. His biographer and editor C. Horstman relates that Rolle was 'sitting one day in a church, rapt in meditation, when he felt in his breast a strange and pleasant heat, as of a real sensible fire, so that he kept feeling of his breast to see if the heat was caused by some exterior cause. He often *heard* heavenly music.' The descriptions of Rolle's mystical life are mostly to be found in two Latin treatises: *Melos Contemplativorum* (*c.*1330) and the *Incendium Amoris* (*c.*1340). 'Heat', 'song' and 'sweetness' are the characteristics of Rolle's mystical experiences and in the *Incendium* he describes how, after a period of moral and spiritual trial, he came to a decisive point in his spiritual development as a result of such sensations:

When I was in the sour-sweet flower of youth, and the time had come of awakening to life, the grace of my Creator came to me . . . I was sitting in a certain chapel, and while I was taking pleasure in the delight of some prayer or meditation, I suddenly felt within me an unwonted and pleasant fire. When I had for long doubted whence it came, I learned by experience that it came from the Creator and not from creature, since I found it ever more pleasing and full of heat. Now from the beginning of that fiery warmth, inestimably sweet, till the infusion of the heavenly, spiritual harmony, the song of eternal praise, and the sweetness of unheard melody, which can be heard and experienced only by one who has received it, and who must be purified and separated from the earth, nine months and some weeks passed away.

For when I was sitting in the same chapel, and was reciting psalms as well as I might before supper, I heard above me the noise of harpers, or rather of singers. And when with all my heart I attended to heavenly things in prayer, I perceived within me, I know not how, a melody and a most delightful harmony from heaven, which abode in my mind . . . Meanwhile wonder seized me that I was taken up into such joy, and that God should have given me gifts which I knew not how to ask for, nor had thought that any, even the most holy, would receive such in this life.[48]

Rolle, like many before him, insisted that what he described could not be understood by the learned, by those whose business it was to analyse and dispute; who were, as he said, 'expert in all knowledge, but inexpert in the love of Christ'. In order to attain the supreme gifts of contemplation a person must turn away from the outer world and devote himself entirely to the thought and love of God, for while the love of temporal things still holds sway in the heart the inestimable rewards of inward devotion to God are withheld. The movement inwards and Godwards involves severe discipline and the unceasing exercise of prayer and meditation, during which time the body is sustained by the barest physical necessities. 'It is well known', says Rolle, 'that contemplation is attained after much time and much labour, and not given straightway and broadcast to any who may come, for it is not within a man's power to receive it, nor does a man's toil, however long he spend, merit it, but it is given of God's goodness to His true lovers.'[49]

Thus contemplation is a gift from God; but it is also a predestined gift, according to Rolle: 'As in the house of God there are many mansions, and as in our fatherland there are diversities of reward in a single state of joy, some souls being more glorious, sublime, and nearer to God than others, so here below some are dear friends of Christ and some more dear . . . and each one of the elect is fittingly placed in his degree, nor can anyone go further than the degree to which the King has predestined him from eternity.'[50] The provisions of grace are emphasized in the treatise *Ego Dormio*, when Rolle describes to a 'dear sister in Christ' the 'third degree of love':

> For I do not say that you or any one else who reads this shall accomplish it all; for it is according to the will of God whom He chooses to do what is said here, whom He wishes to do other things in other ways, as He gives grace to men to have their salvation. For different men obtain different graces from our Lord Jesus Christ, and all shall be placed in the joy of heaven who end their life in love.

This third degree of love is what Rolle calls the contemplative life:

> At the beginning, when you come to this degree, the eye of your spirit is taken up into the bliss of heaven, and there it is illumined with grace and kindled with the fire of Christ's love, so that you shall truly feel love burning in your heart more and more, raising your thoughts to God, and feeling such great love and joy and sweetness that no sickness or anguish or shame or penance may afflict you, but all your life shall be turned into joy; and then, because your heart is so exalted,

your prayers shall turn into joyful song and your meditations into melody. Then Jesus shall be all your desire, all your delight, all your joy, all your solace, all your comfort; I know that all your song shall be about Him and all your rest be within Him.[51]

The contemplative life, Rolle taught, was composed of reading, prayer and meditation. In reading God speaks to the mystic; in prayer the mystic speaks to God; to meditation belongs 'the inspiration of God, understanding, wisdom and aspiration'. When the highest degree of love is attained the mystic acts with true charity towards others: 'Therefore if our love be pure and perfect, whatever our heart loves it is God . . . Truly in the love of God is the love of thy neighbour. Therefore as he that loves God knows not but to love man, so he that truly knows to love Christ is proved to love nothing in himself but God.'[52]

Throughout his writings Rolle exhibited a passionate devotion to Christ and to the holy name of Jesus – a typical preoccupation of English mystics in the fourteenth century. He advised pondering on the name of Jesus day and night: 'Love it more than thy life, root it in thy mind'. In the *Form of Living* he writes:

If thou wilt be well with God and have grace to rule thy life and come to the joy of love, fix the name of Jesus so fast in thy heart that it be never out of thy thought. And when thou speakest to him and sayest 'Jesus' through habit, it shall be in thy ear joy, in thy mouth honey, and in thy heart melody . . . If thou dost think 'Jesus' continually and hold it firmly, it purges thy sin and kindles thy heart, it cleanses thy soul, it removes anger, it does away with sloth. It wounds in love and fulfils in charity . . . It opens heaven and makes a contemplative man.[53]

We are far here from the mysticism of Eckhart and the Pseudo-Dionysian tradition. Rolle's mysticism avoids all abstractions and is rooted in the *humanity* of Christ, in the mystery of the Word being made flesh; but his experiences, as most scholars are agreed, were representative of the middle reaches of the mystical life, of the illuminative rather than of the unitive way. Rolle was widely read and venerated (he died, so tradition has it, administering to victims of the Black Death). He is now perhaps more valued as a literary figure than a mystic; but he retains his importance in the tradition of English spirituality, and though he had his failings and errors he deserves the title 'The Father of English Mysticism'. The following quotation clearly shows the unpretentious eloquence and sincerity of Rolle at his best:

> In what state may men most love God? I answer: In whatever state it be that men are in the greatest rest of body and soul and least occupied with the needs or business of this world. For the thought of Jesus Christ and of the joy that lasts for ever, seeks rest without, that it be not hindered by comers and goers and occupation with worldly things. And it seeks within great silence from the noise of covetings and of vanities and of earthly thoughts. And all those especially that live of the contemplative life seek rest in body and soul. For a great doctor says that they are God's throne who dwell still in one state and are not running about, but are established in the sweetness of God's love.
>
> And I have loved to sit, not for penance, nor for fancy that I wished men to speak of men, nor for any such thing: but only because I loved God more ... For sitting I am most at rest and my heart is most upward.[54]

The Cloud of Unknowing

The Cloud of Unknowing is without doubt one of the great books of the Middle Ages and one of the greatest devotional classics in English. Its author, however, remains unidentified and it is now assumed that it was the writer's firm intention from the first to remain anonymous. Six other works are usually attributed to the author of *The Cloud: Dionise* [or *Denis*] *Hid Divinite* (a translation of the Pseudo-Dionysius' *Mystical Theology*); the *Benjamin Minor* (a free translation of Richard of St Victor's book of that name); *The Epistle* [or *Book*] *of Privy Counselling; The Epistle of Prayer; The Epistle of Discretion in the Stirrings of the Soul*; and *The Treatise of Discerning of Spirits*, the latter a paraphrase of two sermons by St Bernard.

In the fourteenth century, the author of such a work as *The Cloud* could easily have been a woman; but it seems safe to assume that the writer was a man, not only because of the sense of masculinity that pervades the book, but principally because the final paragraph, in which the author speaks of dispensing 'God's blessing and mine', points to him being a priest. Opinion is divided on the writer's status and sphere of activity: it is not at all obvious from the text whether he was a hermit or solitary, a religious or ex-religious (Dominican or Carthusian), or a parish priest: Dom Justin McCann pictured him as a country parson; Dom David Knowles as a solitary, perhaps an ex-Dominican.

Linguistically, the evidence points to an East Midlands provenance for *The Cloud* and its associated writings – i.e. Nottinghamshire, Leicestershire and parts of Northamptonshire and Lincolnshire. The oldest extant manuscript dates from the early years of the fifteenth century (or perhaps the last years of the fourteenth), but the original source was older. It is clear that the author knew Rolle's writings and *The Cloud* was known to Walter Hilton (see p. 142) *c.*1380. These and other considerations point to *The Cloud* being written between *c.*1349 (the year of Rolle's death) and *c.*1395.

As to the authorship, some have put forward Walter Hilton, and indeed there are some resemblances of language and doctrine; but the differences are far greater. Though Hilton's *Scale of Perfection* shows a knowledge of *The Cloud of Unknowing*, the author of the latter shows no familiarity with Hilton's work; but more than any specific evidential factor is the sense that all readers of *The Cloud* and *The Scale* must have that they are encountering two distinct personalities.

If Rolle showed relatively little literary and doctrinal indebtedness, the author of *The Cloud* develops the teaching of several authorities into a highly original synthesis. One of his sources is Richard of St Victor; another is St Augustine, and there is some affinity between *The Cloud* and the *De Adhaerendo Dei*, attributed to Albertus Magnus. But the primary influence is Dionysius the Areopagite, in particular the *Mystical Theology*, which the author translated as *Denis Hid Divinite*. 'Truly,' he says, 'whoso will look in Denis's books, he shall find that his words will clearly confirm all that I have said or shall say, from the beginning of this treatise to the end.' But as David Knowles pointed out, this is not strictly true. To begin with, the outlook of this medieval author was far removed from that of the Pseudo-Dionysius: all those who followed the Dionysian teachings adapted them to the times and theological climate in which they lived, and this author was no exception. Nor did the author of *The Cloud* read Dionysius in the original Greek: he came to him via two medieval Latin translations, those of Johannes Sarracenus (d.1160) and Thomas Gallus (d.1240), the abbot of St Andrew's, Vercelli, a Victorine canon and a mystical theologian in his own right. David Knowles wrote of Gallus that he 'had displayed even more than the customary medieval skill in noiselessly adapting a work of ancient thought to medieval conditions, and had made love rather than understanding the characteristic occupation of the contemplative, thus rendering Denis viable among Thomists* and Bonaventurans. The author of *The Cloud* follows Gallus in this respect and elsewhere also; whatever may have been his sincere belief that he was following Denis, his doctrine is something quite other than that of *Hid Divinity* [sic].'[55] Added to the influences already mentioned are those of Thomist theology in general and of Rhineland mysticism, particularly the teaching of Tauler; the result, however, is far from being a derivative hotch-potch. On the contrary, *The Cloud of Unknowing* shows its author to have been a powerful original thinker who tested everything he had found in his authorities by referral to his own mystical experience.

In all his writings, the author addressed himself to specified individuals who were engaged in following a life of solitude and contemplative prayer. Thus, in the opening of *The Book of Privy Counselling*, he writes:

> Spiritual brother in God, I speak now particularly to you, about your disposition towards contemplation as I think it to be, and not to all those others who shall hear what I write. For if I were to address myself to everyone, then what I write should be applicable to everyone; but since now I write particularly to you, I therefore write nothing but what seems to me most profitable and suitable to your disposition. If some other man share your disposition, so that he may gain as much from what I write as you, so much the better, for I shall be well satisfied. None the less as I now write, it is your own inward disposition, so far as I am able to understand it, which is my only object of attention.[56]

In *The Cloud*, the advice the author gives focuses on the complete concentration on God, to the exclusion of all else, so that 'thou loathe to think on aught but Himself'. This instruction is intended for someone who has dedicated his life to spiritual attainment and the Prologue emphasizes this.† In the first chapter he speaks directly to his disciple: 'Seest thou not how sweetly and how graciously he hath privily pulled thee to the third degree and manner of living, the which is called singular?', showing that the disciple was already well advanced in mystical experience.

*Followers of St Thomas Aquinas.

†His instructions, the author says, are directed solely to 'such a one as doth all that in him is, and hath done long time before, for to able him to contemplative living, by the virtuous means of active living. For else it accordeth nothing to him.'

The author of *The Cloud*, like the Pseudo-Dionysius, propounds a mysticism of darkness. The human mind cannot possibly comprehend God, and yet union with Him is the ultimate object of our existence. Such a union is beyond the ability of the intellect as we know it, but there is another way of knowing God – through what Eckhart called the spark of the soul and Gallus termed the higher will (*principalis affectio*). The same reasoning is found in the Victorine mystics, St Bernard, and St Bonaventura, who saw the union as one of love: 'Love knocks and enters, but knowledge stands without.' The cognitive experience of contemplation is so unlike what is normally termed knowledge that it may more properly be termed 'unknowing'. Thus the aspiring contemplative is placed between a cloud of forgetting and a cloud of unknowing. In the latter state,

> thou knowest not what, saving that thou feelest in thy will a naked intent unto God . . . this darkness and this cloud . . . hindereth thee, so that thou mayest neither see him clearly by light of understanding in thy reason, nor feel him in sweetness of love in thy affection. And therefore shape thee to bide in this darkness as long as thou mayest, evermore crying after him whom thou lovest. For if ever thou shalt see him or feel him as it may be here, it must always be in this cloud and in this darkness . . . Smite upon that thick cloud of unknowing with a sharp dart of longing love.[57]

The terms used her prefigure those employed by St John of the Cross (see p. 164), who wrote that those who attained to union with God 'must not walk by understanding, neither lean upon experience or feeling or imagination, but he must believe in His Being, which is not perceptible to the understanding, neither to the desire nor to the imagination nor to any other sense, neither can it be known in this life at all . . . and thus a soul must pass beyond everything to unknowing.'[58]

The 'cloud of forgetting' necessitates the total elimination from thought of all created things, not just the creatures therein: 'There is no exception whatever, whether you think of them as physical or spiritual beings, or of their states or actions, or of their goodness or badness. In a word, everything must be hidden under this cloud of forgetting.' It is even necessary to cease *thinking* about God, Christ, the Virgin Mary and the saints, for although it is good 'to think on the kindness of God, and to love Him and praise Him for it; yet it is far better to think on the naked being of Him, and to love Him and praise Him for Himself.' Even though meditations on the surpassing goodness of God must form part of the preparations for contemplation, yet at the last they must be put aside: the mystic must 'hold them far down under the *cloud of forgetting*, if ever he shall pierce the *cloud of unknowing* betwixt him and his God'.

Nothing must be at work in the mind of the contemplative but God. All knowledge and feeling of anything less than God must be suppressed, including the consciousness of the self. This is the final barrier that must be overcome; for when everything else has been forgotten 'there still remains between you and God the stark awareness of your own existence. And this awareness, too, must go, before you experience contemplation in its perfection.'

The awareness of the contemplative's own existence can only be destroyed through God's special grace and the complete willingness of the contemplative to receive it. Such willingness demands 'true sorrow, perfect sorrow', which is yet full of 'holy longing': 'Everyone has something to sorrow over, but none more than he who knows and feels that he is [i.e. that he is 'other than', apart from, God]. All other sorrow in comparison with this is a travesty of the real thing. For he experiences true sorrow, who knows and feels not only what he is, but that he is.'

The author of *The Cloud* is at pains to point out to his disciple the dangers of spiritual straining and false illumination – 'For I tell you truly', he says, 'that the devil has his contemplatives as God has his.'

A young man or woman, just starting in the school of devotion hears someone read or speak about this sorrow and longing: how a man shall lift up his heart to God, and continually long to feel his love. And immediately in their silly minds they understand these words not in the intended spiritual sense, but in a physical and material, and they strain their natural hearts outrageously in their breasts! And because they are without grace, and are proud and spiritually inquisitive, they strain their whole nervous system in untutored, animal ways, and thus they quickly get tired with a sort of physical and spiritual torpor.[59]

This self-deception may result in unusual physical phenomena, such as unnatural heat (cf. Rolle), which is taken to be 'the fire of love, lighted and fanned by the grace and goodness of the Holy Ghost'. From this, many evils can spring – hypocrisy, heresy and error. The dangers of such enthusiasm have already been made clear in the accounts of continental movements such as the Beghards and the Brethren of the Free Spirit and the author of *The Cloud* is forthright in his denunciation of the unseemly excesses of 'counterfeit contemplation'.

The Cloud of Unknowing is concerned with the contemplative *life* and how it may be best ordered; it is not an extended description of 'phenomena' or indeed of the experience of contemplation, which is beyond all description. This restraint is, perhaps, an aspect of the book's Englishness. On one occasion, though, a glimpse is given of what the experience consists of:

> At such a time, he may, perhaps, send out a shaft of spiritual light, which pierces this cloud of unknowing between you, and shows you some of his secrets, of which it is not permissible or possible to speak. Then will you feel your affection flame with the fire of his love, far more than I can possibly say now. For I dare not take upon myself with my blundering, earthly tongue to speak of what belongs solely to God.

The 'exercise' of the *Cloud of Unknowing* is described again in the *Book of Privy Counselling*: 'This exercise is that which puts you to silence, silence of thought as well as of word.'

> This truly is what a perfect lover must always do, utterly and entirely despoiling of himself for the sake of the thing that he loves, never allowing or suffering himself to be clothed except only in that thing which he loves; and that not only for a time, but to be everlastingly enfolded in it, in a full and final forgetting of himself. This is the exercise of love, which no one can know but he who feels it. This is what Our Lord teaches when He says: 'Whoever wishes to love Me, let him forsake himself', as if to say: 'Let him despoil himself of himself if he will be truly clothed in Me, Who am the ample garment of love, a lasting love that never shall have an end.'[60]

The Cloud is a practical book for those few in every age who are able to understand it and follow its precepts. In the opinion of Dom David Knowles: 'The real significance of *The Cloud* is that it is the earliest instance in any vernacular literature of a direct, practical, non-schematic instruction in the entrance and progress in the contemplative life understood (as it has been ever since) as the life of mystical, infused prayer.'[61] For those unable to put its teaching into practice, there is still much in *The Cloud of Unknowing* of value and inspiration; and in this work and its companion treatises there is abundant evidence of literary as well as spiritual accomplishment – for instance, the following passage from the *Epistle of Discretioin in the Stirrings of the Soul*:

> For silence is not God, nor speaking is not God; fasting is not God, nor eating is not God; onliness is not God, nor company is not God, nor yet any of all the other such two contraries. He is hid betwixt them, and may not be found by any work of the soul, but only by love of thine heart. He may not be known by reason. He may not be thought, gotten nor traced by understanding. But he may be loved and chosen with the true, lovely will of thine heart. Choose thee him.

Walter Hilton

Walter Hilton (d.1395) was an Augustinian Canon of Thurgarton in Nottinghamshire. It is likely that he spent most of his life as a solitary, joining the priory at Thurgarton some time after 1375. Apart from this, little is known of Hilton, who remains almost as shadowy a figure as the author of *The Cloud of Unknowing*.

Hilton's principal work is *The Scale of Perfection* (*Scala Perfectionis*), written, like *The Cloud*, for the spiritual guidance of one person – in this case, an unnamed anchoress. Among other works usually attributed with confidence to Hilton are the *Epistola Aurea* (Golden Letter), dated *c.*1375 and addressed to Hilton's friend Adam Horsley; the *De Imagine Peccati* (Of the Image of Sin); and the *De Utilitate et Prerogatiuis Religionis* (of the Profit and Prerogatives of Religious Life).

The Scale is in two parts; the first part is addressed to the anchoress; the second does not appear to have been intended for any particular individual and the more advanced teaching it contains reinforces the idea that it was written some years after the first part. Like *The Cloud of Unknowing, The Scale* is part of the Pseudo-Dionysian tradition and also reflects the schematic approach of Richard of St Victor; it differs from *The Cloud*, indeed, in its methodical approach, though like all medieval writers, Walter Hilton was prone to digression. Hilton is a practical teacher whose writings are relevant to the leading of a spiritual life in the world as well as to the life of the advanced contemplative: for Hilton, the contemplative life is a continuation and development of the 'normal' life of grace begun at baptism.

The foundation for both the spiritual life in general and the contemplative life in particular is what Hilton calls the reforming, or re-establishment, of God's image in the soul. The soul cannot be conformed to God until it is reformed, until, that is, virtues are transformed into affection – 'when a man loves virtue because in itself it is good'. Many people, says Hilton, possess virtues such as humility, patience and love towards their fellow-men; but they are a function only of reason and will: 'they have not the love of them in affection':

> But when, by God's grace and through spiritual and intellectual exercise, their reason is turned into light and their will into love, then they possess virtues in affection. For such a man has then bitten so well on the nut's bitter shell that he has broken it, and he feeds upon the kernel. That is, the virtues which at first were so laborious to exercise are now turned into pure delight and savour, when a man takes pleasure in patience, in humility, in purity, in sobriety and in charity, as he does in any other delight.[62]

There is for Hilton a distinction between the soul that is simply restored in faith and the soul restored in faith *and* feeling. Restoration by faith places the soul in a state of grace; but restoration by faith and feeling makes the soul, by the power of the Holy Ghost, aware of the workings of grace in it. The soul apprehends God and spiritual truths 'in the higher parts of its reason', and when this happens the state of contemplation has been attained. 'Feeling', for Hilton, does not imply a mere emotional response: it is his word for the inward awareness of grace at work. He is careful, in fact, to warn against sensible phenomena in the spiritual life – glancing, perhaps, at Rolle as he does so: 'Thou mayst understand that visions or revelations . . . in bodily appearing or in imagining . . . or else in any other feeling in bodily wits . . . as any sensible heat as it were fire glowing and warming the breast . . . are not very contemplation, nor are they but simple and secondary, though they be good, in regard of ghostly virtues, and of ghostly knowing and loving of God.'[63]

> You ought not to allow your heart deliberately to rest or completely to delight in any physical sensation deriving from spiritual consolations or sweetnesses, however good they may in themselves be: in your own estimation you should consider them as nothing or little in comparison with your spiritual aspirations, nor must you set your heart upon them, but forget them if you can, and always try your best to attain to a spiritual feeling of God. You would attain to that feeling if you could know and feel God's wisdom. His endless power, and His

great goodness in Himself and in the beings He created. For this is contemplation, and the other is not.[64]

The ascent from reform in faith to reform in feeling can only be undertaken gradually: 'Reform in faith is the lowest state of elect souls . . . and reform in feeling is the highest state that a soul can come to in this life. But a soul cannot suddenly jump from the lowest to the highest, any more than a man who will climb a high ladder and put his foot in the lowest rung can at the next moment be on the top one.'

To reform the image of God in itself the soul must 'recollect' itself: it must know itself. Before the Fall the three powers of the soul – recollection (memory), reason (understanding) and will – were directed completely at God. In this way, says Hilton, 'man's soul, which may be called a created trinity, was made perfect in its mind and vision and love by the uncreated Blessed Trinity Who is the Lord God. This is the dignity, the degree and the honour of the human soul according to its nature as it was first created.' But Adam's sin, choosing love of himself before love of God, plunged the soul into a forgetfulness of God. Adam lost this prelapsarian honour and dignity, 'and you lost it in him, and you fell away from the Blessed Trinity into a foul, dark, wretched trinity – into oblivion of God, into ignorance of Him and into animal pleasure in yourself.' But through Christ the soul may recollect itself and its true nature:

> I shall give you one word to express everything which you have lost: and this word is 'Jesus'. I do not mean the letters 'IHS' painted on a wall or written in a book, I do not mean the sounds of the word which you can form with your tongue, I do not mean the name as it can be fixed in the heart by the effort of recollection: through such exercises man in love may find Him, but here by 'Jesus' I mean all goodness, everlasting wisdom, love and sweetness, your joy, your dignity and your eternal happiness, your God, your Lord and your salvation.[65]

Hilton recognized three degrees of contemplation, the second of which he subdivided into a higher and lower stage. The first degree consisted of a knowledge of God and spiritual things acquired through reason, reading and study, a knowledge however, that is without 'spiritual affection and that interior savour which is experienced by a special gift of the Holy Spirit'. The second degree consists in affection of spiritual things without understanding, and this is often found, says Hilton, 'in simple and uneducated people who give themselves up entirely to devotion'. In the lower stage of this degree, those leading an active life experience fervent affection for God only fleetingly and it comes and goes 'according to the will of Him who gives it'; in the higher stage, through long physical and spiritual effort, the affective life is lived continuously, by which those who attain to this stage are 'comforted and strengthened against every sin, and greatly relieved of bodily distress'. The third degree of contemplation is as perfect as it can be in this life and consists of 'cognition and affection':

> It consists in knowing God and loving Him perfectly; and this comes when a man's soul is first cleansed from all sins, and formed again, through the fullness of virtues, into the image of Jesus. Then, next, when that man is visited by grace, he is taken up, away from all earthly and carnal affections, from empty thoughts and idle speculations about all physical matters, and he is as it were ravished out of his bodily senses, and then by the grace of the Holy Spirit he is illumined, to see through understanding that truth, which is God, and also to see spiritual things, with a soft, sweet, burning love which is so perfect in him that by the power of this love to ravish him the soul is united and made conformable to the image of the Trinity.[66]

The beginnings of this degree of contemplation may be experienced in this life; but Hilton says that its perfection is reserved for Heaven. 'About this union and conformity of the soul with God,' he continues, 'St Paul says this: *Qui adhaeret Deo, unus spiritus est cum illo*: "Whoever" by the ravishing of love "is united with God, then God and his soul" are not two, but they "both are one", not one in flesh, but in one spirit. And truly in this union a marriage is made between God and the soul which shall never be dissolved.' Like the author of *The Cloud of Unknowing*, Hilton does not elaborate on the ultimate perfection of the soul: his style and his approach are sober and free from morbid introspection and self-advertisement. But there can be no doubt that he counsels from the actual experience of the contemplative life in its higher stages:

> Understand that when you desire Jesus and wish to think of nothing but Him, but cannot do so properly because of worldly thoughts crowding into your mind, you have in fact left the false daylight and

are entering this darkness. But you will not find this darkness peaceful because it is strange to you, who are not yet enlightened and cleansed. Therefore enter it often, and by the grace of God it will gradually become easier and more peaceful. Your soul will become so free, strong, and recollected that it will have no desire to think of anything worldly, while no worldly thing will prevent it from thinking of nothing . . . This darkness and night, then, springs solely from the soul's desire and longing for the love of Jesus, combined with a blind groping of the mind towards Him. And since it brings so much blessing and peace to the soul, albeit of short duration, how much better and more blessed must it be to experience His love, to be bathed in His glorious and invisible light, and to see all truth. It is this light which a soul receives as night passes by and day dawns.[67]

Julian of Norwich

If the authors of *The Cloud of Unknowing* and *The Scale of Perfection* revealed little of their personal spiritual experiences, Dame Julian of Norwich addressed herself solely to the task of describing her own mystical 'shewings' and drawing meaning from them.

The copyist of the first, and shorter, version of Julian's book, the *Revelations of Divine Love*, tells us: 'Here is a vision shewn by the goodness of God to a devout woman whose name is Julian. She is a recluse at Norwich and is living yet in this year of our Lord 1413.' According to Julian's own account, she was born in 1342; by about 1404, perhaps earlier, she lived as an anchoress at St Julian's Church in Norwich (she was perhaps originally from Yorkshire) and may have been previously a nun at the nearby Benedictine priory at Carrow. It was in her cell hard by St Julian's Church that about the year 1410 she received a visit from Margery Kempe,* who wrote of herself: 'Then she was bidden by our Lord to go to an anchoress in the same city, named Dame Jelyan . . . for the anchoress was expert in such things and good counsel could give.'

---

*Margery Kempe (b.*c.*1373) was the daughter of John Brunham, five times mayor of (Bishop's, now King's) Lynn. She married John Kempe, the son of a prosperous merchant, *c.*1393 and travelled extensively. Her mystical experiences, of a particularly spectacular kind, were described in *The Book of Margery Kempe*, extracts from which were published in 1501 by Wynkyn de Worde. Opinions differ on Margery's standing as a mystic. On the one side is E. I. Watkin, who calls her 'a woman whose intelligence was mediocre but whose strong will surrendered in loving devotion to her Divine Lord . . . who sought by her words and example to spread the Kingdom of Christ' (*Poets and Mystics*, p. 134). On the other is W. R. Inge, echoing Emily Hope Allen, who wrote in his *Mysticism in Religion*: 'I have not troubled my readers with Margery Kempe . . . This hysterical young woman calls herself a poor creature, and a poor creature I am afraid she was. She is obviously proud of the "boisterous" roarings and sobbings which made her a nuisance to her neighbours. She never quite rings true.' (p. 11). Recently Clarissa Atkinson has written a more sympathetic study of this still controversial figure.

Julian's sixteen 'shewings' were received by her in May 1373 and were described in two separate forms, a shorter and earlier version – written probably soon after the event* – and a longer, later version. She describes herself modestly as 'a simple unlettered creature' and is emphatic in denying that her shewings marked her out as a soul of exceptional holiness: 'Because of the shewing I am not good, but only if I love God the better . . . I am certain there are full many who never had shewing nor sight but of the common teaching of Holy Church, and who loved God better than I.' She is also at pains to emphasize that all her shewings were in complete accordance with Church teaching. 'Never,' she says, 'did I understand a thing therein which harms me or withdraws me from the true teaching of Holy Church.' The longer version of her revelations is indeed an elaboration of this identity between the shewings and the Catholic faith in which personal details are suppressed with the aim of focusing completely on what God has revealed through her.

Of Julian's life before the events of 1373 we know next to nothing, although it is clear that she had always possessed a deep religious temperament, and she had a strong attachment to her mother that seems to have coloured a characteristic aspect of her teaching – the Motherhood of God, an idea that had been developed in Western theology by St Anselm. She calls Jesus 'our Kind Mother, our Gracious Mother, for that he would all wholly become our Mother in all things, he took the ground of his works full low and full mildly in the Maiden's womb'.

> The Mother's service is nearest, readiest and surest: for it is most of truth . . . We wit that all our mother's bearing is the bearing of us to pain and to dying: and what is this but that our Very Mother, Jesus, he – All-Love – beareth us to joy and endless living? . . . The mother may give her child suck of her milk, but our precious Mother, Jesus, he may feed us with himself, and doeth it, full courteously and full tenderly, with the Blessed Sacrament that is precious food of very life . . . This fair lovely word *Mother*, it is so sweet and kind itself that it may not verily be said of none but him; and to her that is very Mother of him and of all.[70]

Julian had desired three favours of God: to be granted 'bodily sight' of Christ's Passion; to have 'of God's giving, a bodily

---

*The earliest surviving copy is dated 1413.

sickness', so that through suffering she might be purged of a love for earthly things; and to receive three wounds – the wound of contrition (for sin), the wound of compassion (for Christ's sufferings), and the wound of wilful longing for God. The illness duly came upon her, on 3–8 May 1373, when she was thirty and a half years old, and became the fulfilment of her desire to be purified 'so as afterwards to live more according to the worship of God'. Everyone around her, including her mother, expected her to die and on the fourth night she was given the last rites of the Church: 'After this I lingered on two days and two nights, and on the third night I weened oftentimes to have passed, and so weened they that were with me . . . And they that were with me sent for the parson my curate to be at mine ending.'[71] Her breath and eyesight were failing, but when the priest held a crucifix before her face the pain ceased and the crucifix itself began to change:

> And in this suddenly I saw the red blood trickling down from under the garland of thorns hot and fresh and right plenteously . . . like to the drops of water that fall off the eaves of a house after a great shower of rain . . . and for the roundness, they were like to the scale of herring.

Then came the shewings, one after another, the first beginning early in the morning, about four o'clock, the last the following night, after which the pain returned and Julian doubted, in true Petrine fashion, the reality of her visions: 'I said I had raved during the day . . . And straightway I was sore ashamed and abashed at my recklessness . . . by saying I raved I shewed myself not to believe our Lord God . . . Alas, what a wretch I was! This was a great sin and a great unkindness.'[72]

Though Julian considered herself to be 'unlettered', she was an instinctive theologian and as one commentator, James Walsh, has observed, she speaks the same language as Hilton and the author of *The Cloud of Unknowing*, both of whom were steeped in the literature of mystical theology. Parts of the *Revelations*, for instance, are distinctly Dionysian in flavour and the Christological approach of *The Scale* and *The Cloud* is echoed by Julian's account of her first shewing: 'The Trinity is our endless joy and our bliss, by our Lord Jesus Christ and in our Lord Jesus Christ. And this was shewed in the first sight and in them all. For where Jesus appeareth the blessed Trinity is understood.'

The great underlying theme of the *Revelations* is love:

Thus was I learned that love is our Lord's meaning. And I saw full surely in this, and in all, that before God made us, he loved us. Which love was never slaked, nor ever shall be. And in this love he hath done all his works. And in this love he hath made all things profitable to us. And in this love our life is everlasting. In our making we had beginning: but the love wherein he made us was in him from without-beginning. In which love we have our beginning. And all this shall we see in God without end.[73]

This theme is first focused on the sufferings of Christ, as a means of comprehending how completely the crucifixion was an act of love. Behind this first part of the Revelations stand two Pauline texts:

Him I would learn to know, and the virtue of his resurrection, and what it means to share his sufferings, moulded into the pattern of his death.

(Philippians 3:10)

My old self has become dead to the law that I may live to God; with Christ I hang upon the Cross, and yet I am alive; or rather not I; it is Christ that lives in me. True, I am living, here and now, this mortal life; but my real life is my faith in the Son of God, who loved me and gave himself for me.

(Galatians 2:20)

After being shown the dying Christ Julian sees Christ glorified: in Him, she says, the plenitude of the Deity is embodied, and in Him the individual soul finds its completion. But with this comprehension of divine love at work in the reformed soul appears a parallel mystery – the destiny of the reproved, those who shall not be saved. For Walter Hilton, mystical knowledge included an elucidation of this mystery, of 'how rightfully he forsakes them [the reproved] and leaveth them in their sin and doth them no wrong; how he rewardeth them in this world, suffering them for to have fulfilling of their will, and after this for to punish them endlessly.' Julian's vision does not encompass such knowledge, and she admits her confusion and dismay: how, she asks, can all be well 'in face of the great harm that is come by sin to thy creatures?' If wicked angels (and Julian, conversely, believed in the holy ministrations of good angels) and those that die 'out of charity' are damned eternally, as the Church taught, it seemed to her that, in spite of her shewing, it was impossible 'that all manner of things should be well . . . But I had no other answer to the difficulty in this shewing of our Lord's except this: "What is impossible to thee is not impossible to me; I shall save my word in all things – I shall make all things well".'[74] As for the corporation of the saved, Julian saw that in these souls – in the Church – lay the way to God:

> God shewed the very great pleasure that he taketh in all men and women who mightily and wisely receive the preaching and teaching of Holy Church. For he is Holy Church. He is its ground. He is its substance. He is its teaching. He is its teacher. He is the end and the reward towards which every kind soul travelleth.

Julian's mysticism combines homeliness and simplicity with a true sense of the transcendent. Finely attuned though she was to the abiding totality of God's presence, she yet retained the human touch in the description of her shewings: 'In this same time our Lord showed me a ghostly sight of His homely loving. I saw that He is to us everything that is good and comfortable for us; He is our clothing that for love wrappeth, claspeth us and all becloseth us for tender love, that He may never leave us . . .'

Julian is the most approachable of the medieval English mystics, and she demonstrates clearly how an individual relationship with God is sustained and nurtured by the collective environment of the Church:

> From the beginning to the end, I had two manners of beholding. The one was endless, continuant love, with secureness of keeping and blissful salvation, for of us this was all the shewing. The other was of the common teaching of Holy Church in which I was afore informed and grounded, and with all my will having in use and understanding. And the beholding of this went not from me: for by the shewing I was not stirred nor led therefrom in no manner of point, but I had therein teaching to love it and like it: whereby I might, by the help of our Lord and His grace, increase and rise to more heavenly knowing and higher loving.[75]

6. The Spanish Mystical Tradition

FOR most people the mystical spirit of Spain is represented by two supreme figures: St Teresa of Avila and St John of the Cross. This is entirely as it should be; but there were many precursors of these two religious geniuses who provided the soil out of which these two outstanding personalities were to grow to perfection.

The religious temper of Spain was – is – characterized by intensity. For the mystics, this national characteristic resulted in a kind of spiritual militancy – a self-negating pursuit of love. There is no merit in enjoyment, said St Teresa, only in work, suffering and love. 'He who would see the face of that most powerful Wrestler, our boundless God,' maintained Orozco, 'must first have wrestled with himself.' Activity, austerity and ceaseless striving are the hallmarks of the Spanish mystical tradition, expressed in the challenging dictum of St Ignatius Loyola: 'Let each one reflect that just so much does he advance in all spiritual things, as he goes out from self-love, self-will, and self-interest.'

St Ignatius Loyola

Mystical consciousness begins to emerge in Spain in the early years of the sixteenth century; and with it grew up the Society of Jesus, founded by St Ignatius Loyola (1491–1556) in 1534 to support the Catholic Church against the Reformers of northern Europe and to evangelize the heathens in every corner of the world. After being wounded at the siege of Pampeluna in 1521, Ignatius had been fired by the examples of St Dominic and St Francis and he exchanged the uniform of a Spanish soldier for the sackcloth of a soldier of Christ. He embarked upon a pilgrimage to the shrine of Montserrat near Barcelona and later, with the Pope's permission, undertook another to Jerusalem. In between the two pilgrimages he spent several months in retirement at Manresa, the outcome of which was the first draft of his *Spiritual Exercises*.

After studying in Barcelona and at the University of Alcalá, and having been briefly imprisoned for heresy, he migrated to Paris, where he found the first six members of his future order, amongst them Francis Xavier and Peter Faber.

Loyola's principal work, the *Spiritual Exercises*, is primarily a religious manual, a series of carefully organized instructions on holy living that appear to have little direct link with the heights of mystical experience. And yet the object of the *Exercises*, in their author's words, is 'to allow the Creator to work directly on the creature, and the creature with her Creator and Lord'. In other words, this precisely ordered system is designed to facilitate first-hand experience of God, to teach the soul to speak to God 'as a friend with a friend', to bring about the state of illumination and 'the achievement of love divine'. At the end of the *Exercises* is a section entitled 'Contemplation for Obtaining Love', which is in effect a definition of the authentic Christian mystical life. The mystical union between man and God is one of love: each gives, and each receives. For love, says Loyola, 'consists in mutual interchange on either side, that is to say in the lover giving and communicating with the beloved what he has or can give, and on the other hand, in the beloved sharing with the lover.'

The Jesuit Order founded by Ignatius Loyola, and the *Spiritual Exercises* of the founder, were responsible for nurturing an impressive number of contemplatives, among them **Alphonsus Rodriguez** (1533–1617), who entered the Society of Jesus at the age of thirty-eight after losing his wife and his children. In describing his own mystical experience of God, Alphonsus draws heavily on the language and imagery of the *Spiritual Exercises*: 'Then the soul loves God and enjoys Him, because it is so absorbed and as it were bathed in the divine love. The state at which it has arrived is that of a very perfect union with God, and, so to speak, of a transformation into God. At this point, each gives to the other all he has and all he is.'[1]

St Teresa's Precursors and Contemporaries

Outside the Jesuit Order **Alonso de Orozco** (1500–1591) began writing at the behest of the Virgin Mary, who he claimed visited him in a dream. He obeyed the call with determination, leaving over fifty treatises of various kinds, some semi-mystical in spirit, such as the *Mount of Contemplation,* others, like the *Treatise on Confession,* less so. The *Mount of Contemplation* distinguishes four stages (jornadas) in the mystical life and is written in dialogue form; but it does not seem inspired by the fullest type of mystical illumination.

The greatest of St Teresa's precursors was **Francisco de Osuna** (d.*c.* 1540), whose *Third Spiritual Alphabet* (*Tercer Abecedario Espiritual*), which appeared in 1527, was Teresa's earliest mystical guide. It was Osuna who formulated the prayer of 'recollection'; indeed his book was principally written 'to bring to the general notice of all the exercise of recollection'. Of this book St Teresa said: 'I delighted in [it] exceedingly, and determined to follow the mystic road with all my strength.' Osuna's goal was to mark out a way for those 'who in purity of spirit would attain to God', and he addressed himself particularly to the struggles of the aspirant.

The prayer of recollection – which is sometimes used by Osuna to describe the mystic life as a whole as well as a specific stage in it – is described as 'the coming of the Lord to the soul ... the opening of the devout heart to Christ ... a spiritual ascension with Christ ... the third heaven to which the contemplative soul is caught up'. It is the 'art of love':

> For once we have learned by faith that God is to be desired and loved, and is wholly love – then, if our affections be purged and prepared and exercised, I know not how we shall be hindered from being thus transformed, inflamed and raised to a state which knows all to be one clod, one fragment, or (to speak better) one fount of love.

The culmination of recollection is union, when man attains to God, becoming one spirit with Him through an exchange of will. Man wills nothing in this state but that which God wills, 'neither does God withdraw Himself from the will of man, but in all things they are one, like things that are perfectly united, which lose their own natures and are wholly transformed in a third.' And so, says Osuna, if God and man before had diverse wills, now they agree in one without dissatisfaction of either. And hence it results that the man is at unity with himself, and with his fellows; were we all so the multitude of the faithful would be one heart and mind together in the Holy Spirit, the beginning of Whose generation is formed by the Father and the Son. He it is who makes us to be one in love, that He may beget us in grace, and bring us all to be made one together with God, that He may not have to bring us to Him singly.[2]

Bernardino de Laredo (1482–1540), the author of the *Ascent of Mount Zion* (*Subida del Monte Sion por la Via Contemplativa*), was another mystic whose experiences illuminated and guided those of St Teresa. He graduated as a doctor of medicine from the University of Sevilla, but in 1510 he turned his back on the world and was admitted to the Franciscan Convent of San Francisco del Monte near Sevilla. The *Ascent of Mount Zion* was first published anonymously, an indication of the author's humility, although the 1617 edition did bear his name.

The 'practice of quiet', according to Bernardino, teaches the soul to rise 'on wings of love', and he speaks of 'a sudden and momentary uplifting of the mind' in which the soul, by divine instruction, is raised 'of a sudden to be united with its most loving God, without the interposition of any thought or of any intellectual working or of the understanding or of natural reason'. This divine operation, surpassing all reason and understanding, unites the soul with its God 'so often as it pleases the Divine condescension, without the interposition of any thought of created thing'. Bernardino stresses that what he calls facility in 'this blessed uplifting of the soul' is a result, not of the soul's own solicitude and efforts, but of the continual visitations of God:

> And thereto it [the soul] disposes itself with the disposition of a pure intention, for the oftener it is visited by its great Reviver, so much the more reluctant is it to ask and receive this love further. So often does our Lord and loving Physician visit the soul that is faint for His love, that the soul reaches a point at which it cannot and would not escape the arrows of love, never lacking the Physician Who with a glance heals it. And this He does so completely that the soul has but to cry out of a sudden concerning its grievous sickness, and straightway it has its remedy, and the visit of its Beloved Physician. No sooner is it afflicted with love, and with the affliction it has the remedy.[3]

St Peter of Alcantara (1499–1562) studied philosophy at Salamanca before entering the Franciscan Order, becoming superior of his convent at Badajoz, and, in 1538, was appointed to the rank of provincial. He was deeply committed to the task of re-establishing the primitive Rule of St Francis and in time, in spite of opposition, he succeeded in founding several houses in which the strictest form of the Franciscan Rule was observed. Peter of Alcantra was one of St Teresa's spiritual advisors: the 1623 English edition of his *Treatise of Prayer and Meditation* (entitled *A Golden Treatise of Mentall Praier*) refers to Teresa as his 'ghostly child'. He was, besides being an active reformer (as Teresa also was), an unrelenting and ferocious ascetic, as indicated by one of his reputed sayings: 'My body and I have made a compact: while I live in this world it is to suffer without intermission, but when I reach Heaven I will give it eternal rest.'

In the *Treatise of Prayer and Meditation* the important distinction is made between meditation and contemplation. The function of meditation is to consider divine things studiously, with the intention of moving the heart to feeling and emotion for them: the image he uses is drawing a spark from a flint by striking it.

> But contemplation is as though the spark were already struck, – that is to say, that the feeling and emotion which were sought have been attained. The soul is enjoying repose and silence, not by many reasonings and speculations of the understanding, but simply by gazing at the truth ... The one [meditation] seeks, the other [contemplation] finds; the one chews its food, the other tastes it; the one reasons and considers, the other is content with nought but looking upon things, since already it has the taste and love for them. In short, the one is a means, the other an end; the one is a path and a movement, the other is the end of this path, and yet is movement.[4]

Juan de Avila (1500–1569), the 'Apostle of Andalucia', also studied at Salamanca (jurisprudence), though also at Alcalá (theology). He belonged to no religious order, devoting himself instead to evangelical work in the south of Spain. His writings aroused the suspicions of the Inquisition, who saw heretical possibilities in them, and he spent some months in prison. Juan was a powerful and charismatic preacher and a noted spiritual director – he, too, gave spiritual counsel to St Teresa, who sent the text of her *Life* (*Libro de su Vida*) to him for his approval. His best known work is probably the *Tratado del 'Audi Filia'* (1588), translated into English (as *The 'Audi Filia'; or a Rich Cabinet Full of Spirituall Jewells*) in 1620. The *Epistolario Espiritual* (1579) were published in English eleven years later, in 1631, as *Certain Selected Spirituall Epistles*. He was beatified in 1894.

Juan de Avila's practical missionary spirit imparts a certain reserve to his writings: being principally concerned with the spiritually immature he is always careful to observe restraint in his descriptions of mental prayer. Even so, he writes with power and passion of the necessity of submitting to the 'bondage' of Christ's love, 'the very bond of salvation':

> Let us then no more resist Him, but allow ourselves to be vanquished by His weapons ... He would fain consume us, that our old man being destroyed, which is in the likeness of Adam, our new man may be born through love, which is the image of Christ. He would fain melt our hard hearts, to the end that, as on metal that is molten by heat the image willed by the artificer may be iprinted, so we, softened by love which causes us to melt as we hear the voice of the Beloved, may be without resistance, and ready for Christ to imprint upon us the image that He wills – that is, the image of Christ Himself, which is the image of love.[5]

Juan's near contemporary **Luis de Granada** (1504–1588) was a mystic of an entirely different type. He was deeply aware of the mystical resonances of the created world: this nature mysticism, indeed, is his great distinction, allying him more with mystically inclined English poets of the seventeenth century, such as Henry Vaughan and Thomas Traherne, than with his contemporaries among the Spanish mystics.*

Fray Luis was a Dominican preacher and eventually became Provincial of the Order in Portugal. He was also the head of a convent near Badajoz and chaplain to the Duke of Medina-Sidonia. His works are devotional in character, rather than overtly mystical; but the ideal of the transformed soul runs through all his writings and he lays great emphasis on discipline and self-mortification as a concomitant of spiritual devotion. As he said: 'That which costs us nothing is worth nothing.' The purgative

---

*He was widely read in England and in the sixteenth and seventeenth centuries there were several translations and abridgements of Fray Luis' writings, particularly the *Libro Llamada Guia de Pecadores* (1556), the *Sinners' Guide*. Allison Peers notes that John Donne probably knew this, at least, of Fray Luis' works.

way, in other words, is another term for the mystic's life in this world; it is an ever-present necessity if the aspirant is to 'give up all but God and to be joined in spirit with Him in continual and most ardent love'. The unitive life, to which few can hope to attain, is described by Fray Luis in the following terms:

> Accordingly, when a man in this mortal life reaches so high a degree of love that he despises all things which perish, taking unlawful content or pleasure in none, but fixing all his pleasure, love, care, desire and thought upon God, and this so constantly that always, or well-nigh always, his heart is set on Him (for in Him alone he finds rest, and apart from Him none*); when in this way a man is dead to all things, and alive only to God, the greatness of his love triumphing over all other affections, then he will have entered the vaults of precious wine of the true Solomon, in which, inebriated with the wine of this love, he will forget all things – even himself – for His sake.[6]

St Teresa of Avila

In St Teresa of Avila (1515–1582), reformer of the Carmelite Order, these various influences were concentrated and developed. She was influenced by the methodology and spirit of St Ignatius Loyola and the Jesuits, on the one hand, as well as by the reforming zeal and Franciscan fervour of St Peter of Alcantara, on the other; Francisco de Osuna introduced her to the art of recollection; and, as we have seen, she also came into contact with Bernadino de Laredo and Juan de Avila. She was, said Evelyn Underhill, 'touched by all the other mystical forces and persons active in sixteenth-century Spain' and was 'the classic example of that complete flowering of personality in which the life of contemplation does not tend to specialism, but supports and enhances a strenuous active career'. E. Allison Peers deftly summed up this extraordinary character by saying that 'Martha and Mary have seldom been so well combined as in the personality of St Teresa.'[7]

St Teresa was born Teresa Sánchez de Cepeda y Ahumada on 28 March 1515, of mixed Jewish and Christian background, her grandfather being a relapsed Jewish convert. Her mother died at the age of thirty-three, 'in a most Christian manner', said Teresa. She had two sisters and nine brothers, one of whom, Rodrigo, was her particular favourite. She recalled in her autobiography:

---

*Cf. St Augustine, 'our heart is restless until it rests in Thee' (*Confessions*).

We used to read the lives of the Saints together, and when I read of the martyrdoms which they suffered for the love of God, I used to think that they had bought their entry into God's presence very cheaply. Then I fervently longed to die like them, not out of any conscious love for Him, but in order to attain, as quickly as they had, those joys which, as I read, are laid up in Heaven. I used to discuss with my brother ways and means of becoming martyrs, and we agreed to go together to the land of the Moors, begging our way for the love of God, so that we might be beheaded there. I believe that our Lord had given us courage enough even at that tender age, if only we could have seen a way. But our having parents seemed to us a very great hindrance.[8]

At the age of sixteen Teresa entered a local school run by Augustinian sisters as a boarder. She stayed there for about eighteen months and was, she said, 'much the better for it'. Though she had resisted the idea of taking the veil, 'for God had not yet been pleased to give me this desire', she was more inclined to do so at the end of her time with the Augustinian sisters. But 'certain devotional practices which prevailed there' – practices she considered excessive – prevented her from taking her vows in that particular house. A more important consideration was that she had a friend, Doña Juana Suárez, in the Carmelite Convent of the Incarnation, which, like the Augustinian convent, was outside the walls of Avila, 'and this made me decide that, if I was to be a nun, it should be nowhere but in the house where she was'.

At the age of twenty-one, on 3 November 1536, Teresa took the Carmelite habit at the Convent of the Incarnation and for the next twenty years her life was a continuous struggle between spirit and flesh, a constant 'strife and contention between converse with God and the society of the world'. Those years, she said, were spent on a stormy sea, 'falling and evermore rising again, but to little purpose as afterwards I would fall once more'.

The change in lifestyle and diet seriously affected her health. She suffered from frequent fainting fits, heart pains and other ailments – to the bafflement of the local doctors. For nearly a year she resided in the town of Becedas in an attempt to recover, suffering worse agonies from the ministrations of the doctors, 'which were so drastic that I do not know how I endured them'.

It was at this time that she was introduced by her uncle, Don Pedro, to Francisco de Osuna's *Third Spiritual Alphabet*, which contained instructions in the prayer of quiet, or recollection. She began to spend time in solitude and embarked upon the way of prayer, with Osuna's book as her guide:

> Utter scrupulousness seemed to me almost impossible. I guarded against committing any mortal sin – and would to God I had always done so – but I paid little attention to venial sins, and that was what undid me. Still the Lord began to be so gracious to me on this path as to raise me sometimes to the prayer of quiet, and ocasionally to that of union, though I did not understand what either of these was, or how highly I should have valued them.[9]

The Carmelite Order had originated in Palestine, at the foot of Mount Carmel, from whence it took its name. In its first form it was composed of hermits dedicated to a life of extreme austerity, but in the thirteenth century members of the Order migrated all over Europe, establishing houses from Cyprus to England, and gradually the primitive Rule became mitigated. The Convent of the Incarnation at Avila, like many others, was lax in its observance of the original Rule, though Teresa says that there were many there who served God 'in absolute sincerity and great perfection'. Teresa considered it did her great spiritual harm not to be in an enclosed convent; for, she said, 'a convent of unenclosed nuns seems to me a place of very great peril, and more like a road to hell for those bent on wickedness than a remedy for their weaknesses'. She was careful not to include the Incarnation in this denunciation, since the convent was only partially unenclosed; but still, the laxity had an effect on her, deepening her sense of spiritual and moral insufficiency.

But she drew comfort and support from reading St Augustine's *Confessions* and at length began to have authentic mystical experiences as a result of practising the prayer of quiet. One of her techniques was to summon up a picture of Christ within her: 'I found myself the better, as I believe, for dwelling on those moments in His life when He was most lonely. It seemed to me that when He was alone and afflicted He must, like anyone in trouble, admit me.' Often during this picturing, and sometimes when she was reading, there would come to her unexpectedly 'such a feeling of the presence of God as made it impossible for me to doubt that He was within me, or that I was totally engulfed in Him'. She goes on:

This was no kind of vision; I believe it is called *mystical theology*. The soul is then so suspended that it seems entirely outside itself. The will loves; the memory is, I think, almost lost, and the mind, I believe, though it is not lost, does not reason – I mean that it does not work, but stands as if amazed at the many things it understands. For God wills it to realize that it understands nothing at all of what His Majesty places before it.[10]

When she finally realized that the contemplative life was her true vocation – her second conversion – her spiritual progress was rapid. The central portion of the *Life* describes in detail the four stages of mental prayer through which she passed, culminating in the ecstatic union of the fourth stage. Here there is no sense of anything but enjoyment, but without any knowledge of what is being enjoyed: 'The soul realises that it is enjoying some good thing that contains all good things together, but it cannot comprehend this good thing.' Because the soul's inward sensations in this condition are beyond understanding, so they are beyond description. 'I was wondering', writes Teresa, '. . . – after taking Communion and experiencing that state of prayer of which I am writing – how the soul is occupied at that time. Then the Lord said to me: "It dissolves utterly, my daughter to rest more and more in Me. It is no longer itself that lives; it is I. As it cannot comprehend what it understands, it understands by not understanding."' Teresa then elaborates on this paradoxical state:

> Anyone who has experienced this will to some extent understand. It cannot be expressed more clearly, since all that hapens is so obscure. I can only say that the soul conceives itself to be near God, and that it is left with such a conviction that it cannot possibly help believing. All the faculties are in abeyance, and so suspended, as I have said, that their operations cannot be followed. If the soul has previously been meditating on any subject, it vanishes from the memory at once, as completely as if it had never been thought of. If it has been reading, it is unable to remember it or dwell on the words; and it is the same with vocal prayer. So the restless little moth of the memory has its wings burned, and can flutter no more.[11]

After the prayer of union the soul is left with a great feeling of tenderness. Occasionally Teresa would find herself in two minds about whether her experiences had been a dream or a reality: 'But when I have seen myself drenched with tears, which have flowed painlessly, yet so quickly and with such violence that they might have fallen from a cloud in heaven, I have realized that it was no dream.' The soul is also left with so much courage 'that if it were to be torn asunder at that moment for God's sake, it would be greatly comforted'. The soul sees clearly that it has not achieved union with God through its own efforts; it understands, indeed, that it hardly gives its consent to what happens to it. Once the soul understands that the fruit of mystical experience is not its own it can begin to share it with others:

> It begins to show signs that it is a soul which guards heavenly treasures, and that it desires to distribute them freely. It prays to God that it may not be rich alone, and begins to benefit its neighbours, almost unconsciously, and without any deliberate purpose. They understand how things are, because the flowers now smell so sweet that they are eager to come near them. They realize that the soul has virtue in it, and, seeing how delicious the fruit are, long to share in the feast.[12]

Teresa goes on to distinguish a state beyond union, which she calls 'rapture, or elevation, or flight of the spirit or transport . . . these are all different names for the same thing, which is also called ecstasy'. Rapture, she says, is even more beneficial than union and its results are much greater. The soul no longer seems to animate the body and when rapture comes its effects are irresistible, as against union, in which resistance is almost always possible – though at the cost of pain and effort. Rapture comes as a sudden and violent shock: Teresa compares it to being borne up on the wings of an eagle:

> We have to go willingly wherever we are carried, for in fact, we are being born off whether we like it or not . . . Sometimes with a great struggle I have been able to do something against it. But it has been like fighting a great giant, and has left me utterly exhausted. At other times resistance has been impossible; my soul has been carried away, and usually my head as well, without my being able to prevent it; and sometimes it has affected my whole body, which has been lifted from the ground . . . once in particular during a sermon . . . I lay on the ground and the sisters came to hold me down, but all the same the rapture was observed. Then I earnestly beseeched the Lord to grant me no more favours if they must have outward and visible signs.[13]

Apart from the *Life*, from which the quotations in this section have been taken, Teresa's mystical experiences are described in *The Way of Perfection* (*Camino de Perfección*, 1565) and *The Interior Castle* (*Las Moradas*, 1577). In the latter, which contains the fullest account of Teresa's spiritual life, she describes in detail the transforming union of the soul with God known in Christian mysticism as the 'spiritual marriage'. As always with St Teresa, the highest level of mystical experience generated in her a dedication to the active service of God. The trances, visions, locutions and ecstasies were unimportant by comparison with this complete realization of Christian spirituality:

> What is the good, my daughters, of being deeply recollected in solitude, and multiplying acts of love, and promising our Lord to do wonders in His service, if, when we come out of our prayer, the least thing makes us do the exact opposite? . . . The repose which these souls enjoy whom I speak of now is inward only; they have, and desire to have, less outwardly. For to what end, do you think, the soul sends from this Seventh Habitation, and as it were from her very deeps, aspirations into all the other habitations of this spiritual castle? Do you think these messages to faculties, senses and body, have no other end but to invite them to sleep? No, no, no! Rather to employ them more than ever . . . If, as David says, one becomes holy with the holy, who can doubt that this soul, who is now become *one thing* with the Mighty God by this high union of spirit with Spirit, shares His strength?[14]

With the extraordinary expansion of her capacity for mystical experience of the highest order (and, often, accompanying physical phenomena) – 'making progress in prayer', as she called it – came a dissatisfaction with life in the Convent of the Incarnation, where, as we have seen, the Bull of Mitigation allowed a relaxed form of the primitive Carmelite Rule.

One day, while at prayer, Teresa had been plunged, as she thought, into hell: 'I understood that the Lord wished me to see the place that the devils had ready for me there, and that I had earned by my sins. All this happened in the briefest second; but even if I should live for many years, I do not think I could possibly forget it.' She goes on to describe her vision in detail:

> The entrance seemed to me like a very long, narrow passage, or a very low, dark, and constricted furnace. The ground appeared to be covered with filthy wet mud, which smelt abominably and contained

many wicked reptiles. At the end was a cavity scooped out of the wall, like a cupboard, and I found myself closely confined in it . . . There is no light there, only the deepest darkness. Yet, although there was no light, it was possible to see everything that brings pain to the sight . . . I was terrified, and though this happened six years ago, I am still terrified as I write; even as I sit here my natural heat seems to be drained away by fear.[15]

The vision caused her great distress on account of the number of souls (Lutherans in particular) who brought damnation on themselves and it gave her a fervent desire to help such souls escape the kind of torment that had been revealed to her. She also longed to do penance for her 'evil' deeds and to become worthy of 'the bliss that awaits the good': 'I wanted to avoid human company, and finally withdraw completely from the world. My spirit was restless, yet not with a disturbing but a pleasant disquiet; I knew quite well that it was of God, and that His Majesty had given my soul this ardour so I might digest other and stronger meat than I was then eating.'

And so the idea began to found a convent of Discalced or Barefoot nuns that would observe the strict original form of the Carmelite Rule; and one day after communion 'the Lord earnestly commanded me to pursue this aim with all my strength. He made me great promises; that the house would not fail to be established, that great service would be done Him there, that its name should be St Joseph's. . . .'

After considerable difficulties she founded the Convent of St Joseph at Avila and in time other Reformed houses were set up, including some for men.* The final years of St Teresa's life were in fact as full of arduous and continuous administrative and physical activity as they were of mystical experiences and she derived spiritual comfort and inspiration from her hardships and deprivations. Of the foundation of a convent in Toledo, for instance, she wrote: 'We were for some days with no other furniture but two straw mattresses and one blanket, not even a withered leaf to fry a sardine with, till someone, I know not who, moved by our Lord, put a faggot in the church, with which we helped ourselves. At night it was cold, and we felt it . . . The poverty we were in seemed to me as the source of a sweet contemplation.'

---

*The story of Teresa's struggles to found the Discalced Carmelite Order is told in her *Book of Foundations* (*Libro de las Fundaciones*, 1573), as well as in her many letters.

Teresa died in 1582 and was canonized in 1622. In 1814, as Spain (with English help) was driving out the French from its soil, Teresa was proclaimed the national saint of her country. The mysterious physical phenomena that had accompanied her mystical experiences during her lifetime were added to after death by the incorruptibility of her body and an accompanying fragrance. But her devotees were not content to wonder: 'In the wild rush to acquire sacred relics, various of her limbs were torn from her corpse. Her old friend Father Gracián, who had only lately so disappointed her by failing to accompany her on a journey, inaugurated her dismemberment by cutting off one of her hands.'[16]

The words of Professor Allison Peers provide a concise and just estimate of St Teresa's importance in the history of mysticism:

> She is bound by some link or other to most of the great ascetics and mystics of her age . . . And just as in this way she is the centre of the greatest mystics of her time, and her life a connecting link or thread which runs through their own, so the mysticism which finds expression in the *Camino de Perfección* and the *Moradas* has something in common with mysticism of every type. It is neither for the beginner alone nor for the proficient; it neither despises asceticism nor enforces it; it avoids the extremes of quietism while extolling the fundamental truths from which that doctrine springs. Thus the works of St Teresa are a legacy to all who call themselves or would fain be called mystics in spirit and in truth, and as such they have never lacked a multitude of readers.[17]

St John of the Cross
Some thirty miles to the north-west of Avila stood the village of Fontiveros and here, in 1542, was born Juan de Yepes, now known to the world as St John of the Cross, in humble circumstances. At about the age of fourteen Juan was adopted by a devout patron, Don Antonio Alvarez de Toledo, who provided for his education. Juan worked for Don Antonio, who was warden of a hospital in Arévalo (to where Juan's widowed mother and her two sons had moved), and he also studied at a Jesuit school. Juan did not, however, enter the Society of Jesus but instead took the Carmelite habit, entering a house of the Order in Medina in 1563.

The following year he entered the University of Salamanca,

then one of the four leading universities in Europe and where Luis de León (1528–1591), an Augustinian scholar and himself a mystic, was a professor. Juan took a three-year arts course at Salamanca, as well as reading theology at the College of St Andrew's, the college of his Order.

He was ordained priest in the summer of 1567 and soon afterwards met St Teresa, then fifty-two years old, an event that would determine the whole course of his life. Teresa had by then obtained a licence from the General of the Carmelite Order to found two Discalced houses for men. The second of her women's houses had been established in Medina and she had been helped in this by the Prior of the convent in which Juan had professed, Fray Antonio de Heredia. Fray Antonio, to Teresa's surprise, offerd to become the first male member of the new Discalced Order and it was not long before Juan de Yepes (known now as Fray John of St Matthias) became the second. However, he returned to university for a year's further study and during the same period Fray Antonio underwent a probationary trial to see if his health and temperament would stand up to the rigours of the reformed Rule.

In May 1568 Fray John returned to Medina and learned that a house had been provided for the new Order in a village called Duruelo – an uninhabited, cramped and dirty building, suitable in every respect, certainly, for anyone wishing to lead an ascetic lifestyle. When Teresa first saw the house, with a sister nun, she recalled that: 'My companion, though a much better person than I am and a great lover of penance, could not bear the thought of my founding a monastery there. "Mother," she said, "I am certain that nobody, however good and spiritual, could endure this. You must not consider this."'[18]

But consider it she did and here, at the end of September 1568, John of St Matthias, henceforth to be known as John of the Cross, arrived to begin putting the house at Duruelo in order. Fray Antonio – known now as Antonio of Jesus – came in November with a third recruit, Joseph of Christ, and on the following morning all three took their new vows. Their time was spent in prayer, study, devotional offices and evangelizing the surrounding country, the latter activity carried out, even in deep winter, literally barefoot. Three months after their arrival in Duruelo their Foundress paid a visit and was moved, though also a little disturbed, by the austerity of their lives, which included corporal penance. But this asceticism did not, as Teresa feared, deter recruitment and in 1570 a larger and more comfortable house was given to them at Mancera, the second reformed foundation for men having been established at Pastrana in July 1569.

In mid-1572 John and another friar were sent as confessors to Teresa's old convent of the Incarnation at Avila, and there he remained for five years. For some of this period Teresa herself returned to the Incarnation as Prioress, ordered there by the Carmelite authorities, who still exercised their power over the Reform. John's presence transformed the lax spiritual life of the Incarnation and after his departure Teresa wrote: 'I have not found another like him in the whole of Castile, nor any that inspires such fervour in those that tread the way to Heaven. You would never believe how lonely I have been since he went . . . He is very spiritual and most experienced and learned. Those who were brought up here under this teaching miss him sorely.'[19]

During these five years dissension between the followers of the Mitigated Rule (the Observance) and the Discalced Reform grew into open and dangerous conflict and John of the Cross was gradually drawn into this struggle – 'this Babylon', as Teresa called it. From 1572 to 1577 he lived quietly in his house near the Incarnation in Avila, but as the conflict deepened the leaders of the Mitigation attempted to persuade him to abandon the Reform. When this failed they resorted to force. During the night of 13 December 1577 John and another friar, Fray Germán of St Matthias, were taken to the monastery of the Observance in Avila and there they were flogged before being confined in separate prisons.

Dressed in the cloth habit of the Mitigation, John was taken eighty miles to Toledo, interrogated and confined once more in a cell ten feet by six, with no outside window. There he remained for eight and a half months, a period that included the hottest part of the Castilian summer, on a diet of bread, water and occasional scraps of salt fish and with no change of clothing. He was also made to undergo the 'circular discipline', a common punishment in religious houses at this time, which involved being whipped in turn by a circle of friars.

The physical pain and deprivations, however, probably caused him less distress, being used to voluntary sufferings, than the mental and spiritual strain, especially as his captors would torment him with stories of the imminent collapse of the Reform.

His incarceration at Toledo was, in fact, the decisive factor in his development as a mystic, for he was for the first time, as one of his biographers has said, 'thrown back entirely upon God'.[20] His jailers allowed him a small amount of paper and ink, with which he began to write the poems that were to make him famous.

He eventually managed to escape from the prison, probably with the help of a friendly jailer, taking refuge first in a nearby house of Discalced Carmelite nuns, to some of whom he recited the stanzas he had composed during his imprisonment. He spent some time after his escape at another Discalced Convent, at Beas de Segura in the Sierra Morena, before journeying to the monastery of Monte Calvario, to which the Reform had appointed him as Vicar during the temporary absence of the Prior.

His four great prose works were all written in quick succession after the escape from Toledo: *The Ascent of Mount Carmel* and *The Dark Night of the Soul* were finished before 1580; *The Spiritual Canticle* and *The Living Flame of Love* were written before 1582 and 1584. They are all in the nature of commentaries on his three greatest poems: the 'Spiritual Canticle', the 'Dark Night' poem ('En una noche oscura' – 'In an obscure night') and 'Living Flame of Love'. The *Ascent of Mount Carmel* treats of 'Dark Night', which some believe to have been written in the Toledo prison but which Professor Allison Peers suggested was more probably composed soon after the escape. *The Dark Night of the Soul* is a continuation of the *Ascent*, whilst *The Spiritual Canticle*, completed by 1584, deals with the poem of the same name. The last commentary, *The Living Flame of Love*, was, apparently, written in a fortnight at Granada.

John of the Cross distinguishes two 'nights of the soul'. The first is the Night of Sense, in which the sensual part of the soul is purged; the second is the Night of the Spirit, which pertains to those who are proficient in spiritual discipline and occurs when God desires to bring the soul to a state of union with Him. The Night of Sense is, he says, a common experience; the Night of the Spirit is undergone by very few.

Both experiences are, literally, terrifying, but the second night incomparably more so. The conduct of beginners, says John, is not greatly to be praised, since they are still ruled by the love of self and bound by 'the low exercise of the senses'; but still, they have in a certain degree 'bridled their love of creatures, and for God's sake are capable of bearing a little heaviness and dryness'. In order that they might be led completely into the way of the spirit and commune with God 'more abundantly and with greater freedom from imperfections' their apparent progress is halted:

> When the sun of divine favour shines, as they think, more brightly upon them, God shuts off from them that light, closing the door, or the fountain, of the sweet spiritual water, which they were wont to enjoy in God as often and for as long as they wished . . . now God leaves them in such darkness that with their sense of imagination and their reasonings they know not which way to turn. They cannot take a step in meditation, as they were wont, their inward sense being overwhelmed in this night, and left in such dryness that they find no pleasure and sweetness in spiritual things and sacred exercises which formerly gave them delight and joy, but instead find only insipidity and bitterness.[21]

This is the passive entry to the Night of Sense; but there is also an active way. First, there must be an habitual desire to imitate Christ and conform to the pattern of His life. Second, every sensual pleasure must be renounced and rejected for the love of Christ, 'Who in this life had no other pleasure, neither desired any, than to do the will of His Father, which He called His meat and food'. In mortifying and calming the four natural passions (joy, hope, fear and grief) the aim is to stimulate desire for 'complete detachment and emptiness and poverty, with respect to everything that is in the world, for Christ's sake'.[22]

The second night, the Night of the Spirit, is called by John 'the most Intimate Purgation'. It is an inflowing of God into the soul, by which it is purged of ignorance and imperfection, 'habitual, natural and spiritual'. God secretly instructs the soul 'in the perfection of love': the soul does nothing 'but waits lovingly upon God, hearing Him and receiving His light, without understanding that this is infused contemplation'. The soul is, thereby, prepared and illuminated for union with God. But, asks John,

> Why should the soul call 'dark night' that divine light which, as we say, illumines it and purges it of its ignorances? To this the reply is that for two reasons the divine wisdom is not only night and darkness to the soul but also pain and torment. The first is the height of divine wisdom, which exceeds all the capacity of the soul, and to it is

therefore darkness. The second is the meanness and impurity of the soul, for which cause the wisdom of God is painful and afflictive to it, besides being dark.[23]

Just as gazing at the sun produces, paradoxically, a sense of darkness, so when the light of contemplation strikes the soul not yet perfectly enlightened it is plunged into spiritual darkness, 'because it not only transcends it, but also blinds it and deprives it of the operation of its natural intelligence'. And so John says: 'When God descends from Himself to the soul not yet transformed, this illuminating ray of His secret wisdom causes thick darkness in the understanding.' The experience is not only of darkness: it is also painful.

Since this infused divine contemplation has many qualities of exceeding goodness, and the soul which receives them, being not as yet purified, has many miseries, hence it follows, since two contraries cannot co-exist in one subject, the soul must of necessity suffer and be in pain . . . For when the pure light strikes the soul, in order to expel its impurities, the soul perceives itself to be so unclean and wretched that it seems as if God is fighting against it – that it has become the adversary of God.[24]

But the soul must accept and desire such pain and such darkness; for 'Man is created for God; and is called to strip off all selfhood and unlikeness to Him.' Even the joys of the spiritual life must be sacrificed to bring about 'diminished satisfaction with self'.

But if this is done, the soul attains to God through love and through exerting the whole capacity of its being. The ultimate goal is to reach the last deep centre of the soul, which is God: 'so long as it [the soul] attains not as far as this, although it be in God, Who is its centre by grace and by His own communication, still, if it has the power of movement to go farther and strength to do more, and is not satisfied, then, although it is in the centre, it is not in the deepest centre, since it is capable of going still farther.'[25]

There is, that is to say, degrees of love and as many centres, 'each one deeper than another, which the soul has in God'. In the last degree of love, God's love will wound the soul in its deepest centre. It will succeed, that is, in transforming and enlightening it as regards all the being and power and virtue of the soul, such as it is capable of receiving, until it be brought into such a state that it appears to be God. In this state the soul is like the crystal that is clear and pure; the more degrees of light it receives, the greater concentration of light there is in it, and this enlightenment continues to such a degree that at last it attains a point at which the light is centered in it with such copiousness that it comes to appear to be wholly light, and cannot be distinguished from the light, for it is enlightened to the greatest possible extent and thus appears to be light itself.[26]

In the final union of the soul with God – the spiritual marraige – the soul lives the life of God. Whereas before this union it understood things in a natural way, it is now informed by the supernatural light of God's understanding: the soul thereby becomes fully divine, for its understanding and God's understanding are the same. Similarly with the will, which is changed into the life of divine love and is moved 'by the Holy Spirit in Whom it now lives, since its will and His will are now only one'. The memory, which formerly acted only upon created things, 'has in its mind the eternal years'; and desire is activated, not by 'creature food that wrought death', but the delight of God: 'And finally, all the movements and operations which the soul had aforetime, and which belonged to the principle of its natural life, are now in this union changed into movements of God. For the soul, like the true daughter of God that it now is, is moved wholly by the Spirit of God.' Though the soul's understanding, will, memory and delight are now God's, its substance is not the Substance of God, for into this it cannot be changed; it is, however, absorbed in Him,

> and is thus God by participation in God, which comes to pass in this perfect state of the spiritual life, although not so perfectly as in the next life . . . And for this reason the soul may here say very truly with Saint Paul: 'I live, now not I, but Christ liveth in me.' And thus the death of this soul is changed into the life of God, and the soul becomes absorbed in life, since within it there is likewise fulfilled the saying of the Apostle: 'Death is absorbed in victory'.[27]

This total, ineffable absorption in God is achieved through a life of utter detachment. Even Professor Allison Peers, writing of the impression a first reading of St John of the Cross usually produces, conceded that: 'Few persons, however spiritually minded, will fail to find it repellent. It strikes a deadly chill, not only into the unhealthy heat of sense-affection, but into the glowing warmth of what one had hoped and believed to be pure love of God. It calls on one to go out from God-given light into a black and unknown darkness.' John of the Cross therefore deserves the title 'the mystic's mystic': his way to God is only for supremely dedicated souls. And yet his mysticism – and this is true of all the greatest Christian mystics – is a mysticism of love, and in this respect it cannot be said to be finally life denying. 'Where there is no love, put love in', he wrote, 'and you will draw love out.'

The last years of St John of the Cross were darkened by dissension, not now between the Reform and the Mitigation, but between factions within the Reform itself. He died in December 1591, in his forty-ninth year, after an operation. 'They take him for a saint,' St Teresa had written of him, 'and a saint, in my opinion, he is, and has been all his life.'

PART THREE: ASPECTS OF MYSTICISM SINCE 1600

IT WOULD be impossible to discuss, even in brief outline, the nature and development of mystical experience from the beginning of the seventeenth century to the present day without compiling an account at least as long again as the present book. The tradition we have followed from the New Testament era to the flowering of Carmelite mysticism in sixteenth-century Spain was a living stream that fed, and continues to feed, the spiritual life of the West; but inevitably, the impact of the Reformation, and the growth of scientific rationalism, materialism and secularism produced a host of tributaries to this main stream as those endowed with the mystical sense responded to specific religious, philosophical, cultural and political pressures.

The purpose of this final section is to provide a necessarily inadequate and incomplete sketch of a few of these tributaries and to indicate how the mystical sense has asserted itself since 1600, both in a formally religious context and in those whose perception of Ultimate Truth does not necessarily conform to the language of traditional Christian theology.

7. St Francis de Sales and the French School

FRANCIS DE SALES (1567–1622) was the son of a French nobleman and received a Jesuit education at the College of Clermont in Paris. He was, as Bremond says of him, 'religious and enamoured of perfection from the outset', and de Sales himself records that when he began his studies in Paris he was 'seized by a fervent desire to be perfectly holy'.[1] It was during this period that he experienced an intense temptation to despair that was to colour all his subsequent teaching. He related to Ste Chantal that 'as a student in Paris he fell into ... exceeding agonies of mind, being convinced of himself that he was eternally rejected without hope of salvation, and this made him numb with terror'. The torment lasted for some weeks and was overcome by totally submitting to the will of God, even if this meant damnation; whereupon, said Ste Chantal, 'it came to him all at once that his disease had fallen from him like leprous scales, and he felt himself perfectly and completely whole'.[2]

In 1588 de Sales went to Padua to study law and then returned to his family home at Thorens in Savoy. He was ordained priest in 1593, the fulfilment of a childhood ambition that had been hitherto opposed by his father, and was appointed provost of the cathedral chapter of Geneva that same year. He devoted himself to reconverting the Chablais region to Catholicism and became Bishop of Geneva in 1602.

Francis de Sales achieved his reputation as both a staunch defender of the Catholic faith and as a preacher and spiritual director. His published works reflected both the necessity to explicate Catholic doctrine and the demand for his spiritual counsels. The *Controversies* and the *Defence of the Standard of the Holy Cross* were written between 1594 and 1598; the *Treatise on the Love of God* was begun in 1607 and published in 1616, and the more famous *Introduction to the Devout Life* was first published in 1609, the definitive edition appearing ten years later. He died at Lyons on 28 December 1622 and was canonized by Pope Alexander VII in 1665.

The roots of the *Introduction to the Devout Life* lay in letters on spiritual matters to various dedicated penitents, such as Madame de Chantal, Marie de Charmoisy and Marie de Beauvillier. There were many others, such as the 'gentleman fallen into profound melancholy', to whom de Sales wrote, referring to his own experience of spiritual despair: 'I suspect that your mind is still harassed by some fear of sudden death and Divine judgments. Alas, what torment is that! ... My soul, which endured the like for six long weeks, is qualified to compassionate those thus afflicted.'[3] It was Madame de Charmoisy who was principally responsible for the composition of the *Introduction* as she herself described.

> At the beginning, when I placed my soul in the hands of the said Servant of God [de Sales], occasion arose for my return to court. As I was greatly apprehensive of this, I went to confer with the said Servant of God, declaring to him my apprehensions. He then said to me: 'Have courage, my child; do not fear that on this account you will fall back. For if you are faithful to God, He will never fail you; even though He has to stop the sun and the moon, He will give you enough time to perform your exercises and all else that you must do.' For this reason he determined to give me some instructions in writing upon this subject, and these I communicated to a Jesuit father, who found them so excellent and useful that he urged the blessed Servant of God to have them printed. This was the reason why he composed the *Introduction to the Devout Life*, into which book he inserted them.[4]

The principal aim of the *Introduction* was to show how a life of spiritual devotion could be effectively accomplished without withdrawing from the world. The absolute retirement of the early Christian ascetics and of the more rigorous monastic communities was abandoned in what is essentially a spiritual guide for those who must perforce live in the world. Against the ideals of solitude, withdrawal and isolated communing with God de Sales proposed a spiritual method that defended its practitioners against worldly snares at the same time as it deepened their experience of spiritual realities. 'My intention', he wrote in his Author's Preface, 'is to instruct those who live in towns, in families, or at court.'

By their condition they are obliged to lead, as to outward appearances, an ordinary life. Frequently, under an imaginary pretence of impossibility, they will not so much as think of undertaking a devout life. It is their belief that just as no beast dares taste the seed of the herb called *palma Christi*, so no man ought to aspire to the palm of Christian piety as long as he lived amidst the press of temporal affairs. To such I shall prove that . . . a vigorous and resolute soul may live in the world without being infected by any of its moods, may discover sweet springs of piety amidst its salt waters, and may fly through the flames of earthly lusts without burning the wings of the holy desires of a devout life.[5]

And yet de Sales could not countenance any slackening of the spiritual fibres. Gentle, calming, even emollient at times, he none the less expected much of others, as he expected much of himself. He wrote to Madame de Chantal: 'Cut, sever your friendships, do not amuse yourself by untying them. Scissors and knife are necessary. No, the knots are fine, intricate, tangled . . . your nails are too short to take hole of them. Only the sharp knife will do it. The cords are of no value. Do not spare them.'[6] Drawn towards an ever more total abnegation, Ste Chantal told her director:

My true father, the knife has indeed cut to the quick! Alas, my only father, today I remember how once you commanded me to strip myself. I answered, 'I know not of what more!' and you replied, 'Have I not told you, daughter, that I will strip you all?' Oh God, how easy it is to abandon all around us! But to abandon skin, flesh, bone, down to the very marrow, which is, meseems, that which has befallen us, is a great task, difficult, impossible, were it not for God's grace.[7]

To this de Sales replied: 'Our Lord loves you, my mother; He will have you all His own; take no other arm than His to support you . . . Keep your will so simply united to His that nought may dispart you.'

Francis de Sales believed in the inherent beauty of human nature, a goodness that can never be irredeemably stifled; there is a natural inclination to love God that corresponds to the concept of the spark of the soul: 'This pleasure, this confidence, which the human heart has naturally in God, can assuredly proceed from nought save correspondence existing between Divine Goodness and our souls: a correspondence absolute but secret, of which everyone is aware, but which few comprehend.'[8] In a passage typical of his easy, metaphorical style, de Sales goes on to explain that this natural inclination

> does not exist for nothing in our hearts, for it serves God as an anchor by which He may the more gently seize and draw us to Himself, Divine Goodness holding us in some wise linked by this sentiment with Himself, as little birds by a string, by which He can draw us when it pleases His Compassion to have pity on us. On our side, it is a sign and memorial implanted by our First Principle and Creator of that love to which it incites us, a secret token that we belong to his Divine Goodness. Like stags sometime adorned by great princes with collars bearing their arms, that when the creatures are loosed . . . they shall be known of all who may encounter them.[9]

Madame Acarie

In 1602 de Sales made the acquaintance of an extraordinary and fascinating figure – Madame Acarie (1566–1618), a woman who, like St Teresa, combined an intense spiritual life with a practical reforming zeal. Unlike the Carmelite saint, however, her spiritual experiences co-existed with an unshakeable commitment to a husband and family.

Barbe Avrillot was born in Paris on 1 February 1566. When she was eleven she was boarded with the Franciscan nuns at the Abbey of Longchamps, where her aunt was a resident. The life suited her naturally religious temperament, but her mother had no wish for her daughter to be a nun and at the age of fourteen Barbe was removed from the abbey to live at home. Madame Avrillot determined on a successful marriage for Barbe and in 1582 introduced her to Pierre Acarie. They were married in August that year and went to live in the Acarie mansion in the Rue des Juifs. Barbe was sixteen-and-a-half.

Though she missed the religious life she had experienced at Longchamps, Barbe became a devoted wife and mother. She became known as *'la bella Acarie'* and presented Pierre Acarie with six children between 1584 and 1592. Then one day she came across a phrase from St Augustine, 'He is indeed a miser to whom God is not enough', and her life was instantly changed. According to her eldest daughter Marie, 'She told us that this sentence made so sudden a change in her that she was detached at once from all earthly affections.'

In the late summer of 1590, soon after this experience occurred, Barbe fell into an ecstasy during Mass in the parish church of Saint-Gervais. The ecstasy lasted until the evening, when she was found, motionless and hardly breathing, in a Lady chapel behind the high altar. From this time on she experienced frequent raptures, though she often fought against them, sometimes by playing the spinet. Doctors were called in and her blood was duly let – even though the physicians could see that her ecstasies left her red in the face. She was even in ecstasy during the birth of her sixth child in 1592.

These experiences distressed her deeply. No one could explain them to her. Then, in 1592, she met a Capuchin friar, **Benedict of Canfield**. Benedict, or Benet, was an Englishman from Canfield in Essex who had been converted to Catholicism and had studied at the English College at Douai. He had taken the Franciscan habit in 1587 and soon gave signs of uncommon spiritual gifts. His biographer, Jacques Brousse, wrote: 'As a novice his long ecstasies frightened the friars. They thought he was mad or the victim of the devil's.' But Benedict was far more than a hysteric or an exhibitionist; he has been called by Bremond 'Master of the masters themselves, of Bérulle, Madame Acarie, Marie de Beauvillier and many others', and can be seen as a formative influence on the mystical renaissance in seventeenth-century France. It was Benedict who assured Barbe Acarie that her raptures came from God. In so doing he lifted, as Barbe's biographer Duval put it, 'a stone from off her heart'.

For some time after the siege of Paris, during which she had ministered to the sick and the poor, Barbe lived with her cousin Louise de Bérulle, *née* Séguier. Louise's son, Pierre de Bérulle, had received a Jesuit education and was deeply attracted to Barbe Acarie, whose ecstasies he had witnessed at first hand. He became a prominent member of Madame Acarie's spiritual *salon* in the Rue des Juifs, and he too came under the influence of Benedict of Canfield and his *Rule of Perfection*.

Madame Acarie became the focus of the spiritual life of Paris. She was greatly valued as a spiritual counsellor and her influence began to extend to the reformation of religious houses. In 1601 she was introduced to the works of St Teresa of Avila. In spite of a natural distrust of physical manifestations (though she herself reputedly received the stigmata), she began to be intensely interested by the intrepid energy of St Teresa in founding the Discalced Carmelites. Two visions of St Teresa directed Madame Acarie to establish the Carmelite Order in France, which she did with the help and advice of Bérulle, Francis de Sales and others. Letters patent were issued in 1602 authorizing the foundation of a Carmelite convent in Paris, the site chosen being the ancient priory of Notre Dame des Champs. Spanish nuns formed the core of the new élite, though Madame Acarie immediately set about training a group of French postulants in the pure and rigorous Teresian tradition. Like St Teresa, Barbe Acarie shows how completely a mystic may live in the world. She was endlessly active – tending to the sick, performing works of charity, attending to the construction of the new convent, running her home, training her postulants. As Lancelot Sheppard put it: 'St Teresa provides evidence enough of a dynamic energy combined with, in reality derived from, contemplation. Barbe Acarie was her faithful follower.'[10] At Bérulle's instigation, the new house was named the Incarnation. In due course two further convents were founded, at Pontoise and Dijon, and others followed.

Testimonies to the spiritual sources of Madame Acarie's energy and influence are not wanting, though she herself drew back from writing about her experiences. She said that to speak of God one must forget oneself: 'As soon as I become conscious how high are the things of God and that my words come from so mean and diseased a dwelling, all that I say seems so worthless that I cannot abide it.'[11]

Madame Acarie displayed a rare facility for mystical experience, a continual susceptibility to passive illumination, in spite of herself. One witness wrote that, 'having God so present to her soul . . . had she not practised some distraction, she would often have fallen into ecstasy and been transported out of herself'.

Because [of] her great inwardness and familiarity with God, her countenance, like that of Moses, was wont to become wholly luminous . . . If interrupted while speaking on affairs of business or good works she was instantly silent, and forthwith concentrated herself so eagerly upon God that she would forget what she had been saying just before and had to be helped to remember . . . I have seen this happen many times while I talked with her.[12]

Bremond's verdict on the importance of Madame Acarie in the spiritual life of her time is worth quoting in full:

The contemporaries of Mme Acarie found in her a living type of that sublime life towards which so many souls of the time felt themselves vaguely called. Her ecstasies were but signs, as a light hung out for travellers seeking their way at night. Their attention was caught at first by such extraordinary phenomena, but they soon learned from her truths far simpler and of quite different import. Her message consisted of a sentence from the Gospel, the full sense of which only mystics realize, 'The kingdom of God is within you'. 'One must,' she said, 'penetrate to the depths of the soul, and see if God is, or will be there.'

Ste Chantal

Francis de Sales had, he said, 'infinite respect' for Barbe Acarie and regarded as a 'vessel wholly consecrated by the Spirit to His uses'. But he was never intimately involved with her spiritual life, as he was with Ste Chantal, whom he met in 1604.

Jeanne-Françoise Frémyot, later Baronne de Rabutin-Chantal, was born in Dijon in 1572. Though religious by nature, like Madame Acarie her spiritual inclinations were accommodated within a full and active married life. Those inclinations, however, were persistent and grew in strength. When her husband was away, she said, 'I felt great longing to be altogether devoted to God; but alas, I knew not how to profit by or even recognize the grace God was offering me, nearly all my thoughts and prayers being limited to preservation and return of M. de Chantal.'

M. de Chantal died of a hunting accident in 1601, and it was thus as a widow that Jeanne de Chantal met Francis de Sales three years later. 'From the moment that I had the honour to know him,' she wrote, 'I called him a saint in the depths of my heart.' There was an instant rapport between them, and in due course de Sales became her spiritual director. Together they founded the Order of the Visitation, or Visitandines, in 1610. The Order was conceived in the same spirit as the *Introduction to the Devout Life*: that is to say, it was begun 'with the intent that no great severity shall prevent the feeble and the weak from joining it, there to devote themselves to the perfection of the divine love'. At the head of the new Order, de Sales placed Jeanne de Chantal. It was for the Visitandines in their devotion to 'the perfection of the divine love' that de Sales wrote his great guide to the mystical life, the *Treatise on the Love of God* (1616). The *Treatise* shows clearly that he was no mere theoretician and that he wrote from experience of a high order. Yet for him, as for St Teresa, the steadfast practice of true charity and the moral virtues must flow from the contemplative life; indeed, the exercise of these fundamental Christian duties was preferable to the perhaps vain thirsting for union with God.

What Francis de Sales chiefly cared for and loved best, said one of the early Visitandines, was 'to ground his daughters well in the true inward life of the Spirit . . . so that they sought nothing for themselves but mortification, recollection, silence, and hiddenness in God'. Jeanne de Chantal's method of devotion consisted in 'a simple beholding and realizing of His divine presence, in which I felt utterly lost, absorbed, and at rest in Him'; and this became the characteristic tendency of the Visitation – 'a very simple practice of the Presence of God, by an entire self-abandonment to His holy Providence'.

The doctrine here is completely Salesian and reflects de Sales's conception of 'holy indifference'. 'The whole teaching of our blessed Father,' wrote Ste Chantal, 'aimed at complete deprivation of self.' This deprivation, this indifference, taken together and to their limits, led de Sales to 'imagine the impossible', a state in which a man, knowing his damnation would be more pleasing to God than his salvation, 'would abandon his salvation and run to his damnation'.

Pierre de Bérulle and Pascal
Although Francis de Sales had been involved with Madame Acarie in the introduction of the Carmelite Order to France, he had never come into personal contact with her spiritual director, Pierre de Bérulle (1575–1629). Bérulle, however, exerted an influence on de Sales, as he did on so many others. Of him, de Sales wrote: 'A man to whom God has given much and whom it is impossible to be; never have I known a spirit that haunted me so, in spite of my never having seen nor met him.' Bérulle founded the religious community known as the Oratory in 1611, the purpose being to 'raise the state of the priesthood' in France. It marks, in Bremond's opinion, 'the culminating point of the French Counter-Reformation'.[14]

Bérulle's theology established a distinct school in French spirituality and was based on a minutely detailed cultivation of the interior life. It was profoundly theocentric in character, as demonstrated by the axiom: 'First of all it is needful to regard God and not oneself, and not to act by this regard and desire of oneself, but by the pure regard for God.' The great popularizer of Bérulle and Oratorianism, Père Bourgoing, described how Bérulle wished to renew in the Church 'the supreme cult of the adoration and reverence due to God ... This is the spirit which he so strongly desired to establish among us, that with which he was obsessed and transported'. In the school of Bérulle, Bourgoing continues, 'we are taught to be true Christians, to be religious in that primitive religion professed by us at our baptism; we learn to adore the Divine greatness and perfections, the designs, the intentions and the judgements of God, and the mysteries of His Son'. In particular, Bérulle was obsessed with God as Man – the Word Incarnate, Jesus Christ:

> Thus God Incomprehensible makes Himself comprehended in this Humanity; God Ineffable makes Himself heard by the Voice of His Incarnate Word; God invisible shows Himself through the Flesh united by Him with the nature of eternity; and God Dreadful in the Light of His Greatness has revealed Himself in His Sweetness, His Graciousness, His Humanity ... O Miracle! O Glory![15]

In the middle of the seventeenth century the Oratory became divided into two factions, the anti-Jesuit Jansenists and the Molinists, who followed the concept of grace propounded by the Jesuit Luis de Molina (1535–1600) in his *Concordia liberi arbitrii cum gratiae donis* (1588). The Jansenists adhered to the predestinatory and theologically pessimistic doctrines of Cornelius Jansen (1585–1638), doctrines that were condemned as heretical by Innocent X in the bull *Cum occasione* (1653). A leading centre of Jansenism was the community of Port-Royal, which the philosopher and mathematician **Blaise Pascal** (1623–1662) entered in 1654. A few days after Pascal died, a manservant found the record of a transforming mystical revelation, experienced by Pascal in 1654, sewn inside his master's doublet. Though well known, it remains one of the most moving and convincing documents in the literature of spiritual experience:

> The year of grace 1654,
> Monday, 23 November ...
> From about half past ten in the evening until about half past twelve
> FIRE
> God of Abraham, God of Isaac, God of Jacob, not of the

philosophers and scholars.

Certitude, certitude, feeling, joy, peace.

God of Jesus Christ.

Deum meum et Deum vestrum.

Thy God will be my God.

Forgetfulness of the world and of everything, except GOD.

He is to be found only by the ways taught in the Gospel.

Greatness of the human soul.

O righteous Father, the world hath not known thee, but I have
    known thee.

Joy, joy, joy, tears of joy.

I have been separated from him.

Dereliquerunt me fontem aquae vivae.

My God, wilt thou forsake me?

Let me not be separated from him eternally.

This is the eternal life, that they know thee as the only true
    God, and the one whom thou hast sent, Jesus Christ.

Jesus Christ,

Jesus Christ.

I have been separated from him; I have fled him, renounced
    him, crucified him,

Let me never be separated from him.

He is preserved only by the ways taught in the Gospel.

Renunciation, total and sweet.

Total submission to Jesus Christ and to my director.

Eternally in joy for a day's trial on earth.

Non obliviscar sermones tous. Amen.[16]

Quietism: Madame Guyon

The concept of 'holy indifference' put forward by Francis de
Sales had within it potentialities that were to become known as
quietist. **Quietism** was popularized by the teachings of a Spanish
priest, **Miguel de Molinos** (*c.* 1640–1697), whose *Spiritual Guide*
(1675) advocated an extreme form of contemplative devotion in
which utter spiritual indifference, passivity and extinction of the
will were cultivated. Opposition to this doctrine came from both
the Jesuits and the Dominicans, but it was supported by appeals to
the writings of both St Teresa of Avila and Francis de Sales,
amongst others. The practice of Quietist prayer became
extremely fashionable. It was a mysticism in which all self-
mortification, all painful moral effort and all good works were
regarded as superfluous, indeed were inhibiting to the achievement of passive self-annihilation. It was a true that a form

of passivity had been practised by many pre-eminent mystics – including St Augustine, St Catherine of Siena, St Teresa and St John of the Cross. But in Quietism this state became greatly exaggerated and was not confined to the highest reaches of the spiritual life, as it had been previously, but was proposed as a necessary practice for all believers. Moreover, Molinos, set out a way to God without priestly intervention and this rejection of religious mediation constituted a direct challenge to Church authority, particularly that of the Jesuits. Molinos was arrested in 1685 and his teachings condemned two years later.

The practice of Quietist prayer was pursued and popularized by Jeanne-Marie Bouvier de la Mothe, **Madame Guyon** (1648–1717), an aristocratic, voluble and unstable figure whose best intentions were negated by egoism and self-delusion. She had been married to a man over twenty years her senior who was indifferent to her and her inner longings. She came upon the writings of St Thomas à Kempis and thereafter read nothing but works of religion and reflected constantly on her sins. A single phrase from a Franciscan solitary, bidding her to seek God in her heart, had an extraordinary effect on her and she centred all her considerable energy on the attempt to achieve union with God through the practice of passive prayer. Somewhat in the manner of Suso, she underwent pitiless self-mortification, tearing her flesh with pointed spikes and flogging herself with whips and nettles. For five years she travelled with a Barnabite monk, Père La Combe, evangelizing in the Savoy and the south-east of France. She gained many disciples, including clergymen and members of the highest Parisian society. But La Combe was arrested on a charge of heresy, sentenced to life imprisonment and died insane. Madame Guyon was arrested in 1688 but was later released.

Madame Guyon's teaching was contained in two books, *Moyen court et tres facile de faire oraison* (Short and Very Easy Method of Mental Prayer) and *Les torrents spirituels* (The Spiritual Torrents). The extreme nature of Quietist doctrine can be seen in her assertion that in the 'divine state' – that is, when the soul is lost in God – 'even the most evil actions, should they be obliged to perform them, cannot communicate their poison, since for them there exists no longer any evil in anything whatsoever, because of the essential unity which they have with God . . . so that such a soul is in complete ignorance of evil and as it were incapable of committing it'.[17]

Madame Guyon's most notable convert was **François Fénelon** (1651–1715), who became Bishop of Cambrai in 1695 and who was tutor to the grandson of Louis XIV. He placed himself under Madame Guyon's spiritual direction in 1689, the first step in a long and bitter controversy between Fénelon and his former friend Jacques Bossuet, Bishop of Meaux, who had little interest in mystical experience. In his *Explication des maximes des saints sur la vie intérieure* (1697) Fénelon expounded his version of Quietist practice in a series of forty-five articles that distinguished between true and false mysticism.

8. Four Protestant Mystics

THE great Protestant reformers were not indifferent to the Catholic mystical tradition. **Martin Luther** (1483–1546), for example, was deeply familiar with the writings of Eckhart and Tauler and once said of the *Theologica Germanica* that it had taught him more about God, Christ and the human condition than any other book. In Luther, the *experience* of justification – the consciousness of salvation by grace through faith – is akin to mystical intuitions of spiritual progress towards God. Radical Protestantism also had its 'free spirit' enthusiasts, extremists like the millenarianist Anabaptists (the *Schwärmer*, denounced by Luther), typified by the fringe mysticism of Thomas Münzer (*c.*1489–1525), who taught that God's living voice could be heard in the soul and whose views in general had a clear precursor in such as Joachim of Floris.

And yet the post-Reformation Protestant mystics themselves had no settled and determined doctrinal structure, and no developed body of literature, to which their spiritual experiences could be referred. Unlike their medieval Catholic predecessors they lacked the support of tradition and were deeply troubled by sectarianism and controversy within their own Church. Protestant mysticism is thus typically individualist and laid great stress on the value and legitimacy of personal enlightenment, which brought many of them into bitter conflict with the Protestant authorities – as can be seen in the case of one of the greatest, and most difficult, of the early Protestant mystics, Jacob Boehme.

Jacob Boehme
Jacob Boehme (1575–1624) was born at Old Seidenberg, a village near Görlitz in German Silesia, the son of a poor peasant family. A dreamy, introspective boy, he was apprenticed to a

shoemaker. It was while he was working in the master shoemaker's shop alone that a stranger came in, bought a pair of shoes and then, when he had gone out into the street, called to Boehme by name and said: 'Jacob, thou art as yet but little, but the time will come when thou shalt be great, and become another man, and the world shall marvel at thee. Therefore, be pious, fear God, and reverence His Word; especialy read diligently the Holy Scriptures, where thou hast comfort and instruction; for thou must endure much misery and poverty, and suffer persecution. But be courageous and persevere, for God loves and is gracious unto thee.'[1]

As a result of this strange and prophetic encounter Boehme's devotion to spiritual matters intensified, to the annoyance of his fellow-workers in the shoe shop and his master, who dismissed him saying that he would have no 'house-prophet' in his establishment sowing discord and trouble amongst his employees. And so Boehme began a long period of wandering, as a travelling shoemaker and repairer, as devout and spiritually attentive as ever and still diligently searching the Scriptures, as he had been bidden by the stranger, partly to assuage his own doubts and partly to provide some sort of assurance in the face of fierce theological conflicts that were then splitting the Protestant Church.

During his wanderings he was 'lifted into a condition of blessed peace, a Sabbath of the soul, that lasted for seven days'. As he himself said of this transfiguring experience: 'The triumph that was then in my soul I can neither tell nor describe. I can only liken it to a resurrection from the dead.'[2]

He returned to Görlitz in 1595, became a master shoemaker in his own right and married the daughter of a local butcher. In 1600 he had another remarkable experience when he chanced to look at a burnished pewter dish that was reflecting the sunshine. 'He fell', said Bishop Martensen, 'into an inward ecstasy, and it seemed to him as if he could now look into the principles and deepest foundations of things. He believed that it was only a fancy, and in order to banish it from his mind he went out into the green fields. But here he noticed that he could gaze into the very heart of things, the very herbs and grass, and that actual nature harmonized with what he had inwardly seen. He said nothing about this to any one, but praised and thanked God in silence.'[3]

Gradually he began to feel impelled to commit his experiences to paper and he started to write down his recollections early in the morning, before his day's work began. The result was *Dawn Glow*, or *Aurora*, subtitled 'The Root or Mother of Philosophy, Astrology, and Theology on the proper basis; or a Description of Nature'. Unfortunately a copy of the manuscript fell into the hands of the parish priest of Görlitz, Pastor-Primarius Gregorius Richter, an arrogant dogmatist who denounced Boehme by name from the pulpit and threatened to have him arrested. He was indeed taken before the magistrates, who, at Richter's instigation, ordered him to leave Görlitz immediately, which he meekly acquiesced to, saying: 'Yes, dear sirs, it shall be done; since it cannot be otherwise, I am content.' However, the magistrates relented and allowed Boehme to stay in the town, provided he handed over the manuscript of *Aurora* and refrained from writing again.

For five years Boehme obeyed the injunction, though with the utmost difficulty, for he felt that he should obey the God-directed urge to share his experiences with others. At last he decided to follow his conscience: 'I had resolved to do nothing in future, but to be quiet before God in obedience and to let the devil, with all his host, sweep over me. But it was with me as when a seed is hidden in the earth. It grows up in storm and rough weather, against all reason. For in winter-time all is dead, and reason says: "It is all over with it!" But the precious seed within me sprouted and grew green, oblivious of all storms, and, amid disgrace and ridicule, it has blossomed forth into a *lily*!'[4]

From 1619 until his death Boehme poured forth a torrent of writings, among which were *The Three-fold Life of Man*, the *Signatura Rerum*, the *Mysterium Magnum*, *The Incarnation of Christ* and *The Six Mystical Points*. One of his works, *The Way to Christ*, once again drew the wrath of Gregorius Richter, who issued an *Invective* against it. 'There are as many blasphemies in this shoemaker's book', said Richter, 'as there are lines; it smells of shoemaker's pitch and filthy blacking.' Though Boehme issued a defence he submitted to voluntary exile from Görlitz. Richter died in August 1624. Boehme, having fallen ill, returned to Görlitz that year and died on 21 November. His last words were supposed to have been: 'Now I go hence into Paradise.'

Boehme's mystical philosophy is a strange and often incomprehensible synthesis of Lutheran theology, German theosophy (Boehme is in many ways the Protestant counterpart of Eckhart,

Tauler and Suso) and hermeticism – seen in the use of alchemical symbology and terminology and the influence of Paracelsus. The result, for many readers, is a baffling chaos: John Wesley, for instance, described Boehme's writings as the 'most sublime nonsense, inimitable bombast, fustian not to be paralleled'.[5]

Boehme's own mystical experiences had enabled him, as he said, to break through the gates of hell, 'even into the innermost birth and geniture of the Deity, and there I was *embraced* with love, as a bridegroom embraceth his dearly loved bride.' Though the language here is that of Catholic mysticism, Boehme's thought is generally expressed in terms far unlike those of traditional Catholic theology. For instance, he freely used Qabalistic and alchemical symbolism to explain how an invisible, eternal and infinite God could create and pervade a visible, temporal and limited world.

There are, according to Boehme, seven natural properties, each with alchemical and astrological correspondences: (1) introspective desire, which demands only itself; (2) outward-looking desire or movemnt, which seeks expression in multiplicity; (3) restlessness and anguish ('One cannot remain in oneself, and yet can go nowhither!'); (4) the Lightning, the first joyous and completely unexpected contact of Spirit and Nature; (5) Love, or the unity of Wisdom; (6) intelligible sound ('Their voice is gone out through all the earth and their words to the end of the world': Psalm xix); (7) the Essential, the Uncreated Heaven, of which Boehme wrote: 'To describe it I have neither pen nor tongue. Even if this Maiden [Sophia or Wisdom] happen to lead anything of it into our heart, yet the whole man is too cold and dark for us to be able to utter of it even so much as a vestige.'

Through these properties God unfolds and reveals himself in an eternal cycle – the Theogonistic process, which again Boehme despaired of describing in its true nature:*

---

*The first link in the Theogonistic process is what Boehme caled the *Ungrund*, or 'abyss'. This is the eternal stillness, comparable to the Qabalistic *Ain Soph* or the Gnostic *Bythos*. The *Ungrund* is 'an undeveloped totality, wherein nature and spirit repose as yet in complete indifference, where there is neither light nor darkness, good nor evil, and where all varieties and differences are dormant' (Martensen, p. 75).

If I had the tongue of an angel and thou the intelligence of an angel, we should understand one another very well. But now I must speak in an earthly fashion with my half-dead understanding, and since I am only a spark, a particle of the whole, I cannot describe to thee the whole Deity in a circle all at once. I must set one thing *after* another, that thou mayest at last behold the whole. Yes! I must even speak sometimes in a *diabolical* manner, as if the Light were kindled out of darkness, and as if Deity had a beginning! Otherwise I cannot instruct thee. But it is not so: *God has no beginning*; or more truly, He has an eternal beginning and an eternal end.[6]

In spite of his often impenetrable obscurities, Boehme's influence was widespread and profound, from the philosopher Friedrich Schelling (1775–1854) to the theosophist and mystic Louis Claude de St Martin (1743–1803), the 'Unknown Philosopher', and William Law (see p. 196). An early disciple was Johann Scheffler (1624–1677), better known as **Angelus Silesius**, the son of a Polish nobleman and Court Physician to the Emperor Frederic III. It was he who wrote the famous lines:

In water lives the fish, the plant in the earth,
In the air the bird, the sun in the firmament,
In fire the salamander has its dwelling and its birth –
And the Heart of God is Jacob Boehme's element.

Scheffler, however, eventually discarded Boehme's teachings and in 1661 joined the Roman Catholic Church to become a Franciscan friar and a devotional poet in the tradition of Jacopone da Todi. In Germany, Holland and England throughout the seventeenth and eighteenth centuries there sprang up 'Behmenist' sects, the most famous of which were the Philadelphians. Most of Boehme's works were translated and published in England between 1647 and 1663.

George Fox

Protestantism in England in the seventeenth century, for all its avowed hostility to Catholic doctrine and practice, nevertheless demonstrated a need to develop a personal spiritual relationship with God, and even the Puritans exhibited spiritual interests that had definite links with Catholic origins in general and with the mystical tradition of Catholicism in particular: Francis Rous, for example, the author of several works of Puritan devotion, was a student of Dionysius the Areopagite, St Bernard and Tauler.

In the first half of the seventeenth century there sprang up in England many groups of spiritual seekers whose individual propensities were linked by a common renunciation of the forms and practices of external religion and nourished, in many cases, by the influence of Boehme. Of such sects William Penn said that they 'left all visible churches and societies and wandered up and down as sheep without a shepherd . . . *seeking* their Beloved, but could not find Him as their souls desired to know Him'.

It was against this background that Quakerism developed. The Society of Friends, called by Evelyn Underhill 'that great experiment in corporate mysticism', showed ordinary men and women how they might come to a personal apprehension of God. The movement was impelled and initially sustained by the spiritual genius of George Fox (1624–1691). Fox was born at Fenny Drayton in Leicestershire, the son of a Puritan weaver; but at the age of nineteen he left home and became a 'seeker'. 'I was,' he said, 'a man of sorrows in the time of the first workings of the Lord in me.' After three years of wandering and searching for spiritual assurance he had his famous ecstatic revelation, his second birth:

> Then, O then, I heard a voice which said, 'There is one, even Christ Jesus, that can speak to thy condition'; and when I heard it, my heart did leap for joy . . . when God doth work, who shall let it? And this I know experimentally . . . and then the Lord did gently lead me along and did let me see His love, which was endless and eternal and surpasseth all the knowledge that men have in the natural state or can get by history or books.[7]

Righteousness for Fox was a kind of *via negativa*, by which one rids oneself of what the world generally accounts as comfortable and desirable: 'It is the great love of God to make a wilderness of that which is pleasant to the outward eye and fleshly mind; and to make a fruitful field of a barren wilderness.' Fox's language is not that of the Catholic mystical theologian; but it is clear that he was the recipient of genuine mystical insights:

> Now was I come up in Spirit, through the flaming sword, into the paradise of God. All things were new; and all the creation gave another smell unto me than before, beyond what words can utter. I knew nothing but pureness, innocency, and righteousness, being

renewed up into the image of God by Christ Jesus; so that I was come up to the state of Adam, which he was in before he fell . . . But I was immediately taken up in Spirit, to see into another or more steadfast state than Adam's in innocency, even into a state in Christ Jesus, that should never fall.[8]

On another occasion Fox writes that 'the word of the Lord came to me saying, MY LOVE WAS ALWAYS TO THEE, AND THOU ART IN MY LOVE. And I was ravished with the sense of the love of God. . . .'

From these visionary 'openings' Fox passed on to the creative apostolic phase of his life – a peripatetic ministry that lasted forty years and which, like the reforms of St Teresa and the missionary work of St Paul, was distinguished by hardship and persecution.

John Woolman

Quaker spirituality drew not only on the writings of Boehme, but also on traditional Catholic mysticism, as represented, for example, by Thomas à Kempis. A Franciscan compassion for the animal creation is apparent in the writing of the American Quaker John Woolman (1720–1772), who declared: 'as by His breath the flame of life was kindled in all Animals and Sensible Creatures, to say we love God as unseen and at the same time exercise cruelty toward the least creature moving by His life, was a contradiction in itself'.[9]

Woolman was a fervent anti-slavery campaigner, a position that was totally consistent with his mysticism. He proclaimed the sacramental nature of the visible universe, the unity in God of all things. Not long before his death he suffered an attack of pleurisy and could not remember his name:

Being then desirous to know who I was, I saw a mass of matter of a dull gloomy colour, between the south and the east; and was informed, that this mass was human beings in as great misery as they could be, and live; and that I was mixed in with them, and that henceforth I might not consider myself as a distinct or separate being.

He remained in this state for some hours and heard what he believed to be the voice of an angel speaking to other angels, saying: 'John Woolman is dead':

My tongue was often so dry, that I could not speak till I had moved it about and gathered some moisture, and as I lay still for a time, at length, I felt Divine power prepare my mouth that I could speak; and then I said, 'I am crucified with Christ, nevertheless I live; yet not I, but Christ liveth in me; and the life which I now live in the flesh, I live by the faith of the Son of God, who loved me, and gave Himself for me.'

Then the mystery was opened; and I perceived there was joy in heaven over a sinner who had repented; and that that language (John Woolman is dead) meant no more than the death of my own will.[10]

William Law

Boehme's greatest English disciple was William Law (1686–1761), who was acquainted with a leading English Philadelphian, Dr Francis Lee of Cambridge. Law was born at King's Cliffe in Northamptonshire and went up to Emmanuel College, Cambridge, in 1705. Six years later he became a Fellow of Emmanuel and was ordained deacon the same year; but he lost his Fellowship in 1716 as a result of being a Nonjuror* and he thereupon left Cambridge, to become in time tutor to Edward Gibbon, the father of the historian. In 1727 he was ordained priest (by the Nonjuror Bishop Gandy) and from 1740 until his death he remained at King's Cliffe, where he became the centre of a small religious community.

It was in the mid-1730s that Law began to read Boehme ('that wonderful man', as he once called him) and for many English readers Law's transmutations of Boehme's cloudy teachings make the mystic of King's Cliffe as approachable and lucid as his German master is daunting and obscure.

Law is best known for his *Serious Call to a Devout and Holy Life* (1729), which sowed the seed of Methodism in John Wesley, who said of the book that it 'will hardly be excelled, if it be equalled, in the English tongue, either for beauty or expression or for justice and depth of thought'. It also kindled an interest in religion in Samuel Johnson. Later in life Law composed treatises that were more specifically mystical in character, such as *The Spirit of Prayer* (in two parts, 1749 and 1759), *The Spirit of Love* (two parts, 1752 and 1754) and *The Way to Divine Knowledge* (1752), the latter being in effect an exposition of Boehme's teachings.

Law had always been a diligent reader of what he called

---

*i.e. one who refused to take an oath of allegiance to George I and abjure the Stuarts.

'mystical divines' – including Dionysius the Areopagite, Ruysbroeck, Tauler, Suso, and of course Boehme (or Behmen, as Law
called him). Of such as these Law wrote:

> These writers began their office of teaching, as John the Baptist did,
> after they had passed through every kind of mortification and
> self-denial, every kind of trial and purification, both inward and
> outward. They were deeply learned in all the mysteries of the
> Kingdom of God, not through the use of lexicons, or meditating upon
> critics, but because they had passed from death unto life . . . like the
> Psalmist's king's daughter they are *all glorious* within: they are truly
> sons of thunder and sons of consolation; they break open the white
> sepulchres; they awaken the heart and show it its filth and rottenness
> of death, but they leave it not till the Kingdom of Heaven is raised up
> within it. If a man have no desire but to be of the spirit of the Gospel,
> to obtain all that renovation of life and spirit which alone can make
> him to be in Christ a new creature, it is a great unhappiness to him to
> be unacquainted with these writers . . . for in these writers the Spirit
> of God speaks a second time, and everything that can awaken,
> convert, instruct and inflame the heart with the love of God, and all
> holiness and purity of life, is to be found in the most irresistible degree
> of conviction.[11]

Law followed Boehme in asserting the primacy of the will. It is,
Law says, the hunger of the soul, just as St Augustine affirmed
that 'To will God entirely is to have Him', or as Ruysbroeck put it:
'You are as you desire to be'. When the will turns to itself, wishing,
as it were, for a sound of its own, 'it breaks off from the divine
harmony, and falls into the misery of its own discord'. Self is the
root, tree and branches of all the evils of our fallen state, and to
live the life of self is to live without God. The essence and life of
pride are therefore to be found in self-love, self-esteem and
self-seeking, and with pride, for Law, dwells the devil.* But 'To
die to these essential properties of self is to make the devil depart
from us'. In sum, says Law,

> nothing hath separated us from God but our own will, or rather our
> own will is our separation from God. All the disorder and corruption
> and malady of our nature lies in a certain fixedness of our own will,
> imagination, and desire, wherein we live to ourselves, are our own

*Cf. the *Theologia Germanica*: 'Nothing burneth in hell but self-will'.

centre and circumference,* act wholly from ourselves, according to our own will, imagination, and desires. There is not the smallest degree of evil in us but what arises from this selfishness, because we are thus all in all to ourselves.[12]

Our imaginations and desires are the greatest reality we have, 'the true formers and raiser of all that is real and solid in us'. The will rightly applied in prayer is truly creative in Law's view: just as it can generate death, it can also generate life. Here, says Law, lies the ground of the great efficacy of prayer,

> which when it is the prayer of the heart, the prayer of faith, has a kindling and creating power, and forms and transforms the soul into everything that its desires reach after: it has the key to the Kingdom of Heaven and unlocks all its treasures, it opens, extends and moves that in us which has its being and motion in and with the divine nature, and so brings us into real union and communion with God.[13]

Law describes the eternal Word as lying hidden within us all, a spark of the divine nature that will overcome sin and death and hell; that will recreate Heaven in the soul. In the heart the Saviour is to be found, not in 'books, in controversies, in the church, and outward exercises': 'Seek for Him in thy heart, and thou wilt never seek in vain, for there He dwells, there is the seat of His Light and holy Spirit.'

Understanding, will and memory can only reach after God: they are not 'the place of His habitation'. But there is a depth, a centre, an infinity of the soul that Law calls the hidden 'pearl of eternity'. It is this that must be sought out, and this that will bring us to God:

> Awake, then, thou that sleepest, and Christ, who from all eternity has been espoused to thy soul, shall give thee light. Begin to search and dig in thine own field for this pearl of eternity that lies hidden in it; it cannot cost thee too much, nor canst thou buy it too dear, for it is *all*; and when thou hast found it thou wilt know all which thou hast sold or given away for it is as mere a nothing as a bubble upon the water.[14]

*Cf. St Bonaventura: 'God's centre is everywhere, His circumference nowhere'.

9. The Mystical Sense in English Literature

BETWEEN 1480 and 1640 more than two-fifths of the books printed in England were religious in character. The percentage for the period 1600–1640 is even higher; and in William London's *Catalogue of the most Vendible Books in England* (1657–8) the space devoted to books on divinity is equal to that given to all other kinds.[1] This widespread concern is reflected in virtually every form of literature, and a preoccupation with the individual's relationship with God is particularly apparent in many of the major poets.

John Donne

John Donne (1573–1631), perhaps the most intellectually agile of the so-called Metaphysical Poets, was possessed of a deep and disturbing religious consciousness. He was intensely preoccupied with sin and death, with the unutterable distance between God and his sin-spotted soul. And yet the darkness could occasionally be penetrated by light, by those infusions of Grace for which Donne prayed so fervently: 'Thou hast delivered me, O God, from the Egypt of confidence and presumption . . . And from the Egypt of despair by contemplation of thine abundant treasures, and my portion therein; from the Egypt of lust, by confining my affections; and from the monstrous and unnaturall Egypt of painfull and wearisome idleness, by the necessities of domestick and familiar cares and duties.'[2]

In the *Devotions* (1624), which Izaak Walton called 'a Sacred picture of Spiritual Extasies', Donne counterbalances and interweaves physical and spiritual sickness, his own sickness becoming an allegory of the condition of mortality: 'O miserable condition of man! which was not imprinted by God, who, as he is immortal himself, had put a coal, a beam of immortality into us, which we might have blown into a flame, but blew it out by our first sin; we beggared ourselves by hearkening after false riches, and infatuated ourselves by hearkening after false knowledge.'[3] The fundamental mystical concept of the soul's kinship with God is repeated in the succeeding Expostulation:

> If I were but mere dust and ashes I might speak unto the Lord, for the Lord's hand made me of this dust, and the Lord's hand shall re-collect these ashes; the Lord's hand was the wheel upon which this vessel of clay was framed, and the Lord's hand is the urn in which these ashes shall be preserved. I am the dust and ashes of the temple of the Holy Ghost, and what marble is so precious? But I am more than dust and ashes: I am my best part, I am my soul. And being so, the breath of God, I may breathe back these pious expostulations to my God ... Thou hast imprinted a pulse in our soul, but we do not examine it; a voice in our conscience, but we do not hearken unto it ... We are God's tenants here, and yet here, he, our landlord, pays us rents; not yearly, nor quarterly, but hourly, and quarterly; every minute he renews his mercy, but we *will not understand*, lest that we should be converted, and he should heal us.

The intensity of Donne's desire for salvation, for the full knowledge of God, is unforgettably revealed in Holy Sonnet XIV:

> Batter my heart, three person'd God; for, you
> As yet but knocke, breathe, shine, and seeke to mend;
> That I may rise, and stand, o'erthrow mee, and bend
> Your force, to breake, blowe, burn and make me new ...
> Yet dearely I love you, and would be loved faine,
> But am betroth'd unto your enemie:
> Divorce mee, untie, or breake that knot againe,
> Take mee to you, imprison mee, for I
> Except you enthrall mee, never shall be free,
> Nor ever chaste, except you ravish mee.*

And in the nominally secular *Songs and Sonets* he seems to be drawing on the logic of the *via negativa* in the conceit that his love can only be expressed in negatives:

---

*Quotations from Donne's poetry are taken from *Donne: Poetical Works*, edited by Sir Herbert Grierson (Oxford 1933, 1966).

If that be simply perfectest
Which can by no way be exprest
  But *Negatives*, my love is so.
  To All, which all love, I say no.
If any who deciphers best,
  What we know not, our selves, can know,
Let him teach mee that nothing; This
As yet my ease, and comfort is,
Though I speed not, I cannot misse.[4]

Elsewhere, in that curious and difficult poem *The Second Anniversary*, he speaks of the 'essentiall joy' of truly knowing God in the life to come:

Only who have enjoy'd
The sight of God, in fulnesse, can thinke it;
For it is both the object, and the wit.
This is essentiall joy, where neither hee
Can suffer diminution, nor wee;
'Tis such a full, and such a filling good,
Had th'Angels once look'd on him, they had stood.

God, that is to say, is both the *object* of true knowledge and the *means* of knowing. Though such knowledge cannot be fully achieved in this life God can still be approached by striving to restore the Divine Likeness within, as did Elizabeth Drury, whose death the poem allegorizes:

Who kept by diligent devotion,
God's Image, in such reparation,
Within her heart, that what decay was growne,
Was her first Parents fault, and not her owne . . .
Who by a faithful confidence, was here
Betroth'd to God, and now is married there . . .

Such pronouncements as these, and quotations could be multiplied, certainly confirm Donne's capacity for expressing himself in the language of mysticism, and his poetry abounds with echoes of Catholic mystical theology – of St Bernard, for instance. But there is nothing, in either his prose or his poetry, to convince us that Donne was acquainted with the actuality of the contemplative life as it had been described in Catholic theology. Meditative his poetry certainly is; but there was a great deal standing between Donne and genuine mystical experience – not least, for all his sincere agonizing over the sins of his flesh, his fascination with the richness of experience. In Douglas Bush's just estimation: 'His mature faith, if not quite anti-intellectual fideism, was less rational and less mystical than evangelical. The preacher was rather a Christian warrior than a contemplative . . . Donne's vision is of sin, salvation, the earthly road thereto, and the heavenly reward; it is not the vision of the mystic who can leave self and the world behind . . .'[5]

George Herbert
In the second, and posthumous, edition of *Psyche* (1648, 1702), Joseph Beaumont, after praising the lyric poetry of Pindar and Horace, paid tribute to the poems of George Herbert:

> Yet neither of their Empires was so vast
> But they left *Herbert* too full room to reign,
> Who Lyric's pure and precious Metal cast
> In holier moulds, and nobly durst maintain
>   *Devotion in verse*, whilst by the spheres
>   He tunes his Lute, and plays to heav'nly ears.

As a writer, George Herbert (1593–1633),* unlike Donne, confined himself entirely to the composition of religious poetry, with the exception of a few complimentary verses to public figures. He came from a distinguished Welsh family (in his earlier years at Cambridge he was said by Izaak Walton to have 'put too great a value on his parts and parentage') and was the younger brother of Edward, Lord Herbert of Cherbury. His father died in 1596, when George was three and a half; but his mother, the gifted and widely admired Magdalen Herbert, survived to exert a strong influence on him. Donne knew her well and addressed poems to her, including the well-known 'The Autumnall'. George was sent to Westminster School and in 1609 went up to Trinity College, Cambridge. Soon after arriving in Cambridge he sent his mother two sonnets expressing his dedication to sacred poetry; and to his step-father Sir John Danvers he wrote in 1617: 'I want Books extremely: You know, Sir, how I am now setting foot into Divinity, to lay the platform of my future life.'[6]

---

*Quotations from Herbert in this section are taken from *The Works of George Herbert*, edited with a Commentary by F. E. Hutchinson (Oxford, 1941, 1967).

Herbert was ordained deacon by 1626 and he married three years later. In 1630 he was presented to the rectory of Bemerton, near Salisbury, taking priest's orders, as his mother had always wished, in September of that year. His health had never been good. As early as 1609/10 he had written to his mother from Cambridge about 'the heat of my late *Ague*', which, he said, 'hath dryed up those springs, by which Scholars say, the Muses use to take up their habitations'.[7]

In spite of illness (he maintained two curates at Bemerton to help him in his work) Herbert devoted himself to the priesthood. His brother Lord Herbert of Cherbury wrote of him: 'His life was most holy and exemplary; insomuch, that about Salisbury, where he lived, beneficed for many years, he was little less than sainted'.[8] His spiritual life is faithfully and eloquently recorded in *The Temple*, subtitled 'Sacred Poems and Private Ejaculations', published posthumously in 1633; and also in the prose work *A Priest to the Temple, or, The Country Parson His Character, and Rule of Holy Life* (London, 1652). The poems are intimate colloquies with no apparent awareness of an audience; they are overheard self-communings with God. Herbert himself described them to Nicholas Ferrar as forming 'a picture of the many spiritual Conflicts that have past betwixt God and my Soul, before I could subject mine to the will of Jesus my Master in whose service I have now found perfect freedom'.[9] His earlier struggles had arisen from a conflict between worldly ambition and the religious life; at Bemerton, as a result of his failing health, they took the form of frustration at not being able to serve God as he wished to do:

> And then when after much delay,
> Much wrastling, many a combate, this deare end,
> So much desir'd, is giv'n, to take away
> My power to serve thee.[10]

Of the duty of a country parson he wrote: 'Now love is his business and aime', and this ideal was completely fulfilled in his own ministry at Bemerton. As F. E. Hutchinson has said: 'This once proud man, distant with his social inferiors, became accessible to the humblest, made up differences between his parishioners, encouraged them in the habit of reading, and befriended the needy.'[11] He also gave a good deal of time to literary activities. During his years at Bemerton he revised many of his earlier poems, wrote the larger part of *The Temple*, composed *A Priest to the Temple*, and translated a treatise by Cornaro (from the Latin version by Leonard Lessius) on Temperance. There were other writings, according to Walton, that were intended for publication by Herbert's widow but that were destroyed during the Civil War. None of his writings were published in his lifetime, except for a volume of Latin occasional verse and orations.* The English poems were certainly circulated in manuscript before his death, by which time his reputation as a poet was already established. On its publication *The Temple*† was an immediate success, going through four editions in three years, and it made a deep impression on a number of poets, Crashaw and Vaughan in particular (see pp.209, 213).

The Puritan divine Richard Baxter, in the Preface to his *Poetical Fragments* (1681), said of Herbert that he 'speaks *to God* like one that *really believeth a God*, and whose business in the world is most *with God. Heart-work* and *Heaven-work* make up his Book.' In *The Poetry of Meditation* Louis L. Martz showed how deep were the affinities between Herbert and St Francis de Sales, affinities that focus on what was called 'the practice of the Presence of God'. There is no direct evidence to show that Herbert had read St Francis' seminal *Introduction to the Devout Life*, but the probability is that he did. He certainly admired the French ('You live in a brave nation,' he wrote to his brother Henry in Paris in 1618, 'where, except you wink, you cannot but see many brave examples. Bee covetous, then, of all good which you see in Frenchmen'[12]), and in any case he would have had access to the literature from which St Francis' meditative system developed – works such as *The Imitation of Christ*.‡ To take but one of the many examples given by Professor Martz, the following passage from the *Introduction* expresses the essential accent of the poems in *The Temple*:

Memoriae Matris Sacrum (1627).

†The preface, 'The Printers to the Reader', was by Nicholas Ferrar (see p.209), who wrote that the faithful discharge of Herbert's vocation was such 'as may make him justly a companion to the primitive Saints, and a pattern or more for the age he lived in'.

‡The third edition of John Yakesley's English translation of St Francis' *Introduction* was published at Rouen in 1614 as *An Introduction to a Devoute Life*.

As they that be enamoured with humane and natural love, have almost always their thoughts fixed upon the person beloved, their hart full of affection towards her, their mouth flowing with her praises; when their beloved is absent they leese no occasion to testifie their passions by kind letters, and not a tree do they meet with all, but in the barck of it, they engrave the name of their darling: even so such as love God fervently, can never cease thincking upon him, they draw their breath only for him, they sigh and sorrow for their absence from him, all their talk is of him and if it were possible, they would grave the sacred name of our Lord Jesu, upon the brest of all the men in the world.[13]

The Salesian emphasis on the stimulation of 'good thoughts' by meditation on created things is paralleled in Herbert's poem 'Providence':

> All things that are, though they have sev'rall wayes,
> Yet in their being joyn with one advise
> To honour thee . . .

The consecration of familiar objects in this way is alluded to in *A Priest to the Temple*, when Herbert speaks of the 'familiar illustration' in catechism: 'This is the skill, and doubtless the Holy Scripture intends thus much, when it condescends to the naming of a plough, a hatchet, a bushell, leaven, boyes piping and dancing; shewing that things of ordinary use are not only to serve in the way of drudgery, but to be washed, and cleansed, and serve for lights even of Heavenly Truths.'[14] The same method of approaching God was advocated by Hugh of St Victor and St Bonaventura, amongst others, and was disseminated in the popular emblem books of the period. Herbert's use of common imagery and plain language continues and develops this method – in 'The Elixir', for instance:

> Teach me, my God and King,
> In all things thee to see,
> And what I do in any thing,
> To do it as for thee:
>
> Not rudely, as a beast,
> To runne into an action;
> But still to make thee prepossest,
> And give it his perfection.

A man that looks on glasse,
On it may stay his eye;
Or if he pleaseth, through it passe,
And then the heav'n espie.

All may of thee partake:
Nothing can be so mean,
Which with this tincture (for thy sake)
Will not grow bright and clean.

A servant with this clause
Makes drudgerie divine:
Who sweeps a room, as for thy laws,
Makes that and th'action fine.

This is the famous stone
That turneth all to gold:
For that which God doth touch and own
Cannot for lesse be told.

The short Dedication to *The Temple* offers up the ensuing poems to God, an act of sacrifice and thanksgiving, and establishes the note of reverent striving to know God better: 'Lord, my first fruits present themselves to thee;|Yet not mine neither: for from thee they came,|And must return.'

The first poem, after the introductory and didactic 'The Church-porch', is 'The Altar', ingeniously arranged to represent the shape of an altar (just as 'Easter Wings' is shaped like two wings).* The central portion of the design, the 'plinth' of the 'altar', contains the image of the stony heart that only God can cut (cf. Vaughan's Flinty Heart, p. 217); the concluding couplet, through the theme of sacrifice, leads on to the next poem, 'The Sacrifice', a formal, ritualistic monologue on the Passion by Christ Himself, each verse ending with the refrain 'Was ever grief like mine?'. 'The Thanksgiving' takes up the word 'grief' in its opening phrase and asserts the personal note once more after the liturgical lament of 'The Sacrifice'. Herbert pledges his determination to respond to Christ's sacrifice with sacrifices of his own:

---

*This visual conceit relates Herbert to the emblem convention that was so widely practised in the sixteenth and seventeenth centuries (see Rosemary Freeman, *English Emblem Books*, 1948, 1967). Mildmay Fane's *Otia Sacra* (1648), for example, contains emblematic verses arranged in patterns.

But how then shall I imitate thee, and
  Copie thy fair, though bloudie hand?
Surely I will revenge me on thy love,
  And trie who shall victorious prove.
If thou dost give me wealth, I will restore
  All back unto thee by the poore.
If thou dost give me honour, men shall see,
  The honour doth belong to the.
I will not marry; of, if she be mine,
  She and her children shall be thine.

Every poem in *The Temple* draws significance and coherence
from the others in the collection. Every one expresses a
profoundly personal relationship with God, the most dramatic
presentation of which is in that famous poem of temporary
rebellion, 'The Collar':

I Struck the board, and cry'd, No more.
            I will abroad.
  What? Shall I ever sigh and pine?
My lines and life are free; free as the rode,
  Loose as the winde, as large as store.
          Shall I be still in suit?
  Have I no harvest, but a thorn
  To let me bloud, and not restore
What I have lost with cordiall fruit?
            [. . .]
          Away; take heed:
          I will abroad.
Call in thy deaths head there: tie up thy fears.
          He that forebears
          To suit and serve his need,
          Deserves his load.
But as I rav'd and grew more fierce and wilde
          At every word,
Me thoughts I heard one calling, *Child*!
          And I reply'd, *My Lord*.

The sense of sin in *The Temple* is deep; but unlike Donne, Herbert
was not racked with oppressive guilt. He had a calming desire to
submit to God's will, and for him the depths were matched by
occasional glimpses of the heights, enabling him to find God's
hand in despair as well as joy:

How should I praise thee, Lord! how should my rhymes
    Gladly engrave thy love in steel,
  If what my soul doth feel sometimes,
    My soul might ever feel!

Although there were some fourtie heav'ns, or more,
    Sometimes I peere above them all;
  Sometimes I hardly reach a score,
    Sometimes to hell I fall.

                [. . .]

Whether I flie with angels, fall with dust,
    Thy hands made both, and I am there:
  Thy power and love, my love and trust
    Make one place ev'ry where.[15]

That Herbert enjoyed brief mystical intuitions seems to be
implied from such lines as these. In 'The Temper (II)' he asks:
'Where is that mightie joy,|Which just now took up all my heart?';
and in 'The Glance', recalling how the sense of God had first
come upon him as a young man, he describes how he had felt

          a sugred strange delight,
    Passing all cordials made by any art,
  Bedew, embalme, and overunne my heart,
          and take it in.

It is in the mystery of the Eucharist that Herbert seems to come
closest to a pure mystical certainty of God. In 'Peace' he asks 'a
rev'rend good old man' where Peace is to be found. The man
replies with an allegory of Christ's ministry and Passion. He tells
of twelve stalks of wheat, containing 'A secret vertue bringing
peace and mirth|By flight of sinne', that sprang from the Prince's
grave and that were dispersed throughout the world:

    Take of this grain, which in my garden grows,
        And grows for you;
      Make bread of it: and that repose
      And peace, which ev'ry where
    With so much earnestnesse you do pursue,
        Is onely there.

Richard Crashaw

Richard Crashaw (1612/13–1649) was born, as one writer has put it, 'under eminently Protestant auspices',[16] and yet he was to become England's greatest poetic representative of the Counter-Reformation and ended his days a Catholic. He was the son of the Revd William Crashaw, a well-known Yorkshire clergyman, friend of Selden and a stern Puritan who assiduously collected Popish literature in order to expose its diabolic falsity. After his father's death he was sent to Charterhouse and went up to Pembroke College, Cambridge, in 1631. Pembroke had been a High Church college since the mastership of Lancelot Andrewes and the tradition was continued in Crashaw's time by Dr Benjamin Laney, chaplain to King Charles.

Crashaw received his BA degree in 1634 and the following year was elected to a Fellowship at Peterhouse, another bastion of Laudian opinion. By this time Crashaw had probably become acquainted with the religious community at Little Gidding founded by **Nicholas Ferrar** (1592–1637) of Clare. The community consisted of Ferrar, his elderly mother, his brother and brother-in-law and their numerous children. There was a daily system of offices – one for each hour – meals were taken in silence, and, at the suggestion of George Herbert, a friend of Ferrar's, a nightly vigil from nine till one was kept. The life of devotion and meditation was complemented by works of charity in the neighbourhood: a school was founded and visits were made to the poor and the sick.*

Little Gidding attracted many pious visitors, amongst them Crashaw, who participated in the offices and shared in the night watches. He was ordained priest by 1639, in which year he was curate of Little St Mary's, hard by Peterhouse: there, too, he would spend the night in prayer, whilst his sermons, delivered to eager throngs of listeners, 'ravished more like Poems', according to one contemporary, '. . . scattering not so much sentences as Exstasies'.

In 1643 the Parliamentary Commissioners visited Peterhouse and Little St Mary's, leaving in their wake destroyed 'superstitious' decorations. Crashaw was formerly ejected from his Fellowship in June 1644, by which time he had left Peterhouse.

---

*For a succinct account of the Little Gidding community, see A. L. Maycock, *The Story of Little Gidding* (SPCK, 1947).

He took up residence in Paris in 1645, having been converted to Catholicism shortly before his departure. He died in Loreto in April 1649.

He left behind him an extraordinary body of poetry in which sensuality and passion for spiritual realities are fused. There are two volumes of religious poems: *Steps to the Temple* (1646, second edition 1648), and *Carmen Deo Nostro . . . Sacred Poems* (Paris, 1652). The Preface to *Steps to the Temple* (probably by Crashaw's friend Joseph Beaumont) says of Crashaw's poems: 'They shal lift the Reader, some yards above the ground: and, as in Pythagoras Schools, every temper was first tuned into a height by severall proportions of Musick; and spiritualiz'd for one of his weighty Lectures; So maist thou take a Poem hence, and tune thy soule by it, into a heavenly pitch; and thus refined and borne up upon the wings of meditation, in these Poems thou maist talke freely of God, and of that other state.' These poems are, says the writer, 'Stepps for happy souls to climbe heaven by'.

The title of this volume recalls George Herbert's *The Temple*, published thirteen years earlier; but Crashaw is a very different poet to the Rector of Bemerton. Where Herbert is intimate and self-revelatory Crashaw is devotional and emblematic. His work is the prime English example of the Baroque sensibility – pictorial, intricate, symbolic, abundant, audacious; and he expressed a distinctive aspect of Counter-Reformation theology by his yoking of the five senses in the service of spiritual devotion and religious art. The collection opens with 'The Weeper', which adds its own elaborate, not to say grotesque, metaphors to a conventional subject – the figure of Mary Magdalene, whose tears become symbols of the sacrament of penance, through which a way to God can be found:

> Vpwards thou dost weepe,
> Heavens bosome drinks the gentle streame.
> Where th'milky rivers meet,
> Thine Crawles above and is the Creame.
> Heaven, of such faire floods as this,
> Heaven the Christall Ocean is.*

The boldness and palpability of the imagery is typical and is seen again in one of his poems on the wounds of Christ:

*Quotations from Crashaw's poetry are taken from *The Poems, English, Latin and Greek, of Richard Crashaw*, edited by L. C. Martin (Oxford, 1927; second Edition 1957).

Iesu, no more, it is full tide
From thy hands and from thy feet,
From thy head, and from thy side,
All thy *Purple Rivers* meet.

Thy restlesse feet they cannot goe,
For us and our eternall good
As they are wont; what though?
They swim, alas! in their owne flood.

In 'On a prayer booke sent to Mrs M.R.' Crashaw presents his version of the spiritual marriage, when 'the noble Bridegrome' opens up the sacred store 'Of hidden sweets, and holy joyes' to the prepared soul:

Amorous Languishments, Luminous trances,
    Sights which are not seen with eyes,
Spirituall and soule peircing glances.
    Whose pure and subtle lightning flies
Home to the heart, and setts the house on fire;
And melts it downe in sweet desire . . .
Happy soule shee shall discover,
    What joy, what blisse,
    How many heavens at once it is,
To have a God become her lover.

Austin Warren remarked that what is known of Crashaw's life 'gives no ground for suspicion that his poetry is anything save an ingenious expression of his deepest spirit'.[17] What seems to a twentieth-century ear to be artificial and formally rhetorical was for Crashaw a natural mode of sincere self-expression: 'To learn the instruments of his craft, the forms of his workings, the methods of his devotion was but to find the means of expressing himself.'[18] He stands virtually alone amongst the great English poets of his period in the closeness of his relationship with the spirit of the Counter-Reformation and in the way he drew his themes and images from contemporary Catholic devotional literature and art, hagiography and mysticism. This relationship is symbolized by his choice of spiritual heroine: St Teresa, on whom he wrote three poems, two appearing in the 1646 edition of *Steps to the Temple*, and one, 'The Flaming Heart: Upon the booke and picture of Teresa . . .', published with the first two in the 1648 edition.

The first poem, 'In memory of the Vertuous and Learned Lady *Madre de* Teresa', begins by celebrating martyrdom: Love is 'Absolute sole Lord' of life and death (this section of the poem draws on the episode in St Teresa's *Life* that describes her childhood desire to be martyred at the hands of the Moors: see p. 158). The next section turns on the idea that God forbade her childish ambition but fulfilled it in another way:

> Thou art Love's victime; and must dy
> A death more mysticall and high.

St Teresa's most famous ecstasy, or 'transverberation', was when, as recounted in the *Life*, a seraph thrust a golden fire-tipped dart through her heart, the pain of which, she said, 'was so excessive, that it forced me to utter those groans; and the suavities, which that extremitie of paine gave, was also so very excessive, that there was no desiring at all, to be ridd of it'.[19] (It was this ecstasy that inspired Bernini's famous sculpture of Teresa.)

This co-mingling of subtle pain and intolerable joy is the wound of love. So St John of the Cross had written: 'O delicious wound, then, and the more delicious the more the cautery of love penetrates the inmost substance of the soul, burning all it can burn that it may supply all the delight it can give'; so Teresa herself wrote of the soul's consciousness of having received 'a delicious wound': though it cannot discover how nor who gave it, 'yet [it] recognizes it as a most precious grace, and hopes the hurt will never heal'. And so Crashaw writes of a death

> in which who dyes
> Loves his death, and dyes again;
> And would for ever so be slain.
> And lives, and yes; and knows not why
> To live, But that he thus may never leave to Dy.

In 1652 Crashaw added twenty-four lines to his third poem on St Teresa, 'The Flaming Heart', in which he personally addresses the saint in an impassioned hymn of devotion, praise and supplication:

By all thy dowr of *Lights* and *Fires*;
By all the eagle in thee, all the dove;
By all thy lives and deaths of love . . .
By all thy brim-fill'd Bowles of feirce desire
By thy last Morning's draught of liquid fire;
By the full kingdom of that final kisse
That seiz'd thy parting Soul, and scal'd thee his . . .
By all of *Him* we have in *Thee*;
Leave nothing of my *Self* in me.
Let me so read thy life, that I
Unto all life of mine may dy.

Crashaw is often called a mystical poet. He is indeed more mystical in spirit than Donne, though only a handful of poems – including the Teresan poems – deal specifically with mystical experience. He cites only two mystics, St Teresa and the pseudo-Dionysius; but his background and training must have made him familiar with St Augustine and St Bernard, and probably also with St Francis de Sales (see p. 177). Temperamentally, he is allied to 'imagistically minded' mystics like St Teresa and St Catherine of Siena; but one poem, the ode on the Epiphany, assumes a philosophical and metaphysical style that is unusual for Crashaw in order to treat of the *via negativa*:

Now by abased liddes shall [we] learn to be
Eagles; and shutt our eyes that we may see.

There is perhaps no finer summary of Crashaw's poetry and of its place in any history of the mystical spirit than Austin Warren's: 'It is the world of man's inner life at its mystical intensity, the world of devotion expressing itself through the sacraments and ceremonial and liturgy; it is a world of the supernatural, wherein the miraculous becomes the probable; and this world manifests itself to the senses in a rhetoric brilliant, expressive, and appropriate.'[20]

Henry Vaughan
Henry Vaughan (1622–1695), the 'Silurist',* was born into an old Welsh family and spent most of his life in the parish of

---

*Vaughan styled himself thus after the British tribe, called the Silures by Tacitus, who formerly inhabited the area in which he lived.

Llansantffread, at Trenewydd or Newton between the Brecon
Beacons and the Black Mountains. He went up to Jesus College,
Oxford, with his twin brother Thomas, the alchemical writer, but
left without taking his degree. Most of Vaughan's published
writings appeared between 1646 and 1657. They include: *Silex
Scintillans* (1650: the first part); *Olor Iscanus* (1651: poems, with
four short prose translations); *The Mount of Olives; or, Solitary
Devotions* (1652: prose, including a translation, *Man in Glory*, of
the *De Felicitate Sanctorum*, attributed to St Anselm); *Flores
Solitudinis* (1654: translations, including *Primitive Holiness, Set
forth in the Life of blessed Paulinus*); and *Silex Scintillans* (1655: the
unsold sheets of the 1650 edition supplemented by a new Part ii).

The Mount of Olives* was intended to encourage the practice of
Christian meditation, although Vaughan admitted in his Preface
that 'the world abounds with these Manuals'. But:

> It is not then their scarsity that call'd this forth, nor yet a desire to
> crosse the age, nor any in it. I envie not their frequent Extasies, and
> raptures to the third heaven; I onely wish them real, and that their
> actions did not tell the world, they are rapt in some other place. Nor
> should they, who assume to themselves the glorious stile of Saints, be
> uncharitably moved, if we that are yet in the body, and carry our
> treasure in earthen vessels, have need of these helps.*

By contrast with what Vaughan clearly regards as spurious
mysticism are the 'sound directions and wholsome words' of his
own book, which has been published for the good of the
'Peaceful, humble, and pious Reader' and 'for his glory, who in
the dayes of his flesh prayed here himselfe, and both taught and
commanded us to pray'. Eschewing the 'fruitlesse curiosities of
Schoole-Divinity', Vaughan concluded his Preface with a short
exhortation:

> That thou wouldest not be discouraged in this way, because very
> many are gone out of it. Think not that thou art alone upon this Hill,
> there is an innumerable company both before and behinde thee.
> Those with their Palms in their hands, and these expecting them. If
> therefore the dust of this world chance to prick thine eyes, suffer it not

---

*Quotations from Vaughan are taken from *Henry Vaughan. Poetry and Selected Prose*, edited
by L. C. Martin (Oxford, 1963).

to blinde them . . . Look not upon transitorie, visible things, but upon him that is eternal, and invisible. Choose the better part, yea, that part with Saint Hierome, who preferred the poor Coate of Paul the Hermite to the purple and pride of the world.

Vaughan never tires of contrasting the darkness of the world with the light of heaven. For him, the world was a wilderness, 'A darksome, intricate wood full of Ambushes and dangers; a Forrest where spiritual hunters, principalities and powers spread their nets . . .'[21] Again, in the short preface to the Life of Paulinus, he admonishes the reader who wishes to be led 'into that house of light' to forsake the corrupt and poisoned world, 'to look after a better country, an inheritance that is undefiled and fadeth not away':

If thou doest this, thou shalt have a portion given thee here, when all things shall be made new . . . Doat not any more upon a withered, rotten Gourd, upon the seducements and falshood of a most odious, decayed Prostitute; but look up to Heaven, where wealth without want; delight without distast, and joy without sorrow (like undefiled and incorruptible Virgins) sit clothed with light, and crowned with glory . . . Farewel, and neglect not thy own happiness.

Light is Vaughan's central metaphor for the consciousness of God's Image within, his great symbol for paradise lost, man's spiritual inheritance:

> Ah! what time wilt thou come! when shall that crie
>   The *Bridegroome's Comming*! fil the sky?
> Shall it in the Evening run
> When our words and works are done?
> Or wil thy all-surprizing light
>   Break at midnight?
> When either sleep, or some dark pleasure
> Possesseth mad man without measure . . .[22]

In 'The Men of War' he exclaims:

> Were not thy word (dear Lord!) my light
> How would I run to endless night.

In 'Cock-crowing' God is addressed as 'Father of lights!' and

Vaughan asks for 'the cloke|And cloud which shadows thee from me' to be removed:

> O take it off! make no delay,
> But brush me with thy light, that I
> May shine unto a perfect day,
> And warme me at thy glorious Eye!

The image is also present in two of Vaughan's best known lyrics – 'They are all gone into the world of light!' and 'The World', with its memorable opening:

> I saw Eternity the other night
> Like a great Ring of pure and endless light . . .

Vaughan has the true mystical longing to be united with God and to be purged of all earthly attachments. In 'Day of Judgement' he prays against both friends and wealth and asks for three things:

> A living FAITH, a HEART of flesh,
> The WORLD an Enemie,
> This last will keepe the first two fresh,
> And bring me, where I'de be.

But it is the world of men that poisons spiritual sight, not the world of Nature, which Vaughan always endows with deep spiritual significance. (For Vaughan, as for St Bonaventura, Nature, the Bible and the True Self are the three great books by which man can learn to regain the paradise within.) Nature is a perpetual allegory: 'tempests have more in them than a showr':

> Sure, mighty love foreseeing the discent
>   Of this poor creature, by a gracious art
>   Hid in these low things snares to gain his heart,
> And layd surprizes in each element.
>
> All things here shew him heaven; *Waters* that fall
>   Chide, and fly up; *Mists* of corruptest fome
>   Quit their first beds & mount; trees, herbs,
>   flowres, all
> Strive upwards stil, and point him the way home.[23]

The 1650 edition of *Silex Scintillans* has an engraved title page bearing the emblem of the Flashing Flint, a flinty heart that weeps, bleeds and flames as a result of being struck by God's hand. This edition also has a Latin explanation of the emblem, which I give here in the paraphrase of Louis L. Martz:

> *The Author's Emblem (concerning himself)*
> You have often touched me, I confess, without a wound, and your *Voice* without a voice, has often sought to counsel me; your diviner breath has encompassed me with its sacred murmur. I was deaf and dumb: a *Flint*: You (how great care you take of your own!) try to revive another way, you change the Remedy; and now angered you say that *Love* has no power, and you prepare to conquer with *Force*, you come closer, you break through the *Rocky* barrier of my heart, and it is made *Flesh* that was before a *Stone*. Behold me torn asunder! and at last the *Fragments* burning towards your skies, and the cheeks streaming with tears out of the *Adamant*. Thus once upon a time you made the *Rocks* flow and the *Crags* gush, oh ever provident of your people! How marvellous toward me is your hand! In *Dying*, I have been born again; and in the midst of my *shattered means* I am now *richer*.[24]

After this explanation comes 'The Dedication', which restates the theme of sudden spiritual illumination and recalls George Herbert's *The Temple*, which also begins with a short poem called 'The Dedication'. But Herbert is more than simply a literary precedent: he is part of the spiritual history the poems express, as 'The Match' makes clear in its reference to the 'holy, ever-living lines' that have checked Vaughan's 'fierce, wild blood that still heaves, and inclines,|But is still tam'd|By those bright fires which thee inflam'd.'

The first poem in the collection, 'Regeneration', contains an allegorical account of the workings of grace, which leads the pilgrim into an illuminated consciousness of God's presence. The key to the symbolism is given at the end of the poem in the quotation from the Canticle (5:17): 'Arise O North, and come thou South-wind, and blow upon my garden, that the spices thereof may flow out'. The landscape the pilgrim finds himself in is the Garden of the Soul, a pervasive Christian emblem that drew its strength from medieval exegesis of the Canticle (cf. St Bernard, p. 82): 'A garden inclosed is my sister, my spouse; a spring shut up, a fountain sealed'. In Vaughan's poem these images re-emerge to define a specific spiritual experience – the spice-laden air, the garden, the fountain, which contains stones, some bright and round, symbolizing the spiritually reborn, and some 'ill-shap'd and dull', standing for those still held in the bondage of the flesh:*

> The first (pray marke,) as quick as light
> Danc'd through the floud,
> But, th'last more heavy then the night
> Nail'd to the Center stood.

Vaughan's finest poetry, wrote Louis Martz, 'draws its strength from the great central tradition of Platonic Christianity'.[25] Its recurrent theme is the recovery of the Divine Image within. The memory of paradise lingers in us all: a spark of the divine light yet burns in the darkness, 'For there is a dimme glimmering of light yet un-put-out, in men: let them walke, let them walke, that the darknesse overtake them not'.[26] These words from the *Confessions* indicate the extent of Vaughan's debt to Augustinian mysticism and relate directly to the central image and concern of *Silex Scintillans* – the ignition through grace of the Divine Spark:

> All things teach us to die
> And point us out the way
> While we passe by
> And mind it not; play not away
> Thy glimpse of light.[27]

Thomas Traherne

The keynote of the life and writings of Thomas Traherne (1637–1674) is 'Felicity', or Happiness. As he wrote of himself in the *Centuries* (III, 46): 'When I came into the Country, and being seated among silent Trees, had all my Time in mine own Hands, I resolved to Spend it all, whatever it cost me, in Search of Happiness, and to Satiat that burning Thirst which Nature had Enkindled in me from my Youth.'† By Felicity, Traherne principally meant 'to be Good to others', and of his own desire to do good a contemporary wrote that he was 'ready to do all good Offices to his Friends, and Charitable to the Poor almost beyond his ability'.

---

*However, the symbolism of 'Regeneration' is also enriched by hermetic references and is indeed derived directly from Thomas Vaughan's *Lumen de Lumine*.

†All quotations from Traherne in this section are taken from *Thomas Traherne: Poems, Centuries and Three Thanksgivings*, edited by Anne Ridler (Oxford, 1966).

Little is known of Traherne's outward life. He was born the son of a shoemaker in Herefordshire, but his father died when he and his brother Philip were small. He went up to Brasenose College, Oxford, in 1652–3 and was ordained deacon and priest in 1660. A year later he took up residence at Credenhill near Hereford and became the spiritual adviser of a lapsed convert to Roman Catholicism called Susanna Hopton. It was for her and her circle that Traherne wrote the *Centuries*, and it was Susanna Hopton who was instrumental in publishing, anonymously in 1699, the *Thanksgivings*.

Traherne published only one work (*Roman Forgeries*) in his lifetime. His book *Christian Ethicks* (subtitled 'The Way to Blessedness') had been prepared for the press but he died before it was published. Its purpose, the Preface declared, was 'to excite [men's] Desire, to encourage them to Travel, to comfort them in the Journey, and so at last to lead them to true Felicity, both here and hereafter'. Traherne's spirituality is emphatically affirmative and theocentric. He seeks to know God through delight in created things. On the face of it, this is a divergence from the main trend of Christian mysticism, which – as we have seen – maintained that the soul must be free from the love of creatures if it is to approach God. Traherne, by contrast, held that 'Never was any thing in this World loved too much'. It is our duty, he says, to be united to all things, as God is: 'We must lov them infinitly but in God, and for God: and God in them: namely all His Excellencies Manifested in them.'[28] But there is an essential qualification: 'many Things hav been loved in a fals way: and all in too short a Measure'. The true way of love for Traherne, as for St Thomas Aquinas, was the willing of good. And it was more: it was Enjoyment; it was to take joy in creation, as God does. This is the essence of Traherne's 'nature mysticism':

> You shall be Glorified, you shall liv in Communion with Him, you shall ascend into the Throne of the Highest Heavens; you shall be Satisfied, you shall be made Greater than the Heavens, you shall be Like Him, when you enjoy the World as He doth; you shall converse with His Wisdom Goodness and Power abov all Worlds, and therefore shall Know Him. To know whom is a Sublime thing: for it is Life Eternal.[29]

Traherne's prose and poetry are suffused with excitement and barely contained rapture. They are urgent, enthusiastic, exuberant, ecstatic. His writings consist mainly of variations on the primal themes of Felicity, Love, Innocence and Enjoyment – in the specific senses employed by Traherne. There is no tension apparent in his words, no anguish. Whatever spiritual trials he had undergone before the attainment of felicity are now over, and he writes from a serene plateau of assurance. Though the *Centuries* may draw on the methodology of the *Confessions* and the *De Trinitate* of St Augustine, as Louis Martz appears to demonstrate, and though they may also draw on the mystical treatises of St Bonaventura, they are essentially one man's 'good news': they constitute the outpourings of a profoundly simple vision of man's relationship to the world and to God. The sense of grateful wonder in being part of the immense living unity of the creation is therefore always present in Traherne:

> A Stranger here
> Strange Things doth meet, Strange Glories See;
> Strange Treasures lodg'd in this fair World appear,
> Strange all, and New to me.
> But that they mine should be, who nothing was,
> That Strangest is of all, yet brought to pass.[30]

Paradise, for Traherne, was a spiritual state. It was for him, as it was for the Platonist Peter Sterry, 'the Similitude and Presence of God in the whole Creation'.[31] Paradise, therefore, can be re-entered by Fallen Man: this Similitude and this Presence can yet be apprehended. But how?

At the outset of the *Centuries* Traherne writes: 'I hav found, that Things unknown have a Secret Influence on the Soul: and like the Centre of the Earth unseen, violently attract it . . . So is there in us a World of Lov to somewhat, tho we know not what in the world that should be.'[32] This inviolate instinct to love is the impulse by which the soul advances to glory, by which it regains Paradise; and it does so by valuing the elements of creation as they should be valued – that is, as God values them: 'The End for which you were Created is that by Prizing all that God hath don, you may Enjoy your self and Him in Blessedness.'[33] And therefore, as the celebrated passage in the *Centuries* proclaims:

You never Enjoy the World aright, till the Sea it self floweth in your Veins, till you are Clothed with the Heavens, and Crowned with the

Stars: and perceiv your self to be the Sole Heir of the whole World: and more than so, becaus Men are in it who are evry one Sole Heirs, as well as you ... Till your Spirit filleth the whole World, and the Stars are your Jewels, till you are as Familiar with the Ways of God in all Ages as with your Walk and Table: till you are intimately Acquainted with that Shady Nothing out of which the World was made: till you lov Men so as to Desire their Happiness, with a Thirst equal to the zeal of your own: till you Delight in GOD for being Good to all: you never Enjoy the World.[34]

For himself, Traherne, wrote in the *Third Century* of 'Those Pure and Virgin Apprehensions I had from the Womb, and that Divine Light wherewith I was born':

The Corn was Orient and Immortal Wheat, which never should be reaped, nor was ever sown. I thought it had stood from Everlasting to Everlasting. The Dust and Stones of the Street were as Precious as GOLD. The Gates were at first the End of the World, The Green Trees when I saw them first through one of the Gates Transported and Ravished me; their Sweetnes and unusual beauty made my Heart to leap, and almost mad with Exstasie ... I knew no Churlish Proprieties,* nor Bounds nor Divisions: but all Properties and Divisions were mine ... So that with much adoe I was corrupted; and made to learn the Dirty Devices of this World. Which now I unlearn, and becom as it were a little Child again, that I may enter into the Kingdom of God.[35]

The Cambridge Platonists
The seventeenth century was an age of rational enquiry, a period impelled to 'explain' the physical and moral universe. But it was also, as the preceding sections have indicated, an age when the religious sense found full expression. The two streams – 'philosophy' and religion – met in the so-called rational theologians, those thinkers for whom the old beliefs still held a central place in their world-view but who were conscious of the need to justify Christian tenets in modern terms. Such men were religious modernists, fully alive to the necessity of separating blind dogmatism and authoritarianism from the living core of Christian belief and to redefine this core in 'rational' terms.

'Reason', however, did not mean mechanistic reduction. Leading this trend of rational theology were the Cambridge

*i.e. properties, possessions.

Platonists, a group of mainly Puritan divines associated with Emmanuel College, Cambridge, a staunchly Puritan foundation. A key member of the group, **Benjamin Whichcote** (1609–1683), never tired of quoting the phrase from Proverbs (10:27): 'The spirit of man is the candle of the Lord'. For Whichcote and the others right reason and true faith were not incompatible because God Himself is perfect reason, and Whichcote defined the true improvement of the rational faculties as 'the exercise of the several virtues of sobriety, modesty, gentleness, humility, obedience to God, and charity to men'.[36]

The Platonist group at Cambridge were, in the words of Basil Willey, 'the modern analogues of the Alexandrian Fathers, Clement and Origen, with this significant difference – that the Fathers came between a declining philosophy and a rising Christianity, while the seventeenth-century theologians came between a declining Christianity and a rising philosophy. The resemblance between the two schools lies in their effort to maintain religion and philosophy as allies, not as strangers or enemies.'[37]

So the Cambridge theologians – learned, pious, sober men all – sought to break away from fideism and polemic and focus on the abiding truths of their religion. It was necessary for them to think of these truths in different terms and to express them afresh. A system already lay to hand by which this could be done – Platonism and Neoplatonism, or rather the eclectic Platonism inherited by the seventeenth century, which had many fundamental affinities with Christian theology (such as the immortality of the soul) and which had indeed become a part of that theology.

John Smith (1618–1652), a pupil of Whichcote, was an Emmanuel man, though he later became a Fellow of Queens'. His *Select Discourses* were published posthumously in 1660. The first Discourse, 'Concerning the True Way or Method of attaining to Divine Knowledge', affirms the reality of spiritual knowledge. Such knowledge of God is absolutely real: it is neither theoretical nor abstract, but is described metaphorically from sensation. Divine knowledge – knowledge of the Real – is thus the mystical *experience* of God:

> It is but a thin, aiery knowledge that is got by meer Speculation, which is usher'd in by Syllogisms and Demonstrations; but that which

springs forth from true Goodness . . . brings such a Divine light into the Soul, as is more clear and convincing than any Demonstration. The reason why, notwithstanding all our acute reasons, and subtile disputes, Truth prevails no more in the world, is, we so often disjoyn *Truth* and true Goodness, which in themselves can never be disunited.[38]

Divinity, for John Smith, was not a science but a '*Divine* life', 'it being something rather to be understood by a *Spiritual sensation* than by any *Verbal description*'. To seek this life, this sensation, in books and writings is to seek the living among the dead. No, says Smith: '*intra te quaere Deum*, seek for God within thine own soul . . . David, when he would teach us how to know what the divine Goodness is, calls not for *Speculation* but *Sensation, Taste and see how good the Lord is.*'

The mechanistic philosopher Thomas Hobbes had negated the reality of spirit: the Platonists asserted the opposite, that spirit only was truly real. **Ralph Cudworth** (1617–1688), another Emmanuel man, defined atheism as 'making senseless matter the only self-existent thing, and the original of all things'.[39] Cudworth's self-existent principle is God: 'The true and genuine idea of God in general is this, A perfect conscious understanding being (or mind) existing of itself from eternity, and the cause of all other things.'

Henry More (1614–1687) came from a wealthy Calvinist family and went up to Christ's College from Eton. Amongst his voluminous writings were *An Antidote against Atheism* (1653), *The Immortality of the Soul* (1659), *An Explanation of the Grand Mystery of Godliness* (1660) and *Divine Dialogues* (1668). More created his convoluted ideas from a variety of sources – amongst them occult speculation, Plotinus, hermeticism, and the mysticism of the *Theologia Germanica*. He was the most mystically minded of the Cambridge Platonists and, like Coleridge, sensed the divine presence interpenetrating all things – the eternal presence of 'that bright Idee Of steddie Good'. Brought up in a Calvinist home, he had never had any instinctive affinity for 'that hard Doctrine concerning Fate'. He was possessed instead of 'that exceeding hail and entire sense of God which nature herself had planted deeply in me'. He paints a picture of himself as an ethereal, angelic being, whose body gave off a flower-like fragrance. As a young man he had had a 'mighty and almost immoderate thirst after Knowledge', but nothing he found in his reading could satisfy his inner longing. He remained in dark uncertainty for three or four years, until at last he experienced spiritual illumination:

> Whether the Knowledge of Things was really that supreme Felicity of Man, or something Greater and more Divine was: Or, supposing it to be so, whether it was to be acquir'd by such an Eagerness and Intentness in the reading of Authors, and Contemplating of Things; or by the purging of the Mind from all sorts of Vices whatsoever.[40]

More's illumination showed him that spiritual vision sprang from ethical purification, a fundamental Platonist idea; he saw also that the personal will must be extinguished in favour of the divine. True holiness, he realized, was 'the only safe entrance into divine knowledge:

> When this inordinate Desire after the Knowledge of things was thus allay'd in me, and I aspir'd after nothing but this sole Purity and Simplicity of Mind, there shone in upon me daily a greater Assurance than ever I could have expected, even of those things which before I had the greatest Desire to know.[41]

Emanuel Swedenborg

One class of 'proofs' adduced by Henry More to prove the existence of spirit concerned ghosts, apparitions and spirits: 'there are other intelligent beings', he wrote, 'besides these that are clad in heavy earth and clay'. For More, as for Milton, 'Millions of spiritual creatures walk the earth'.* Just such a universe was revealed through the visions of Emanuel Swedenborg (1688–1772), born in Stockholm, the second son of the Lutheran Bishop of Skara, who because of his influence on William Blake is perhaps best dealt with here.

As a young man Swedenborg devoted himself to scientific studies, he travelled widely, and while in England met the astronomers Sir Edmund Halley and John Flamsteed. In 1716 he was made a special assessor to the Swedish Royal College of Mines and he published several notable works on scientific subjects: *Opera Philosophica et Mineralia* (3 volumes, 1734), in which he developed a pioneering theory to account for the formation of planets: *Oeconomia Regni Animalis* (1740), on

---

Paradise Lost, IV, 677.

anatomy; *Miscellaneous Observations on Geology and Mineralogy* (1743) and *On the Infinite and Final Cause of Creation* (1744). But it was not until 1745, in *Worship and the Love of God*, that Swedenborg turned his full attention to the subject of religion, which from this point became the ruling influence in his life.

In 1747, when he was fifty-nine, he resigned his assessorship in order to devote himself entirely to the visionary revelations he was now subject to. He believed that he was in direct communication with spiritual beings and remained unmoved by sceptical responses to his accounts of what he had experienced: 'I am well aware', he said, 'that many persons will insist that it is impossible for anyone to converse with spirits and with angels during his lifetime in the body; many will say that such intercourse must be mere fancy; some, that I have invented such relations in order to gain credit; whilst others will make other objections. For all these, however, I care not, since I have seen, heard and felt.'

In spite of this contention, Swedenborg was a modest, simple scholarly man who had no thought of founding a new religious sect.* He simply believed that his own mystical experience of God and his visions of heaven *and* hell qualified him to speak out in assured tones of what others had simply speculated upon. In fact he believed himself to be a divinely appointed messenger: he was the mouthpiece of God, by Whom he had shown the true nature of heaven, hell, their inhabitants and the soul of man. The particularity and concreteness of Swedenborg's visions is shown in the following quotation concerning 'The Grievous Punishment of Revenge':

> The spirit is then whirled around with something filthy, as if it were arms, stretched out and immovable; they are not arms, but only rags, somewhat white. The body, being stretched out in this way and continually rotated, is carried towards heaven, and, that he may be struck to the inmosts with shame, it is proclaimed before all that he is of such a quality.[42]

William Blake

In the estimation of Caroline Spurgeon, William Blake (1757–

---

*A Swedenborgian Church, or New Church, did, however, spring up. An interesting literary treatment of Swedenborgianism is to be found in J. S. Le Fanu's *Uncle Silas* (3 vols, 1864), in which Swedenborgian doctrine is skilfully woven into the structure of the novel.

1827) was 'one of the great mystics of the world'.[43] Many would
agree with her; but though Blake's perception of spiritual realities
was extraordinarily acute his mysticism was of a highly
unorthodox type and of a complexity, at least in its expression, that
allows him to be many things to many men – a Rosicrucian initiate
to W. B. Yeats, a pioneer prophet of revolution to Marxists.

Blake saw himself as a prophet in the Old Testament sense: his
visions had a collective as well as a personal reference through
their relationship to the national spirit, the 'Giant Albion'. His
visions came to him spontaneously; his poems were largely
'dictated'. Of his *Milton* he says: 'I have written this poem from
immediate dictation, twelve or sometimes twenty or thirty lines at
a time, without pre-meditation and even against my will. The time
it has taken in writing was thus rendered non-existent, and an
immense poem exists which seems to be the labour of a long life,
all produced without labour or study.' 'I may praise it,' he also said
of *Milton*, 'since I dare not pretend to be any other than the
Secretary; the Authors are in Eternity.'

As a young man Blake espoused Swedenborgianism. Besides
the influence of the Swedish seer he had read Boehme and
Paracelsus, and he was conversant with Hinduism and Qabalism.
He saw the world as being perceived in the image of
consciousness: 'As a man is, so he Sees. As the Eye is formed,
such are its Powers. You certainly mistake, when you say that the
Visions of Fancy are not to be found in This World. To Me This
World is all One continued Vision of Fancy or Imagination.' The
world of Imagination, he said, is the world of Eternity: 'There
Exist in that Eternal World the Permanent Realities of Every
Thing which we see reflected in this Vegetable Glass of Nature.
All Things are comprehended in their Eternal Forms in the
divine body of the Saviour, the True Vine of Eternity . . .'[44] With
this transmuted Platonism went a familiar prescription, though
again it is given a distinctively Blakean twist:

> We are told to abstain from fleshly desires that we may lose no time
> from the Work of the Lord: Every moment lost is a moment that
> cannot be redeemed; every pleasure that intermingles with the duty of
> our station is a folly unredeemable, & is planted like the seed of a wild
> flower among our wheat . . . I know of no other Christianity and of no
> other Gospel than the liberty both of body & mind to exercise the
> Divine Arts of Imagination, Imagination, the real & eternal World of
> which this Vegetable Universe is but a faint shadow, & in which we

shall live in our Eternal or Imaginative Bodies when these Vegetable Mortal Bodies are no more . . . What are the Treasures of Heaven which we are to lay up for ourselves, are they any other than Mental Studies & Performances? . . . O ye Religious, discountenance every one among you who shall pretend to despise Art & Science! . . . What is Mortality but the things relating to the Body which Dies? What is Immortality but the things relating to the Spirit which Lives Eternally? What is the Joy of Heaven but Improvement in the things of the Spirit? What are the Pains of Hell but Ignorance, Bodily Lust, Idleness and Devastation of the things of the Spirit?[45]

Is this mysticism? In one sense it undoubtedly is, for such passionate utterances confirm the piercing clarity of Blake's spiritual vision and his confidence in the reality of those visions. Thus Blake is a mystic if mysticism is understood as a transforming first-hand experience of a greater – a spiritual – Reality. But Blake was an artist as well as a mystic; more than this, he was an artist *first*, unlike St John of the Cross, great poet though he was, who most assuredly was a mystic before all things. Blake never uses the word 'mysticism'; but he does use the word 'vision'. The visionary who habitually dwells in a world of abiding spiritual reality is able to re-perceive created things and endow them with a symbolism that directly relates back to this reality: visionary experience, that is to say, is perfectly consistent with artistic expression. True mysticism, on the other hand is not, since – as we have already established – mystical experience is by its very nature ineffable. This tension between artist and mystic in Blake was identified by Northrop Frye:

[Mysticism] is a form of spiritual communion with God which is by its nature incommunicable to anyone else, and which soars beyond faith into direct apprehension. But to the artist, *qua* artist, this apprehension is not an end in itself but a means to another end, the end of producing his poem. The mystical experience for him is poetic material, not poetic form. From the point of view of any genuine mystic this would be somewhat inadequate, and one who was both mystic and poet . . . might be rather badly off. If he decided for poetry, he would perhaps do better to use someone else's mystical experiences, as Crashaw did St Teresa's.[46]

Blake did not use someone else's experiences. As he said:

I am in God's presence night & day,
And he never turns his face away.[47]

But still he seems to inhabit a far country in relation to the orthodox tradition of Christian mysticism, and the principal reason is because for him, as Frye perceptively observed, the spiritual world was a source of energy; he was 'a spiritual utilitarian': 'He had the complete pragmatism of the artist, who, as an artist, believes nothing but is looking only for what he can use.'[48] This view does not diminish Blake, who was a visionary of exceptional stature; it simply defines him in terms of his achievement as an artist, for it is his art – the pictures and the poetry – that, for good or ill, stands between us and the world of spirit in which he continually dwelt.

Wordsworth and Coleridge

Like Blake, William Wordsworth (1770–1850) believed in the primacy of the imagination in conducting us to a vision of unchanging Reality:

> Imagination! Lifting up itself
> Before the eye and progress of my Song
> Like an unfather'd vapour; here that Power,
> In all the might of his endowments, came
> Athwart me; I was lost as in a cloud,
> Halted, without a struggle to break through.
> And now recovering, to my Soul I say
> I recognise thy glory; in such strength
> Of usurpation, in such visitings
> Of awful promise, when the light of sense
> Goes out in flashes, that have shewn to us
> The invisible world, doth Greatness make abode,
> There harbours whether we be young or old.
> Our destiny, our nature, and our home
> Is with infinitude, and only there;
> With hope it is, hope that can never die,
> Effort, and expectation, and desire,
> And something evermore about to be.[49]

The essence of Wordsworth's mysticism is contained in these lines from *The Prelude*, subtitled 'Growth of a Poet's Mind'. There are several echoes of Catholic mysticism: the phrase 'without a struggle to break through' recalls the state of 'unknowing', and the image of the cloud itself refers us back to *The Cloud of Unknowing* and the Pseudo-Dionysius; the recognition that it is the soul's nature, impelled by effort and desire, to seek its true home in an eternal Reality – in 'something evermore about to be' – is also central to Christian mysticism. But of course there are also significant differences between Wordsworth's vision and the experiences of the Church mystics of the Christian tradition. Like Blake, Wordsworth was a poet; but for him poetry *was* mysticism: the poet follows his calling because he intuitively apprehends the divine life in all things and gives expression to his intuition through the power of the imagination.

Wordsworth's philosophy and his religion, for they are indeed one, were founded in a spiritualized adaptation of the empiricist, sensationist philosophy of the eighteenth century, in particular the ideas of David Hartley. But in Wordsworth, as in Coleridge, these ideas were significantly modified, in Wordsworth's case by a profound visionary experience of Nature. The moral and intellectual nature, he held, was shaped by sense impressions. Through the proper exercise of the senses is aroused 'extrinsic passion' – 'Those hallow'd and pure motions of the sense':

> In Nature and the language of the sense
> The anchor of my purest thoughts, the nurse,
> The guide, the guardians of my heart, and soul
> Of all my moral being,

And yet, paradoxically, the highest revelations come when 'the light of sense goes out', when the poet is conscious of nothing but God's presence within him: when he knows only that

> one interior life
> In which all beings live with God, themselves
> Are God, existing in the mighty whole,
> As indistinguishable as the cloudless east
> Is from the cloudless west, when all
> The hemisphere is one cerulean blue.[50]

As Ernest de Selincourt commented: 'How far this intense mystical experience is compatible with Christianity let theologians determine.'[51] Although Wordsworth had no affinities with dogmatic Christianity he never strayed far from orthodoxy, and with age he drew closer to the central Christian truths, so that he modified his poetical autobiography, *The Prelude*, to exclude all traces of his earlier tendencies towards pantheism. In the 1805 version he writes:

> Wonder not
> If such my transports were; for in all things
> I saw one life, and felt that it was joy.

The 1850 version has this significant addition:

> Communing in this sort through earth and heaven
> With every form of creature, as it looked
> Towards the Uncreated with a countenance
> Of adoration, with an eye of love.

Similarly in Book IX,

> I worshipped then among the depths of things
> As my soul bade me . . .
> I felt and nothing else.

becomes in 1850:

> Worshipping then among the depths of things
> As piety ordained . . .
> I felt, observed, and pondered.

Wordsworth had always been more than a 'nature mystic', more than a simple pantheist. Like Vaughan and Traherne he had experienced a transfigured Nature; but he, like them, had from the first accurately sensed the First Cause of the divine life that flowed through all things:

> Gently did my soul
> Put off her veil, and self-transmuted, stood
> Naked as in the presence of her God.[52]

Of Wordsworth's friend **Samuel Taylor Coleridge** (1772–1834), Walter Jackson Bate wrote: 'If we wish to understand and assess Coleridge's career, we must do so at least partly in terms of what mattered most to him: the hope that his life, whatever its failings, might ultimately be religious in shape, intention, meaning.'[53] On the one hand, Coleridge sensed, like Wordsworth, the divinity of Nature; on the other, he was instinctively attracted to the Christian view of God's transcendence. His later years were dedicated to trying to reconcile the 'dynamic philosophy' of Nature, dismissed by the orthodox as pantheism, and what he saw as the inherent dualism of the Christian God and the created universe.

In his earlier years Coleridge had spoken of his intention to

> discipline my young and novice thought
> In ministeries of heart-stirring song,
> And aye on Meditation's heaven-ward wing
> Soaring, aloft I breathe the empyreal air
> Of Love, omnific, omnipresent Love,
> Whose day-spring rises glorious in my soul
> As the great Sun, when he his influence
> Sheds on the frost-bound waters . . .[54]

In the same poem (*Religious Musings*, 1794), which is replete with biblical images and phrases, Coleridge describes the ministry of the incarnated Logos:

> Lovely was the death
> Of Him whose Life was Love! Holy with power
> He on the thought-benighted Sceptic beamed
> Manifest Godhead . . .
> And first by Fear uncharmed the drowséd Soul.
> Till of its nobler nature it 'gan feel
> Dim recollections; and thence soared to Hope.
> Strong to believe whate'er of mystic good
> The Eternal dooms for His immortal sons.
> From Hope and firmer Faith to perfect Love
> Attracted and absorbed: and centred there
> God only to behold, and know, and feel,
> Till by exclusive consciousness of God
> All self-annihilated it shall make
> God its identity: God all in all!
> We and our Father one!

The mystical ascent through faith to love brings us to the experience of divine unity:

There is one Mind, one omnipresent Mind,
Omnific. His most holy name is Love.
Truth of subliming import! with the which
Who feeds and saturates his constant soul,
He from his small particular orbit flies
With blest outstarting! From himself he flies,
Stands in the sun, and with no partial gaze
Views all creation; and he loves it all,
And blesses it, and calls it very good!
This is indeed to dwell with the Most High!
Cherubs and rapture-trembling Seraphim
Can press no nearer to the Almighty's throne.[55]

Amongst Coleridge's many influences were the 'inner light' mystics, Boehme and George Fox, of whom he spoke with gratitude in *Biographia Literaria*: 'One assertion I will venture to make, as suggested by my own experience, that there exist folios on the human understanding, and the nature of man, which would have a far juster claim to their high rank and celebrity, if in the whole huge volume there could be found as much fulness of heart and intellect, as burst forth in many a simple page of GEORGE FOX, JACOB BEHMEN, and even of Behmen's commentator, the pious and fervid WILLIAM LAW.'[56] The writings of such mystics helped to keep Coleridge from dogmaticaly embracing a single religious or philosophical system:

> They contributed to keep alive the *heart* in the *head*; gave an indistinct, yet stirring and working presentiment, that all the products of the mere *reflective* faculty partook of DEATH, and were as the rattling twigs and sprays in winter, into which a sap was yet to be propelled from some root to which I had not penetrated, if they were to afford my soul either food or shelter. If they were too often a moving cloud of smoke to me by day, yet they were always a pillar of fire throughout the night, during my wanderings through the wilderness of doubt, and enabled me to skirt, without crossing, the sandy deserts of utter unbelief.[57]

By the end of his life Coleridge was expressing his spiritual intuitions in the unequivocal language of Christian belief:

> God's child in Christ adopted, – Christ my all, –
> What that earth boasts were not lost cheaply, rather
> Than forfeit that blest name, by which I call
> The Holy One, the Almighty God, my Father? –

Father! in Christ we live, and Christ in Thee –
Eternal Thou, and everlasting we.
The heir of heaven, henceforth I fear not death:
In Christ I live! in Christ I draw the breath
Of the true life! – Let then earth, sea, and sky
Make war against me! On my heart I show
Their mighty master's seal. In vain they try
To end my life, that can but end its woe. –
Is that a death-bed where a Christian lies? –
Yes! but not his – 'tis Death itself there dies.[58]

Shelley and Keats

No such Christian certitude ever came to Percy Bysshe Shelley (1792–1822), who remained a Platonist inspired by Ideal Love and Ideal Beauty. Love was 'the bond and the sanction which connects not only man with man, but with everything which exists. We are born into the world, and there is something within us which, from the instant that we live, more and more thirsts after its likeness.'[59] Shelley defines this 'something' as 'a soul within our soul'; it is 'a mirror whose surface reflects only the forms of purity and brightness'. His constant desire was to be mystically fused with what he called in *Prometheus Unbound* 'the deep truth', which, he said, was 'imageless'. The yearning for such a union was given personal and metaphysical expression in *Epipsychidion*, that strange allegory of earthly and spiritual love:

> We shall become the same, we shall be one
> Spirit within two frames, oh! wherefore two?
> One passion in twin-hearts, which grows and grew,
> Till like two meteors of expanding flame,
> Those spheres instinct with it become the same,
> Touch, mingle, are transfigured; ever still
> Burning, yet ever inconsumable:
> In one another's substance finding food,
> Like flames too pure and light and unimbued
> To nourish their bright lives with baser prey,
> Which point to Heaven and cannot pass away:
> One hope within two wills, one will beneath
> Two overshadowing minds, one life, one death,
> One Heaven, one Hell, one immortality,
> And one annihilation.[60]

Given Christian reference points this could be an orthodox

expression of mystical ecstasy; but there is no trace of Christian theology in Shelley's passionate quest for the Ideal, which remains, as in the famous verse from his elegy on Keats, the unidentified and unidentifiable One:

> The One remains, the many change and pass;
> Heaven's light forever shines, Earth's shadows fly;
> Life, like a dome of many-coloured glass,
> Stains the white radiance of Eternity,
> Until Death tramples it to fragments.[61]

The subject of Shelley's elegy, **John Keats** (1795–1821), found such a unifying principle in the idea (or, more accurately, the Idea) of Beauty. As he wrote to his brother George: 'The mighty abstract Idea I have of Beauty in all things stifles the more divided and minute domestic happiness.' It is this ruling Idea that gave rise to the famous conclusion of the *Ode on a Grecian Urn*:

> Beauty is truth, truth Beauty, that is all
> Ye know on earth, and all ye need to know.

Keats believed that we approach truth progressively, by stages. Of a passage in *Endymion* he said: 'When I wrote it, it was a regular stepping of the Imagination towards a truth.' The passage in question (I, 774 ff) describes the ecstasy of spiritual vision, which, when the mind is ready, can be triggered by a variety of stimulii:

> Feel we these things? – that moment have we stept
> Into a sort of oneness, and our state
> Is like a floating spirit's.

In *Endymion* the moon symbolizes the eternal Idea, the one essence of which all life partakes:

> And as I grew in years, still didst thou blend
> With all my ardours: thou wast the deep glen;
> Thou wast the mountain-top, the sage's pen,
> The poet's harp, the voice of friends, the sun;
> Thou wast the river, thou wast glory won;
> Thou wast my clarion's blast, thou wast my steed,
> My goblet full of wine, my topmost deed:
> Thou wast the charm of women, lovely Moon![62]

And wherein lies happiness, asks Keats?

> In that which becks
> Our ready minds to fellowship divine,
> A fellowship with essence; till we shine,
> Full alchemiz'd, and free of space.[63]

10. Mysticism in the Modern World: Two Responses

THOUGH this survey has been strictly historical, as well as acritical, in its approach, the idea that mystical aspirations and mystical attainment are things of the past must be firmly rebutted. The living stream of Western spirituality flows ever on, though threatened on all sides by the clogging silt of opposing cultural and political trends. For Teresa of Avila, the soul was an interior castle of which humanity at large was unaware: the truth still holds. Herein lies one of the functions of spirituality. Those with a developed spiritual sense in every period of history show their contemporaries and all who follow how necessary, how vital it is to acknowledge the spiritual component of our constitution, for to deny or disregard our spiritual resources is to close ourselves to a vivifying sense of purpose and meaning. And so the mystical quest – whether it is overlaid with the terminology of twentieth-century psychology or quantum physics, or conflated with the language of Eastern metaphysics – continues, and must continue.

This final chapter concentrates principally on two responses to spiritual realities in the modern world – the world of science, unbelief, popular materialistic cultures and widespread rejection of traditional structures of belief.

First, we should perhaps remind ourselves of the range of personalities and spiritual types a detailed examination of spirituality in the nineteenth and twentieth centuries might include. On the one hand there is the enclosed, intense, suffering world of **St Thérèse of Lisieux** (1873–1897), who once said: 'I do not believe I have ever been more than three minutes at a time without thinking of [God].' The language by which she expressed her wholly Catholic form of spirituality is often overpoweringly cloying; but it also has a concentrated power that can be reminiscent of Crashaw's Baroque fervours, as in the poem *Vivre d'amour*:

> Burning arrow, burn me away until nothing is left,
> Take my heart, here in this sad sojourn, here below.
> Jesus, my Lord, let me live my dream,
>   Let me die of love!
>   [. . .]
> I am impassioned with his love;
> Oh, that he would come at last to inflame me forever!
> There lies my heaven, there rests my destiny:
>   TO LIVE IN LOVE!

More disciplined – and to many more convincing – is the language used by '**Lucie-Christine**' (1844–1908) to describe the consciousness of God's presence in the posthumously published *Spiritual Journal*:

> For two days now God gives me each time that I go into church a sense of His Presence that I cannot express, finding it above all ideas. It is a full sight, although it has no form; it is at the same time sight and union. I am plunged into God. I see Him so intensely that my soul is more certain and more possessed by the sight than my bodily eyes by the light of day; and at the same time He is in me, He is one with me, penetrates me, is closer to me than the air I breathe, is more united to me than the soul is united to the body which lives by it; I am absorbed by Him. I no longer know by what existence I exist, it seems to me that I am transported into another life, a region that is no more this earth; and this detachment is ineffable, it is a rapture and inebriation. Therein the soul knows God as no speech could make Him known to her, and there results from this an ardent thirst to abase all other souls before Him.[2]

In contrast to both Thérèse of Lisieux and Lucie-Christine is **Charles de Foucauld** (1858–1916), soldier, explorer, ascetic and contemplative. Foucauld passed from loss of faith and dissipation to a life of total abasement and sacrifice. The turning point came in 1886, under the influence of the Abbé Huvelin, the spiritual director of Baron von Hügel. Eventually Foucauld entered the Trappist monastery of Akbès in Syria. He wrote: 'God makes me find in the solitude and silence a consolation on which I had not counted. I am constantly, absolutely constantly, with Him and with those I love.' But even the rigours of the

Trappist Order did not satisfy Foucauld, and in 1897 he migrated to Palestine and became a servant for the Poor Clares at Nazareth. He was ordained in 1901 and from 1905 devoted himself to a life of prayer and ascetic discipline, in the manner of the Desert Fathers, in the solitudes of North Africa. Of the heights of his spiritual experiences Foucauld wrote: 'I see all things in the light of the immense peace of God, of his infinite happiness, of the immutable glory of the blessed and ever tranquil Trinity. Everything loses itself for me in the happiness that God is God.'

Other figures – some more, some less concerned with the traditional patterns and images of the religious life – press for inclusion: **Evelyn Underhill** (1875–1941) herself; **Dag Hammarskjöld** (1905–1961), the former Secretary-General of the United Nations, who summed up his religious experience in the short but powerful phrase, 'Not I, but God in me'; and **Simone Weil** (1909–1943), a Jew who was profoundly influenced by the poetry of George Herbert and who placed great emphasis on the Passion of Christ. She wrote with the clarity born of experience about the apparent absence of God in times of affliction:

> A kind of horror submerges the whole soul. During this absence there is nothing to love. What is terrible is that if, in this darkness where there is nothing to love, the Soul ceases to love, God's absence becomes final. The soul has to go on loving in the emptiness, or at least to go on wanting to love, though it may be with an infinitesimal part of itself. Then, one day, God will come to show himself to the soul and to reveal the beauty of the world to it, as in the case of Job. But if the soul stops loving it falls, even in this life, into something almost equivalent to hell.[2]

Of the many possible figures, I have chosen Pierre Teilhard de Chardin and Thomas Merton to illustrate in more detail how mystical insights have interacted with the experience of modernity. In the former, the concepts of science and of traditional theology mingle to produce a uniquely personal and complex synthesis; in the latter, a sympathetic awareness of Eastern spirituality becomes drawn into a robust, individualistic outlook that yet has deep roots in the tradition of Catholic mystical theology and experience.

Teilhard de Chardin

The vision of Pierre Teilhard de Chardin (1881–1955) embraced both science and personal mystical experience. It also accommodated certain aspects of Eastern thought, those aspects that fascinated Teilhard by their emphasis on the ultimate unity of the universe, in spite of a fundamental conviction that 'the two of us, the East and I, have two diametrically opposed conceptions'.[3] This highly individual, syncretic vision placed Teilhard outside the main stream of orthodox Christian thought, even though he remained a loyal member of the Jesuit order from 1901 until his death in April 1955 and never attempted to break free from the intellectual constrictions this loyalty demanded. His reputation as a geologist and paleontologist was high and he was offered a chair in prehistory at the Collège de France; but his Jesuit superiors frowned upon his amalgamation of natural science and theology, with the result that none of his writings on religion and philosophy, including the seminal *The Phenomenon of Man*, was published during his lifetime. (*The Phenomenon of Man* did not appear in English until 1959, with a foreword by the agnostic Sir Julian Huxley.)

The personal experiences were formative and came early. Teilhard was born at Sarcenat, near Clermont-Ferrand in the Auvergne. From his father he received encouragement to pursue his scientific interests, whilst through his mother he became familiar with the Catholic mystics. As a child Teilhard had several experiences of the numinous in which he *realized* the oneness of all things, a kind of Wordsworthian pantheism of which he said: 'all I shall ever write will only be a feeble part of what I feel'. This nature mysticism was developed and intensified during his time in Jersey, 1901–5, and by his first contact with the East – teaching at a Jesuit school in Cairo from 1905 to 1908. Yet the sense of overwhelming awe he felt on confronting the vastness of the desert also brought with it a recognition of the negative aspects of pantheistic absorption in an impersonal One. The temptation to turn away forever from the world of men was great and resulted in a severe religious crisis for Teilhard during the period in Egypt.

After leaving Egypt Teilhard studied theology at a Jesuit house in Hastings from 1908 to 1912. Of these years he wrote:

All that I can remember of those days . . . is the extraordinary solidity and intensity I found then in the English countryside, particularly at sunset, when the Sussex woods were charged with all that 'fossil' Life which I was then hunting for, from cliff to quarry, in the Wealden clay.

There were moments, indeed, when it seemed to me that a sort of universal being was about to take shape suddenly in Nature* before my very eyes.[4]

It was at Hastings that Teilhard first began to incorporate the concept of evolution into his spiritual vision, under the influence of Henri Bergson's book *Creative Evolution*. In particular, his formulation of the cosmic Christ had its origins in this period.

Ordained in 1911, Teilhard served during the First World War as a stretcher-bearer, rather than as an ordinary chaplain. It was, as he said, 'a baptism of the real'. His first essay, 'Cosmic Life', was a product of the war years and was intended to be his intellectual testament if he did not survive. This was followed by other essays – 'The Mystical Milieu' (1917), 'The Soul of the World' (1918) and 'The Great Monad' (1918).

Teilhard's experience of front-line war was catalytic and transforming. It helped him to overcome an aversion to interpersonal relationships, which he had seen as intrusions into the inner world of vision. By 1916 he had conquered the temptaion to immerse himself totally in matter and beyond his ecstatic experience of nature he perceived an even greater one, 'that through all nature I was immersed in God'. What he described as the 'true summons of the cosmos' was defined as 'a call consciously to share in the great work that goes on within it; it is not by drifting down the current of things that we shall be unified with their one, single, soul, but by fighting our way, with them, towards some term still to come'.[5] Pantheism was not enough; religious aspirations that shut out human affairs and the

---

*It is interesting to compare this with the famous incident described by Wordsworth in *The Prelude*:

> I dipp'd my oars into the silent Lake,
> And, as I rose upon the stroke, my Boat
> Went heaving through the water, like a Swan;
> When from behind that craggy Steep, till then
> The bound of the horizon, a huge Cliff,
> As if with voluntary power instinct,
> Uprear'd its head. I struck, and struck again,
> And, growing still in stature, the huge Cliff
> Rose up between me and the stars, and still,
> With measur'd motion, like a living thing,
> Strode after me. With trembling hands I turn'd,
> And through the silent water stole my way
> Back to the Cavern of the Willow tree.

natural world were also incomplete. The way forward was through a synthesis of both approaches. As Teilhard put it in 'Cosmic Life': 'There is a communion with God, and a communion with earth, and a communion with God through earth.' In other words, mystical experience must be related to action and effort: God must be related to His world.

After the war Teilhard lived in Paris until 1923, when he went on a scientific mission to China at the invitation of a fellow-Jesuit. The experience of Asia proper, together with that of the war, had a decisive effect on the development of his thought. In Mongolia he was led 'to the heart of the unique greatness of God', and it was here that he formulated a prayer that became the famous 'Mass on the World'. God was seen as 'the universal *milieu* in which and through which all things live and have their being'; the world is 'the glorious living crucible in which everything melts away in order to be born anew'.[6] Of his own spiritual development Teilhard wrote, in words addressed to God: 'I have been brought to the point where I can no longer see anything, nor any longer breathe, outside that *milieu* in which all is made one.' He describes a state in which all opposites are united – 'The excitement of action and the delight of passivity; the joy of possessing and the thrill of reaching out beyond what one possesses; the pride in growing and the happiness of being lost in what is greater than oneself.'[7]

For Teilhard God was inseparable from the universe. He could not accept the idea of God as pure Spirit. He saw instead, and praised steadfastly and passionately, God's 'incarnate Being in the world of matter'.

In *The Heart of Matter* Teilhard reaffirms the realization that 'God truly waits for us in things' – that at the heart of matter is the heart of God, and that God cannot be loved without loving the world. The supreme focus of such a love is the universal Christ, the Incarnation of God, the unique feature of the Christian revelation that provides the impetus to truly worship and love the material creation. This theme is explored in the essay 'The Christic', written a few weeks before Teilhard's death.

The fundamental uniqueness of Christianity was, for Teilhard, unassailable. In *The Divine Milieu* he elaborated upon the distinction between the processes of Christian mysticism and both 'the errors of a pagan naturalism' and 'the excesses of quietism and illuminism'. The essential point is that in Christian mysticism the personal 'I' is never extinguished:

> Pantheism seduces us by its vistas of perfect universal union. But ultimately, if it were true, it would give us only fusion and unconsciousness; for, at the end of the evolution it claims to reveal, the elements of the world vanish in the God they create or by which they are absorbed . . . Christianity alone . . . saves . . . the essential aspiration of all mysticism: to be united (that is, to become the other) while remaining oneself . . . We can only lose ourselves in God by prolonging the most individual characteristics of beings far beyond themselves: that is the fundamental rule by which we can always distinguish the true mystic from his counterfeits.[8]

Teilhard's time in the Far East fell into two periods: 1923 to 1931, and 1932 to 1946. These years gave his writings a host of new reference points and, overall, were profoundly enriching, despite his reservations about the Eastern way. As he put it in a letter written soon after his arrival in China:

> I do not believe . . . that the majority of oriental thought-patterns are anything but outmoded and obsolescent . . . But I do say that by taking these forms, decayed though they be, into account, we discover such a wealth of 'potentialities' in philosophy, in mysticism, and in the study of human conduct that it becomes scarcely possible to be satisfied with an image of a mankind entirely and definitely enveloped in the narrow network of precepts and dogmas in which some people think they have displayed the whole amplitude of Christianity.[9]

Teilhard returned from the East in 1946 and spent his last years in Paris, from 1946 to 1951, and in 'exile' in New York, from 1951 until 1955. The pattern and quest of his life have been well summed up by Ursula King:

> Throughout his life, Teilhard was a wanderer between different worlds. His life and thought are interwoven like the parts of an immense symphony with ever new variations on a basic theme. This theme is the supreme adventure of man's ascent to the spirit, and the continuous breakthrough of God's presence in the world of matter and flesh. Teilhard's vision, like that of other seers before him, was one of consuming fire, kindled by the radiant powers of love. It was a mystical vision deeply Christian in origin and orientation; yet it broke through traditional boundaries and grew into a vision global in intent.[10]

The shift from monistic pantheism – 'communion with earth' – to a mysticism that embraces the personal as well as the cosmic is described in 'The Mystical Milieu', written in 1917. Mystical experience is seen as progressing through a series of expanding circles – an image not dissimilar to that used by Teresa of Avila in *The Interior Castle*. The movement is from an experience of homogeneity – the oneness of the universe – to an experience of heterogeneity and individuality. This process culminates in what is essentially Christian pantheism, a union of a transcendent Reality beyond the world with an immanent, ever-present, *intimate* divinity centred in Christ – the pan-Christ – and operative at the personal and interpersonal levels. In this figure of Christ, the personal is combined with the universal – 'communion with God through earth'.

This figure of the universal Christ goes far beyond the traditional Christian conception of Christ and was part of Teilhard's vision of the 'confluence' or 'convergence' of world religion and civilizations on unity. This evolutionary perspective was a consequence of Teilhard's scientific background. Evolution, for him, was not merely a theory: it was 'a general condition to which all theories, all hypotheses, all systems must bow . . . Evolution is a light illuminating all facts, a curve that all lines must follow'.[11] He held that religion and evolution should be neither confused nor divorced: they are destined to form 'one continuous organism', and he saw it as the task of both himself and his age to effect this synthesis. With this view of evolution went a dynamic conception of God. As Teilhard noted in his diary in 1950: 'God is not dead – but HE CHANGES.'

Nearly all Teilhard's writings, as Ursula King has said, have a mystical matrix and contain experiential referents. But unlike the majority of Christian mystics, Teilhard nowhere provides a connected descriptive account of his personal experiences: they remain embedded in wider cultural and philosophical concerns. He had no interest in the merely historical development of mysticism *per se* or in the academic study of mystical theology. He attempted to articulate a completely *new understanding* of mysticism, a new recognition of its cultural and personal function. His evolutionary perspective meant that he could not accept that the nature of man's spiritual quest remained static and immune to development. As man changes, as the human organism adapts and develops, so do his mystical aspirations and the processes by which he attempts to realize them. Nor was mysticism for Teilhard solely a quest of the individual – in terms we have already encountered, of the alone for the Alone. If that had been generally true of the past, present and future conditions demanded a more comprehensive definition.

Isolated contemplation (what Teilhard called the *via secunda*, where nature mysticism, 'communion with earth', was the *via prima*) was seen as world-excluding. The synthesis he sought was the *via tertia*, by which man is united with the Absolute through a unifying experience of the world – 'communion with God through earth'.

Teilhard's spirituality is thus essentially active and Christocentric. Mystical knowledge of God is not achieved by withdrawing from the world, but by being actively absorbed in it, by being wholly aware of the processes of divine evolution – that controlled moving towards the ultimate Pleroma, or Omega Point:

> In attaining it and merging myself in it, I have the whole universe in front of me, with its noble endeavours, its entrancing search for knowledge, with its myriads of souls to be perfected and healed. I can and must plunge breathlessly into the midst of human labour. The greater share I take, the more weight I will bring to bear on the whole surface of the real, the nearer I will attain to Christ and the faster I shall grapple myself to him.[12]

Summing up his own spiritual insights, Teilhard wrote: 'Throughout my life, by means of my life, the world has little by little caught fire in my sight until, aflame all around me, it has become almost luminous from within . . . Such has been my experience in contact with the earth – the diaphany of the Divine at the heart of a universe on fire.'[13]

Thomas Merton

Merton was born on 31 January 1915, at Prades in the eastern Pyrenees, to an American mother and a New Zealander father. His domineering mother died of cancer when Merton was six, leaving him deprived of an emotional centre to his life, which was thereafter characterized by wanderings in search of an abiding focus. Not that Ruth Merton had been a particularly doting parent. As Merton remarked in later life, 'perhaps solitaries are made by severe women'.

In 1929 he entered Oakham School and in due course

proceeded to Cambridge, which he disliked, and continued to dislike all his life. He drank heavily, ran up bills and, it would seem, made one of several casual girlfriends pregnant. In 1935 he left England for good and enrolled at Columbia University, which was much more to his taste.

One day, in Scribners on Fifth Avenue, he came across a copy of Etienne Gilson's *The Spirit of Medieval Philosophy*. His imagination was immediately seized by the concept of *aseitas*:

> In this one word, which can be applied to God alone, and which expresses His most characteristic attribute, I discovered an entirely new concept of God – a concept which showed me at once that the belief of Catholics was by no means the vague and rather superstitious hangover from an unscientific age that I had believed it to be . . . *Aseitas* – simply means the power of a being to exist absolutely in virtue of itself, not as caused by itself, but as requiring no cause, no other justification for its existence except that its very nature is to exist. There can be only one such Being: That is God . . . This notion made such a profound impression on me that I made a pencil note at the top of the page: 'Aseity of God – God is being *per se*'.[14]

Merton now had an intellectual concept of God to which he could assent. It remained for him to locate spiritual motivation, to discover his vocation. He began to think more and more about the mystical process and about the power of what he called 'Christian virtue', even as he continued to get drunk and pursue girls: 'I was already dreaming of mystical union when I did not even keep the simplest rudiments of the moral law'.

He was also, just as inexorably, moving towards Catholicism. He was baptized into the Catholic Church in November 1938, a momentous step of which he wrote in his autobiography: 'Now I had entered into the everlasting movement of that gravitation which is the very life and spirit of God: God's own gravitation towards the depths of His own infinite nature, His goodness without end. And God, that centre Who is everywhere, and whose circumference is nowhere, finding me . . . And He called out to me from His own immense depths.'[15]

He applied for admission to the Franciscan Order, but was advised to withdraw his application, probably after confiding the existence of his illegitimate child. He eventually found what he was searching for in the Abbey of Our Lady of Geth-semani in Bardstown, Kentucky, a monastery of the Cistercians of the Strict Observance – better known as Trappists.

The severe Trappist regime (Gethsemani was known as the strictest of all the Trappist houses) enraptured him at first sight, though he came to long for a kind of solitary life that was unavailable at Gethsemani: 'Now the church was full of light, and the monks stood in their stalls and bowed like white seas at the ends of the psalms . . . The whole earth came to life and bounded with new fruitfulness and significance in the joy of their simple and beautiful chanting.' And so he entered the medieval world of the Gethsemani Trappists, a world of silence, white robes, prayer and a minutely ordered ascetic discipline. His new life was hard physically, but mentally and spiritually it uplifted him and set him free.

In 1946 he began writing his autobiography, *The Seven Storey Mountain* (the image is from Dante). The following year he wrote *Seeds of Contemplation*, in which he first revealed his gift as a spiritual teacher; and in 1948 he produced *The Waters of Siloe*. In spite of the security and happiness he found at Gethsemani, doubts began to build up in him as the time to take his final vows approached. Could the Trappist Order ever provide him with the life of complete peace and solitude he desired? 'The Cistercian Life is energetic,' he wrote. 'There are tides of vitality running through the whole community that generate energy even in people who are lazy.' In spite of his doubts, the final vows were taken and he remained at Gethsemani.

In *Seeds of Contemplation*, which draws on Pascal and St John of the Cross, Merton insists that self-will and appetite must be renounced if we are to develop spiritually. Joy consists only in seeking to know and do the will of God:

> The only true joy is to escape from the prison of our own selfhood . . . and enter by love into union with the Life Who dwells and sings within the essence of every creature and in the core of our minds.

This is the essence of Merton's spirituality. We become more like God the more we are ourselves – our *true* selves. We must discover, with God's help, our real identity: 'The perfection of each created thing is not merely in its conformity to an abstract type but in its own individual identity with itself . . . We can be ourselves or not, as we please. But the problem is this: since God alone possesses the secret of my identity, He alone can make me who I am or rather, He alone can make me who I will be when I at last fully begin to be.' The problem resolves itself to this: 'To discover myself in discovering God. If I find Him, I will find myself; and if I find my true self, I will find Him.'

The Seven Storey Mountain, published by Harcourt Brace in 1948, was a huge success, the original edition selling some 600,000 copies. Merton showed himself to be a naturally gifted writer, and the passage from rake to religious was an inherently fascinating human theme. Throughout the book the community at Gethsemani is painted in glowing colours; but there is as well a detectable note of disappointment, a regret that the heroism of embracing the Trappist ideals had not been enough. There remained a deeper, more terrifying ideal, evoked in a meditation in which God speaks to him concerning true solitude:

> When you have been praised a little and loved a little I will take away all your gifts and all your love and all your praise and you will be utterly forgotten and abandoned and you will be nothing, a dead thing, a rejection. And in that day you shall begin to possess the solitude you have so long desired. And your solitude will bear immense fruit in the souls of men you will never see on earth.
>
> Do not ask when it will be or where it will be or how it will be: On a mountain or in a prison, in a desert or in a concentration camp or in a hospital or at Gethsemani. It does not matter. So do not ask me, because I am not going to tell you. You will not know until you are in it.

After ordination Merton experienced a period of poor health and nervous exhaustion, which incapacitated him as a writer. He found himself face to face 'with a mystery that was beginning to manifest itself in the depths of my soul and to move me with terror'. The workload at Gethsemani physically exhausted him ('You are lucky', he noted rather acidly, 'if you can get a minute to kneel down before the tabernacle and say a Hail Mary'). But this suffering, as is so often the case, brought a pivotal clarification of his yearning for solitude. Solitude, he came to recognize, is not something to be hoped for in the future: it is a deepening of the present. Unless it is looked for in the present, it will never be found. He wrote: 'The peace I had found, the solitude of the winter of 1950, deepened and developed in me beyond measure.'

In *The Ascent to Truth* (1951) Merton attempted to outline a method of contemplative prayer that could be used by contemporary readers, although he restricted the application of the method by basing it on the formidable prescriptions of St John of the Cross. Whilst preaching a mysticism of detachment, Merton also maintained that one did not have to make a choice between affirmation and denial:

> We have to take both. We must affirm and deny at the same time. We have to start with a concept of God, but we have simultaneously to know that it is quite inadequate as a description of him. Corresponding with these are the *via negationis* or *negativa*, the way of unknowing on the one hand, and the *via amoris*, the way of love on the other.

Merton then goes on to define the experience of Christian contemplation:

> Christian contemplation is precipitated by crisis within crisis and anguish within anguish. It is born of spiritual conflict. It is a victory that suddenly appears in the hour of defeat. It is the providential solution of problems that seem to have no solution. It is the reconciliation of enemies that seem to be irreconcilable. It is a vision in which Love, mounting in the darkness which no reasoning can penetrate, unites in one bound all the loose strands that intelligence alone cannot connect together, and with this cord draws the whole being of man into a Divine Union, the effects of which will some day overflow into the world outside him.

Though all Merton's writings reveal a deep familiarity with the literature of Catholic mystical theology – for example, St Augustine, William of St-Thierry, Aquinas, and of course St Bernard – he also became deeply read in Eastern religion, to which there are many references in his later writings. For instance, in a letter explaining *Hagia Sophia* – the feminie, 'wisdom' aspect of God – he writes:

> The wisdom of God, 'reaching from end to end mightily', is also the Tao, the nameless pivot of all being and nature, the centre and meaning of all . . .

He also corresponded with the Hindu yogi Patanjali and came to know the Zen master D. T. Suzuki and, at a conference in Bangkok in 1968, Chogyam Trungpa Rinpoche, whose spirituality deeply moved Merton.

Merton saw the contemplative vision as a supreme restorative principle in the modern world – a world of depersonalizing institutions and potential thermonuclear destruction. The task of the contemplative is one of self-emptying so that God can take possession of him. It is a total, unconditional surrender to emptiness and nakedness:

> A real 'transformation of consciousness' occurs in the individual subject from an awareness of his false self, or empirical ego, to the true self or person. Now the individual is no longer conscious of himself as an isolated ego, but sees himself in his inmost ground of being as dependent on Another or as being formed through relationships, particularly his relationship with God. By forgetting himself both as subject and as object of reflection, man finds his real self hidden with Christ in God. And so, as his self-consciousness changes, the individual is transformed; his self is no longer its own centre; it is now centred on God.[16]

On the 1968 trip to the Far East Merton met the Dalai Lama and several other holy men. One hermit particularly impressed him:

> He said he had meditated in solitude for thirty years or more and had not attained to perfect emptiness and I said I hadn't either.
>
> The unspoken or half-spoken message of the talk was our complete understanding of each other as people who were somehow *on the edge* of great realization and knew it and were trying somehow or other, to go out and get lost in it.'[17]

In Bangkok Merton lectured on 'Marxism and Monastic Perspectives'. After he had given his paper he retired to his room in a cottage at the Red Cross Center. He died that afternoon, 10 December 1969, apparently as a result of an accident with an electric fan, though his death is still a mystery: murder is not ruled out by a recent biographer.

Of Merton's spiritual stature there can be no doubt. Few in our time have spoken in such classic and inspiring terms of the 'deep movements of love' that come in the highest reaches of contemplation and of the immensity of the gulf between what we truly are and the hollow shell of our self-image:

And when God allows us to fall back into our own confusion of desires and judgments and temptations, we carry a scar over the place where that joy exulted for a moment in our hearts.

The scar burns us. The sore wound aches within us, and we remember that we have fallen back into what we are not, and are not yet allowed to remain where God would have us belong. We long for the place He has destined for us and weep with desire for the time when this pure poverty will catch us and hold us in its liberty and never let us go, when we will never fall back from the Paradise of the simple and the little children into the forum of prudence where the wise of this world go up and down in sorrow and set their traps for a happiness that cannot exist.[18]

*   *   *

I began this book with reference to the idea of 'proving God on the pulses'. This kind of proof is not susceptible to scientific, repeatable analysis; but then neither is the love of a parent for his children. To those who have experienced such love, it is a fact, a fundamental pivot in their life. For those who have claimed direct experience of God, the same is true. They have the certitude of knowing, of *realization*.

It can come to us all. At any time. As it came to an ordinary English priest, Anthony Duncan, one day in the latter half of the twentieth century:

I will tell you how it was with me on that day.

It was my normal time for prayer, and I was sitting in my stall in the Lady Chapel of the Church at Highnam. If my memory serves me right I had just read part of the Daily Office, and the time had come for me to begin to recollect myself in preparation for silent prayer.

My preparations had scarcely begun when, quite suddenly, I became aware of two points of light, one to the left and one to the right, some little way in front of me. Almost at once I knew what they were. Almost at once I knew *who* they were, for they were persons of great intensity. In my seeing of them, they formed themselves into beings, beings of light.

Don't ask me what they looked like. Don't ask me how I knew who and what they were. Don't even ask me with what eyes I saw them. I know no answers to these questions and I wonder indeed if there are answers to questions like that.

Don't ask me how long I was confronted by these two angels – for angels they were, I know no other term to describe them. Time did not seem to be involved in the encounter. It was, in some way, timeless, and yet there was some sense of duration because there was an unfolding of events.

First came the angels, fellow-creatures, brothers in Creation with me, but of another order of being. It was given to me to perceive them and know them for who and what they were. But they were only the beginning. They were heralds, I suppose. They alerted me, and brought me into a Presence.

Quite sudenly, between them, there stood my Lord and my God. Christ stood there, Risen, Ascended, Glorified. And I knew Him. And throughout my whole being, and throughout the whole Universe, there reverberated a single Word. It was a Word which was spoken to me and it told me my vocation. I knew what I had to do and what I was for. This Word reverberated on and on throughout all ages and I knew that there was no other Word that could be uttered to me. My Lord stood there for ever and ever and the whole of Creation trembled. There was no other than Him, and I was called into His Presence.

Are you going to ask me what he looked like? I cannot tell you. He came, recognisably to my whole being. It was His Humanity that made it possible for me to know Him and relate to Him as man to Man. But His Light was too bright for my perception, and he appeared as a darkness. In the darkness in which the two angels had shone like beacons he came as a man-shaped darkness which was darker than the darkness. And yet it was not dark with the absence of light but rather Dark with the excess of it. It was the darkness of Compassion, for it was the Uncreated Light and had I seen that I should have been destroyed utterly.

Once, many years before, I saw the Uncreated Light and I was destroyed. Like St John on Patmos, 'I fell at His feet as though dead.' And I was re-created and forgiven in that 'peace of God which passeth all understanding.' I know these things for I have been through them by the Grace of God.

But on this occasion I did not fall down. I was rather called to look my Lord in the face and hear what He had to say to me. He came as a Friend. And my encounter with the Uncreated Light now was as a man-shaped darkness, darker than the surrounding dark. This, at any rate, was how it was given me to perceive it.

This was ten years ago, almost exactly. The image implanted in my consciousness has returned to me many times since and I have come to a small measure of understanding of it.

Of His great courtesy, our Lord came to me and called me into His Presence. He, my Lord and my God, is the Uncreated, and all Creation abides in Him and He is everywhere within it, in a personal relationship with all His hands have made. I perceived my two brothers, the angels, because, like me, they are creatures. Whatever continuum it is which forms the context of their lives, a bridge was made between it and the time-space continuum in which I abide in this mortal life. And I perceived them and we knew each other as brothers.

But my Lord is the Uncreated. There is no way by which He may be perceived other than through His Humanity. And to me, that day, the Uncreated showed Himself man-shaped. Through the Humanity-taken-into-God, the Humanity of Christ, I am able to know, to relate to, to touch the Divinity. In my understanding, as it has grown over the years, He stood before me as a gateway through which I am beckoned. 'Behold, I stand at the door and knock' He said in Holy Scripture. He is the Door, and He knocks for me to enter! He is the Way, the Truth, the Life. That is my experience of Him. And it is through that gateway of His Humanity that I am called to go. That is the Way, that is the Truth, and that is the Life. 'No man comes to the Father but by me', He said. His Humanity is the only access to the Uncreated.

Ten years ago, in the Lady Chapel of Highnam Church, I was wholly overcome by the Word of command that had been spoken to me. Ever since then I have been struggling to find ways of obeying and understanding it. But there was another Word, unspoken at that time, which has uttered itself more and more insistently within me as the years have passed. It is a Word which was left for me to utter and articulate for myself and for any who will hear it.

For I have personally encountered and experienced The Incarnation. I have encountered, recognised and known the Risen Humanity, Ascended and in Glory. It has been given me to encounter the Uncreated within the confines of created humanity. I have known myself to be called and beckoned through that Humanity into the Uncreated.

Human nature ascended into Heaven in Christ. I now know that for I have seen it and this is my personal experience of it. But there is but one Human Nature. Mankind images its Creator in that Man is one Being with an infinitude of persons. And therefore I, and the totality of mankind, are partakers of that one Human Nature which, in Christ, has been taken up into the Uncreated.

I know that the Word became flesh and dwelt among us. I have seen His glory, the glory as of the only-begotten of the Father; the Uncreated, my Lord and my God.[19]

Appendix: Chronological List of Selected Mystics and Mystical Theologians

Ignatius of Antioch	*c.*35–*c.*107
Justin Martyr	*c.*100–*c.*165
Irenaeus	*c.*130–*c.*200
Clement of Alexandria	*c.*130–*c.*215
Tertullian	*c.*160–*c.*225
Origen	*c.*185–254
St Antony	*c.*251–356
St Athanasius	*c.*296–373
Gregory of Nazianzus	329–389
Basil the Great	*c.*330–379
Gregory of Nyssa	*c.*330–*c.*395
John Cassian	*c.*360–435
Palladius	*c.*365–425
Methodius	d.*c.*311
St Augustine	354–430
Dionysius the Areopagite	*fl.c.*500
John Scotus Erigena	*c.*810–*c.*877
St Anselm	*c.*1033–1109
St Bernard of Clairvaux	1090–1153
William of St-Thierry	*c.*1085–1148
St Hildegard of Bingen	1098–1179
Hugh of St Victor	d.1142
Richard of St Victor	d.1173
St Francis of Assisi	1181/2–1226
Albertus Magnus	1193–1280
Joachim of Floris	d.1202
Mechthild of Magdeburg	*c.*1210–*c.*1280
St Bonaventura	*c.*1217–1274
St Thomas Aquinas	*c.*1225–1274
Jacopone da Todi	*c.*1230–1306
Mechthild of Hackborn	1240–1298
Angela of Foligno	*c.*1248–1309

St Gertrude the Great	1256–*c.*1302
Meister Eckhart	*c.*1260–1327/8
Margery Kempe	*c.*1290
John Ruysbroeck	1293–1381
Henry Suso	*c.*1295–1366
Richard Rolle	1300–1349
Johann Tauler	*c.*1300–1361
Rulman Merswin	b.*c.*1310
Gerard Groote	1340–1384
Julian of Norwich	1342–*c.*1413
St Catherine of Siena	1347–1380
The Cloud of Unknowing author	*c.*1349–*c.*1395
Theologia Germanica author	*c.*1350–1400
Walter Hilton	d.1395
St Catherine of Genoa	1447–1510
Bernardino de Laredo	1482–1540
Francisco de Osuna	d.*c.*1540
St Ignatius Loyola	1491–1556
St Peter of Alcantara	1499–1562
Juan de Avila	1500–1569
Alonso de Orozco	1500–1591
Luis de Granada	1504–1588
St Teresa of Avila	1515–1582
Alphonsus Rodriguez	1533–1617
St John of the Cross	1542–1591
Madame Acarie	1566–1618
St Francis de Sales	1567–1622
Ste Chantal	1572–1641
Pierre de Bérulle	1575–1629
Jacob Boehme	1575–1624
Augustine Baker	1575–1641
Brother Lawrence	*c.*1605–1691
Blaise Pascal	1623–1662
Angelus Silesius	1624–1677
George Fox	1624–1691
Madame Guyon	1648–1717
François Fénelon	1651–1715
William Law	1686–1761
Emanuel Swedenborg	1688–1772
John Wooolman	1720–1772
'Lucie-Christine'	1844–1908
Charles de Foucauld	1858–1916
St Thérèse of Lisieux	1873–1897
Evelyn Underhill	1875–1941
Pierre Teilhard de Chardin	1881–1955

Dag Hammarskjöld	1905–1961
Simone Weil	1909–1943
Thomas Merton	1915–1968

References

Chapter 1: The Nature of Mysticism

1 William Wordsworth, *Lines Composed a Few Miles Above Tintern Abbey.*
2 Butler, *Western Mysticism*, pp. xx3–4.
3 Inge, *Mysticism in Religion*, p. 8.
4 Lasson, quoted by Inge, *Christian Mysticism*, p. 242.
5 Jones, *Studies in Mystical Religion*, xv. Author's italics.
6 Harkness, *Mysticism: Its Meaning and Message*. p. 21.
7 Ibid., pp. 23–4.
8 Quoted in Happold, *Mysticism*, p. 50.
9 Robert Browning, *Paracelsus*, I, 1, 726.
10 Underhill, *Mystics of the Church*, p. 22.
11 Inge, *Christian Mysticism*, p. 7
12 1 John 3:2–3
13 *Phaedo*, translated by Hugh Tredennick, Penguin (1969), pp. 110–111.
14 Ibid., p. 112.
15 *Theologia Germanica*, translated by Susanna Winkworth, xxxiv.
16 Happold, *Mysticism*, p. 60.
17 *The Vision of God*, XIII.
18 Sermon on St John the Baptist, quoted in Underhill, *Mysticism*, pp. 338–9.
19 Underhill, *Mystics of the Church*, p. 27.
20 *Medieval Mystical Tradition*, p. 112
21 *The Living Flame of Love*, II.
22 *The Adornment of the Spiritual Marraige*, III, 1, translated by C. A. Wynschenk; Happold, *Mysticism*, p. 293.
23 Collins, *Christian Mysticism in the Elizabethan Age*, p. 51.
24 *The Names of God*, quoted in Collins, op. cit., p. 53.
25 *Mystical Theology*, quoted in Happold, *Mysticism*, p. 212.
26 Inge, *Christian Mysticism*, p. 140, note 2.
27 *Imitatio Christi*, I, translated by Leo Sherley-Price.

28 *Timaeus*, translated by F. M. Cornford, in *Greek Philosophy: Thales to Aristotle*, edited by Reginald E. Allen, Collier-Macmillan (1966), p. 244.

29 Romans 1:2

30 *Symposium*, 211. Paraphrase of Jowett's translation by Charles Carrol Albertson; Harkness, *Mysticism: Its Meaning and Message*, p. 65.

31 *Life of Plotinus*; Collins, *Christian Mysticism in the Elizabethan Age*, p. 10.

32 *Enneads*, VI, 9, 10; Harkness, op. cit., p. 67.

33 Ibid., VI, 9, 9.

34 Underhill, *Mystics of the Church*, p. 12.

35 Ibid., p. 14.

Chapter 2: Mysticism in the Bible

1 Jones, *Studies in Mystical Religion*, p. 3.

2 Ibid., p. 4.

3 Isaiah 6:1–3.

4 Ezekiel 1:26–8.

5 Jeremiah 1:4–7, 9

6 Inge, *Christian Mysticism*, p. 43.

7 Psalm 139.

8 2 Corinthians 12:2–4.

9 1 Corinthians 9:27.

10 Hebrews 11:6.

11 Philippians 1:21.

12 1 John 4:7–13.

13 John 6:51–56.

Chapter 3: The Patristic Age

1 *Adversus Haereses* (Against Heresies), V, i, 1.

2 Ibid., VI, xx, 5–7.

3 *De Testimonio Animae* (On the Evidence of the Natural Christianity of the Soul), i.

4 *Paedagogus* (Tutor), III, i.

5 Acts 7:54–5.

6 *Epistle to the Ephesians*, vii, 2; Bettenson, *Early Christian Fathers*, p. 41. (References throughout this chapter are to the 1969 paperback edition of Bettenson's selection of early patristic writings.)

7 *Epistle to the Trallians*, ix; Bettenson, op. cit., p. 44.

8 *Epistle to the Smyrneans*, vi; Bettenson, p. 49.

9 Ibid., iv.

10 *Epistle to the Romans*, ii; Bettenson, p. 45.

11 Ibid., iv–vii, Bettenson, pp. 45–6.

12 Bettenson, p. 3.

13 *Adversus Haereses*, IV, xx, 1; Bettenson, op. cit., p. 66.

14 *De Carne Christi* (On Christ's Human Nature), 5; Bettenson, p. 14.

15 *Adversus Praxean* (Against Praxeas), 9; 12;' Bettenson, p. 121.

16 *Adversus Marcionem* (Against Marcion), iv, 2; Bettenson, p. 131.

17 *Stromateis* (Miscellanies), V. xii.

18 Ibid., V, i; Bettenson, p. 171.

19 Ibid., VI, xii; Bettenson, 184.

20 Bettenson, p. 18.

21 De Principiis (On First Principles), III, iv, 1; Bettenson, p. 198.

22 Ibid., I, i, 5–7; Bettenson, p. 186.

23 *Exhortatio ad Martyrium* (A Call to Martyrdom), 30; Bettenson, p. 223.

24 *Natural History*, VI, 17.

25 Jean Steinmann. *St John the Baptist and the Desert Tradition*, translated from the French by Michael Boyes (1958), p. 49.

26 Anson, *The Call of the Desert*, p. 6.

27 Ibid., p. 9.

28 Underhill, *Mystics of the Church*, pp. 56–7.

29 *De Anima et Resurrectione* (On the Soul and Resurrection).

30 *Enarrationes in Psalmos* (Explanations of the Psalms), Psalm xli.

31 *Confessions*, VII, x, 16.

32 Ibid., VII, xvii, 23.

33 Ibid., X, vi.

34 Ibid., IX, x, 24–5.

35 Ibid., I, iv, 4.

36 *On the Divine Names*, ii, 11.

37 *Mystical Theology*.

38 Ibid., ii, 1; Jones, *Studies in Mystical Religion*, p. 109.

39 Ibid., i, 3; Jones, op. cit., p. 110.

40 Jones, pp. 110–11.

41 Ibid., pp. 111–12.

42 Lossky, *Mystical Theology of the Eastern Church*, p. 8.

43 Ibid., p. 9.

44 *Theophanes*; Lossky, p. 37.

45 Homily LXXIX, 2; Lossky, p. 218.

Chapter 4: Early Medieval Mysticism

1 *De Divisione Naturae;* Jones, *Studies in Mystical Religion*, p. 113

2 Quoted in Underhill, *Mystics of the Church*, p. 85.

3 Butler, *Western Mysticism*, p. 97; Harkness, *Mysticism: Its Meaning and Message*, p .91.

4 Harkness, op. cit., pp. 92–3.
5 *On the Love of God*, x, translated by T. L. Connolly; Harkness p. 94.
6 Underhill, *Mystics of the Church*, p. 88.
7 Ibid., p. 76.
8 Ibid., pp. 77–8.
9 Ibid., p. 82.
10 *Laude*, 60.
11 *Little Flowers*, xv; Jones, *Studies in Mystical Religion*, p. 160.
12 *Little Flowers*, x.
13 Quoted by Jones, op. cit., p. 165.
14 Underhill, op. cit., p. 94.
15 Jones, op. cit., p. 173.
16 Ibid., p. 194.
17 Graef, *The Story of Mysticism*, pp. 167–8.

Chapter 5: The Later Middle Ages
(i) The Continental Mystics

1 Clarke, *The Great German Mystics*, pp. 5–6.
2 Jones, *Studies in Mystical Religion*, p. 219.
3 Ibid., p. 226.
4 Sermon, XII, in Clarke, *Meister Eckhart*, p. 184.
5 Walshe, *Meister Eckhart*, No. 94; Introduction, xxvi.
6 Clarke, *Meister Eckhart*, p. 137.
7 Ibid., p. 138.
8 Sermon I: a sermon preached at Christmastide; Happold, p. 278.
9 Jones, op. cit., pp. 256–7.
10 *The Book of the Two Men*.
11 Jones, op. cit., p. 217.
12 Sermon XXXIV.
13 *Theologia Germanica*, tr. Winkworth.
14 Underhill, *Mystics of the Church*, p. 139.
15 *Theologia*, tr. Winkworth.
16 Sermon for the 15th Sunday after Trinity.
17 Jones, op. cit., p. 278.
18 Underhill, op. cit., p. 142.
19 *Life of the Blessed Henry Suso*, tr. T. F. Knox.
20 *Life*; Underhill, op. cit., p. 143.
21. Ibid., p. 144.
22 *Life of the Blessed Henry Suso*; Jones, op. cit., p. 284.
23 Underhill, op. cit., p. 147.
24 Walsh (ed.), *Spirituality Through the Centuries*, p. 202.
25 *Book of the Sparkling Stone*, tr. Jane T. Stoddart.
26 *The Adornment of the Spiritual Marriage*.
27 *The Book of True Contemplation*.

28 *Book of the Sparkling Stone.*
29 *Treatise of Perfection of the Sons of God*, tr. Edmund Colledge; in Walsh (ed.), op. cit., p. 207.
30 Letter to Guillaume de Salvavarilla, Archdeacon of Liège; Jones, op. cit., p. 219. This was writen during the Great Schism.
31 Jones, p. 320.
32 Quoted in Sherley-Price (tr.), *The Imitation of Christ*, pp. 22–3.
33 De Montmorency, *Thomas à Kempis*; Jones, op. cit., p. 324.
34 George Eliot, *The Mill on the Floss*, IV, 3.
35 Sherley-Price, op. cit., p. 23.
36 Brother Azarias, *The Culture of the Spiritual Sense* (1884); Sherley-Price, p. 14.
37 *Imitation of Christ*, II, 31.
38 Ibid.
39 Jones, op. cit., p. 326.
40 *Imitation of Christ*, III, 58.
41 Ibid., III, 13.
42 Underhill, *Mystics of the Church*, p. 157.
43 Letters; Jones, op. cit., p. 303.
44 Jones, p. 302.

(ii) The English Mystics

45 *Ancrene Riwle*, tr. Salu, Introduction, p. xi.
46 Ibid., Part III, p. 62.
47 *Medieval English Lyrics*, ed. Davis, p. 108–9.
48 *Incendium*, xv, 187–90; Knowles, *English Mystical Tradition*, p. 58.
49 Ibid., xxxi, 234; Knowles, p. 60.
50 *Melos*, ed. Arnould, xlix, 157.
51 *Ego Dormio*, tr. Hope Allen; Colledge, *Medieval Mystics of England*, pp 151–2.
52 *Incendium*; Conrad Pepler, 'Richard Rolle', in Davis (ed.), *English Spiritual Writers*.
53 Pepler, ibid., p. 28.
54 Ibid., p. 29.
55 Knowles, *English Mystical Tradition*, p. 74.
56 *Book of Privy Counsel*, tr. Hodgson; Colledge (ed.), *Medieval Mystics of England*, p. 157.
57 Knowles, op. cit., p. 77.
58 *Ascent of Mount Carmel*, tr. Allison Peers, II, iv.
59 *Cloud of Unknowing*, tr. Wolters, 45.
60 *Book of Privy Counsel*, tr. Hodgson; Colledge (ed.), op. cit., p. 181.
61 Knowles, op. cit., p. 99.
62 *Scale of Perfection*, I, 14; tr. Colledge, *Medieval Mystics of England*, pp. 211–12.

63 Ibid., I, 52; Knowles, op. cit., p. 107.
64 Ibid., I, 12, Colledge, op. cit., p. 208.
65 Ibid., I, 46.
66 Ibid., I, 8; Colledge, op cit., p. 205
67 Ibid., II, 24, 25; tr. Sherley-Price.
68 *Revelations of Divine Love*, ed. Walsh, Introduction, p. 1.
69 *A Shewing of God's Love*, ed. Sister Anna Maria Reynolds, vi, pp 15–16.
70 *Revelations*, ed. Warrack, lx, 149–51.
71 Reynolds, op. cit., ii, pp. 4–5.
72 *Revelations*, ed. Walsh, Introduction, p. 4.
73 Ibid., pp. 17–18.
74 Ibid., p. 23.
75 Underhill, *Mystics of the Church*, p. 132.

Chapter 6: The Spanish Mystical Tradition

1 Graef, *Story of Mysticism*, p. 234.
2 Allison Peers, *Spanish Mysticism*, p. 65.
3 *Ascent of Mount Zion*; ibid., p. 77.
4 *Treatise of Prayer and Meditation*; ibid., p. 82.
5 *Spiritual Epistles*; ibid., p. 90.
6 *Sinner's Guide*; ibid., p. 95.
7 Underhill, *Mystics of the Church*, pp. 172, 173; Allison Peers, op. cit., p. 23.
8 *Life of St Teresa*, tr. Cohen, chapter 1.
9 Ibid., chapter 4.
10 Ibid., chapter 10.
11 Ibid., chapter 18.
12 Ibid., chapter 19.
13 Ibid, chapter 20.
14 Quoted in Underhill, op. cit., pp. 180–1.
15 *Life*, chapter 32.
16 Cohen, *Life*, Introduction, p. 16.
17 Allison Peers, *Spanish Mysticism*, p. 99.
18 St Teresa, *Foundations*; Allison Peers, *Spirit of Flame*, p. 22.
19 St Teresa, *Letters*, CCLXI, December 1578; *Spirit of Flame*, p. 35.
20 *Spirit of Flame*, p. 45.
21 Allison Peers, *Spanish Mysticism*, p. 109.
22 *Ascent of Mount Carmel*, I; Happold, p. 360.
23 *Spanish Mysticism*, p. 111.
24 Ibid., pp. 112–13.
25 *The Living Flame of Love*, I; Happold, p. 362.
26 Ibid., Happold, p. 363.
27 Ibid., Stanza II; Happold, p. 366.

Chapter 7: St Francis de Sales and the French School

1 Bremond, *A Literary History of Religious Thought in France*, vol. 1, p. 67.
2 Ibid., p. 68.
3 Ibid., p. 69.
4 *Introduction to the Devout Life*, tr. John K. Ryan, Introduction, p. ix.
5 Ibid., pp. xxv–xxvi.
6 Bremond, op. cit., p. 83.
7 Ibid.
8 *Treatise on the Love of God*, I, xv; Bremond, op. cit., p. 92.
9 Ibid., I, xviii; Bremond, p. 93.
10 Sheppard, *Barbe Acarie*, p. 112.
11 Bremond, *Literary History of Religious Thought in France*, vol. 2, p. 174.
12 Père Binet, quoted by Bremond, ibid., p. 170.
13 Ibid., p. 193.
14 Ibid., vol. 3, p. 133.
15 Ibid., p. 44.
16 Quoted in Morris Bishop, *Pascal: The Life of Genius* (1937), pp. 172–3.
17 Graef, *The Story of Mysticism*, p. 263.

Chapter 8: Four Protestant Mystics

1 Martensen, *Jacob Boehme*, p. 4.
2 Ibid., p. 5.
3 Ibid., pp. 5–6.
4 Ibid., p. 8.
5 G. C. Cell, *The Rediscovery of John Wesley* (1935), p. 177.
6 Martensen, op. cit., p. 37.
7 Fox, *Journal*.
8 Ibid.; Freemantle, *The Protestant Mystics*, pp. 86–7.
9 Woolman, *Journal*; Underhill, *Mystics of the Church*.
10 Ibid.; Freemantle, op. cit., p. 172.
11 Law, 'Two Answers to Dr Trapp'; Hobhouse, *Selected Mystical Writings of William Law*, p. 34.
12 Law, *The Grounds and Reasons of Christian Regeneration, or the New-Birth* (1759); Hobhouse, pp. 25–6.
13 Law, *An Appeal to All Who Doubt or Disbelieve the Truths of the Gospel,* (1740); Hobhouse, p. 82.
14 Law, *The Spirit of Prayer*, Hobhouse, p. 82.

Chapter 9: The Mystical Sense in English Literature

1 Douglas Bush, *English Literature in the Earlier Seventeenth Century* (1962), p. 310.
2 Donne, *Essays in Divinity*, ed. Evelyn M. Simpson (1952), p. 75.
3 Donne, *Devotions Upon Emergent Occasions*, Meditation I.
4 Donne, 'Negative Love'.
5 Bush, op. cit., p. 326.
6 Letter III, in *The Works of George Herbert*, ed. F. E. Hutchinson (Oxford, 1941, 1967), p. 364.
7 Ibid., Letter I.
8 Lord Herbert of Cherbury, *Autobiography*, ed. Sidney Lee (1906), p. 11.
9 Hutchinson, op. cit., Introduction, xxxvii.
10 Herbert, 'The Crosse'.
11 Hutchinson, op. cit., xxxviii.
12 Ibid., Letter IV, p. 366.
13 *An Introduction to a Devoute Life*, tr. John Yakesley (3rd edition, 1614); Martz, *The Poetry of Meditation*, p. 255.
14 Herbert, *A Priest to the Temple*, XXI, 'The Parson Catechizing'; Hutchinson, op. cit., p. 257.
15 Herbert, 'The Temper (I)'.
16 Austin Warren, *Richard Crashaw. A Study in Baroque Sensibility* (1939), p. 18.
17 Ibid., p. 201.
18 Ibid.
19 *The Flaming Heart* (1624), p. 419 (an English translation of St Teresa's *Life*).
20 Warren, op. cit., p. 206.
21 Vaughan, *The Mount of Olives*, 'Admonitions when we prepare for any farre Journey'.
22 'The Dawning'.
23 'The Tempest'.
24 Martz, *The Paradise Within*, pp. 5–6.
25 Ibid., p. 19.
26 St Augustine, *Confessions* 10:23; from the translation of William Watts (1631).
27 'The Check'.
28 *Centuries*, II, 66.
29 Ibid., II, 18.
30 'The Salutation'.
31 Peter Sterry, 'A Catechism' in *The Appearance of God to Man in the Gospel* (1710), a posthumous collection of Sterry's works. Sterry was chaplain to Cromwell.
32 *Centuries*, I, 3.

33 Ibid., I, 12.
34 Ibid., I, 29–30.
35 Ibid., III, 3.
36 Basil Willey, *The Seventeenth-Century Background* (1934). Quotation taken from Penguin edition (1962), p. 125.
37 Ibid., p. 112.
38 John Smith, *Discourse I*; Willey, op. cit., p. 128.
39 Ralph Cudworth, *The True Intellectual System of the Universe* (1678); Willey, p. 142.
40 *The Philosophical Poems of Henry More*, ed. G. Bullough (1931), Introduction.
41 R. Ward, *Life of More* (1710), ed. M. H. Howard (1911); quoted by Bullough, op. cit., p. 35.
42 Swedenborg, *The Spiritual Diary* (Swedenborg Society, 1962), p. 262.
43 Spurgeon, *Mysticism in English Literature*, p. 129.
44 'A Vision of the Last Judgment'; *Blake: Complete Writings*, ed. Geoffrey Keynes (Oxford, 1966), pp. 605–6.
45 *Jerusalem*, Plate 77, 'To the Christians'; Keynes, op. cit., pp. 716–7.
46 Northrop Frye, *Fearful Symmetry. A Study of William Blake* (1962), pp. 7–8.
47 'I rose up at the dawn of day'; Keynes, op. cit., p. 558.
48 Frye, op. cit., p. 8.
49 Wordsworth, *The Prelude* (1805 text), ed. Ernest de Selincourt, revised by Helen Darbishire (Oxford, 1960), VI, 525–542.
50 Notebook fragment; de Selincourt, op. cit., Introduction,. xxxiii.
51 Ibid.
52 *The Prelude*, IV, 140–2.
53 Walter Jackson Bate, *Coleridge*, 'Masters of World Literature Series' (1969), p. 213.
54 Coleridge, *Religious Musings* (1794); *The Poems of Samuel Taylor Coleridge*, ed. Ernest Hartley Coleridge (Oxford, 1912, 1964), p. 124.
55 Ibid.; p. 113.
56 *Biographia Literaria*, ed. J. Shawcross (Oxford, 1907, 1967), Vol. 1, p. 98.
57 Ibid.
58 'My Baptismal Birth-day' (1833); *Poems* ed. Coleridge, p. 490.
59 Shelley, 'On Love', in *Essays and Letters by Percy Busshe Shelley*, ed. Ernest Rhys (1886), p. 52.
60 *Epipsychidion* (1821), 573–587; *Shelley: Poetical Works*, ed. Thomas Hutchinson (Oxford, 1967), p. 424.
61 *Adonais* (1821), LII.
62 Keats, *Endymion: A Poetic Romance*, III, 162–169; *Keats: Poetical Works*, ed. H. W. Garrod, (Oxford, 1956), p. 109.

63 Ibid., I, 777–780.

Chapter 10: Mysticism in the Modern World: Two Responses

1   *The Spiritual Journal of Lucie-Christine* (1915); Underhill, *Mystics of the Church*, p. 245.
2   Quoted by Holmes, *A History of Christian Spirituality*, p. 152.
3   *Christianity and Evolution* (1971), p. 122.
4   *The Heart of Matter* (1978), p. 25.
5   *Writings in Time of War* (1968), p. 32.
6   *The Heart of Matter*, p. 132.
7   Ibid., p. 126.
8   *The Divine Milieu* (1960), pp. 103, 106, 107.
9   *Lettres Intimes à Auguste Valensin, Bruno de Solages, Henri de Lubac, André Ravier 1919–1955* (1974), p. 104.
10 King, *Towards a New Mysticism*, p. 101.
11 *The Phenomenon of Man* (1959), p. 219.
12 *Christ in Matter*, quoted in Happold, *Mysticism*, p. 139.
13 Happold, ibid., p. 394.
14 *The Seven Storey Mountain* (1948); Furlong, *Thomas Merton*, p. 71.
15 Ibid.; Furlong, p. 79.
16 Brother Patrick Hart, 'The Contemplative Vision of Thomas Merton', *Cistercian Studies* (1978).
17 *The Asian Journal of Thomas Merton*, ed. Naomi Burton, Brother Patrick Hart and James Laughlin (1973); Furlong, pp. 326–7.
18 *New Seeds of Contemplation* (1962), p. 179.
19 Anthony Duncan, 'An Encounter', *New Fire*.

Select Bibliography

THIS bibliography functions as a general indication of the sources on which the text is based and as a guide to further reading and study. It is in two parts: general studies of mysticism and related topics, and studies of individual mystics and spiritual movements.

Abbreviations:
ACW: Ancient Christian Writers series
          (Longman).
CWS: Classics of Western Spirituality series
          (SPCK/Paulist Press).
LCC: Library of Christian Classics series
          (SCM/Westminster Press).
LCL: Loeb Classical Library.
NPNF: Nicene and Post-Nicene Fathers (Parker).

General Studies

Henry Bettenson (tr. and ed.), *The Early Christian Fathers* (1956, 1969).

——, *The Later Christian Fathers* (1956, 1969).

Louis Bouyer, *A History of Christian Spirituality, vol. 1: The Spirituality of the New Testament and the Fathers* (1963).

John Bowker, *The Religious Imagination and the Sense of God* (1978).

Mary Ann Bowman (ed.), *Western Mysticism: Guide to the Basic Works*, American Library Association (1980).

Henri Bremond, *A Literary History of Religious Thought in France*, tr. K. L. Montgomery, vol. 1 (1928), vol. 2 (1930), vol. 3 (1936).

Ruth Burrows, *Guidelines for Mystical Prayer* (1976).

Cuthbert Butler, *Western Mysticism* (1922).

J. B. Collins, *Christian Mysticism in The Elizabethan Age* (1940).
Harold G. Coward and Terence Penelhum (eds.), *Mystics and Scholars: Proceedings of the Calgary Conference on Mysticism, 1976*, Canadian Corporation for Studies in Religion (1979).
Jean Daniélou, *The Origins of Latin Christianity* (1977).
Charles Davis (ed.), *The English Spiritual Writers* (1961).
Robert S. Ellwood, *Mysticism and Religion* (1980).
C. Elsee, *Neoplatonism in its Relation to Christianity* (1908).
Anne Freemantle (ed.) and W. H. Auden (introduction), *The Protestant Mystics* (1964).
Hilda Graef, *The Light and the Rainbow: A Study in Christian Spirituality* (1959).
——, *Mystics of Our Time* (1962).
——, *The Story of Mysticism* (1966).
Peter Grant, *Literature of Mysticism in Western Tradition* (1983).
F. C. Happold, *Mysticism: A Study and an Anthology* (1963).
Georgia Harkness, *Mysticism: Its Meaning and Message* (1973).
Urban T. Holmes, *A History of Christian Spirituality: An Analytical Introduction* (1980).
James R. Horne, *Beyond Mysticism* (1979).
W. R. Inge, *Christian Mysticism* [The Bampton Lectures] (1899).
——, *Mysticism in Religion* (1947).
——, *Studies of English Mystics* (1906).
Martin Israel, *Approach to Mysticism* (1968).
Paul de Jaegher (ed.), *Anthology of Mysticism* (1977).
M. R. James, *The Apocryphal New Testament* (1924).
William James, *The Varieties of Religious Experience* (1902).
William Johnston, *The Way of Christian Mysticism* (1984).
——, *The Inner Eye of Love: Mysticism and Religion* (1978, 1981).
——, *The Still Point: Reflections on Zen and Christian Mysticism* (1970).
Rufus M. Jones, *Studies in Mystical Religion* (1909).
Steven Katz (ed.), *Mysticism and Philosophical Analysis* (1978).
David Knowles, *The English Mystical Tradition* (1961).
——, *The Monastic Order in England* (2nd edn., 1949).
——, *What Is Mysticism?* (1979).
Andrew Louth, *The Origins of the Christian Mystical Tradition* (1981).
Louis L. Martz, *The Paradise Within: Studies in Vaughan, Traherne and Milton* (1964).
——, *The Poetry of Meditation* (1962).

C. F. D. Moule, *The Origin of Christology* (1977).
Herbert Musurillo, *The Acts of the Christian Martyrs* (1972).
Rudolph Otto, *Mysticism East and West* (1957).
E. G. Parrinder, *Mysticism in the World's Religions* (1978).
Coventry Patmore, *The Rod, the Root and the Flower* (1895).
Conrad Pepler, *The English Religious Heritage* (1958).
A. Poulain, *The Graces of Interior Prayer* (English translation, 1910).
E. K. Saudreau, *The Degrees of the Spiritual Life*, tr. Dom Bede Camm (2 vols., 1921).
Ben-Ami Scharfstein, *Mystical Experience* (1973, 1979).
Beryl Smalley, *The Study of the Bible in the Middle Ages* (1952).
Margaret Smith, *Introduction to Mysticism* (1977).
Peter Spink, *Path of the Mystic* (1982).
Caroline Spurgeon, *Mysticism in English Literature* (1913).
F. Staal, *Exploring Mysticism* (1975).
W. T. Stace, *Mysticism and Philosophy* (1961).
D. T. Suzuki, *Mysticism: Christian and Buddhist* (1980).
Michael Talbot, *Mysticism and the New Physics* (1981).
E. M. Thompson, *The English Carthusians* (1932).
Herbert Thurston, *The Physical Phenomena of Mysticism* (1952).
——, *Surprising Mystics* (1955).
Evelyn Underhill, *The Essentials of Mysticism* (1920).
——, *Mysticism: A Study in the Nature and Development of Man's Spiritual Consciousness* (1911).
——, *The Mystic Way* (1913).
——, *Mystics of the Church* (1925).
W. J. Wainwright, *Mystical Experience* (1982).
——, *Mysticism* (1981).
James Walsh (ed.), *Spirituality Through the Centuries: Ascetics and Mystics of the Western Church* (1966).
E. I. Watkins, *The Philosophy of Mysticism* (1919).
——, *Poets and Mystics* (1953).
Rowan Williams, *The Wound of Knowledge: Christian Spirituality from the New Testament to St John of the Cross* (1979).
Richard Woods (ed.), *Understanding Mysticism* (1981).
R. C. Zaehner, *Mysticism, Sacred and Profane* (1957).
——, *Hindu and Muslim Mysticism* (1970).

Individual Studies

MADAME ACARIE
Lancelot C. Sheppard, *Barbe Acarie: Wife and Mystic* (1953).

ANCRENE RIWLE
M. B. Salu (tr.), *The Ancrene Riwle*, Introduction by Gerald Sitwell (1963).

ANGELA OF FOLIGNO
M. Steegman (tr.), *The Book of Divine Consolations of the Blessed Angela of Foligno*, Introduction by Algar Thorold (1908).

ANSELM
Karl Jaspers, *Anselm and Nicholas of Cusa* (1966).

ST ANTONY
D. J. Chitty, *The Letters of St Antony the Great* (1975).

APOCALYPTIC SPIRITUALITY
Bernard McGinn (tr.), *Apocalyptic Spirituality* (treatises and letters of Joachim of Fiore and the Spiritual Franciscans, amongst others), CWS (1979).

AQUINAS
Summa Theologiae, Dominican edition (1964).
H. Pope (ed.), *Thomas Aquinas: On Prayer and the Contemplative Life* (1914).

ASCETISM
Peter F. Anson, *The Call of the Desert: The Solitary Life in the Christian Church* (1964).
D. J. Chitty, *The Desert, a City* (1966).
Owen Chadwick (ed.), *Western Ascetism*, LCC, xii (1958).

ATHANASIUS
A. Robertson (tr.), *Vita Antonii* (Life of St Antony) and other tracts, NPNF, vol. iv (1892).
Robert C. Gregg (tr.), *Athanasius: The Life of Antony and the Letter to Marcellinius*, CWS.

ST AUGUSTINE
Henry Bettenson (tr.), *The City of God* (1972).
Peter Brown, *Augustine of Hippo* (1967).
John Burnaby, *Amor Dei: A Study of the Religion of St Augustine* (1960).

Erich Przywara (ed.), *An Augustine Synthesis* (1977).
John Ryan (tr.), *The Confessions* (1960).
J. E. Sullivan, *The Image of God: The Doctrine of St Augustine and its Influence* (1963).
Augustine of Hippo: Selected Writings, CWS (1984).

AUGUSTINE BAKER
J. McCann (ed.), *Confessions of Venerable Fr. Baker* (1922).

ST BASIL
W. K. L. Clarke, *St Basil the Great* (1913).
E. F. Morrison, *St Basil and his Rule* (1912).

ST BERNARD OF CLAIRVAUX
Etienne Gilson, *The Mystical Theology of St Bernard* (1940).
B. Scott James (tr.), *The Letters of Saint Bernard of Clairvaux* (1953).
Kilian Walsh (tr.), *On the Song of Songs*, Cistercian Fathers Series (2 vols., 1971, 1976).
R. Walton (tr.), *On Loving God*, Cistercian Fathers Series (1973).
Sister Benedicta Ward (ed.), *The Influence of St Bernard* (1976).

BOEHME
Peter Erb (tr.), *The Way to Christ*, CWS (1978).
Hans L. Martensen, *Studies in the Life and Teaching of Boehme*, tr. T. Rhys Evans, with Notes and Appendices by Stephen Hobhouse (1949).

BONAVENTURA
Ewert Cousins (tr.), *The Soul's Journey into God: The Tree of Life: The Life of St Francis*, CWS (1978).

CALVIN
Ford Lewis Battles (tr.), *The Piety of John Calvin* (1969).

CASSIAN
Owen Chadwick, *John Cassian: A Study in Primitive Monasticism* (1950).

ST CATHERINE OF GENOA
Charlotte Balfour and Helen D. Irvine (eds.), *St Catherine of Genoa* (1946).
Friedrich von Hügel, *The Mystical Element of Religion as Studied in St Catherine of Genoa* (2 vols., 1908).
Serge Hughes (tr.), *Catherine of Genoa: Purgation and Purgatory;*

The Spiritual Dialogue, CWS (1979).

ST CATHERINE OF SIENA
Edmund Gardner, *St Catherine of Siena* (1907).
Suzanne Noffke (tr.), *Catherine of Siena: The Dialogue*, CWS (1980).
Vida Scudder (ed.), *St Catherine of Siena As Seen in Her Letters* (1905).

THE CLOUD OF UNKNOWING
Phyllis Hodgson (ed.), *The Cloud of Unknowing* and *The Book of Privy Counselling*, Early English Text Society, orig. ser., 218 (1944), reprinted with additions 1958.
J. McCann (tr.), *The Cloud of Unknowing and Other Treatises* (1924).
Clifton Wolters (tr.), *The Cloud of Unknowing* (1961).
William Johnston, *The Mysticism of 'The Cloud of Unknowing'* (1978).
James Walsh (ed.), *The Cloud of Unknowing*, CWS (1981).

CRASHAW
L. C. Martin (ed.), *The Poems . . . Of Richard Crashaw* (1927, 1957).

DIONYSIUS THE AREOPAGITE
J. Parker (tr.), *The Works of Dionysius the Areopagite* (2 vols., 1897, 1899).
C. E. Rolt (tr.), *The Divine Names and Mystical Theology* (1920).
Shrine of Wisdom (ed.), *Mystical Theology and the Celestial Hierarchies* (1965).
John D. Jones (tr.), *Pseudo-Dionysius: The Divine Names and Mystical Theology*, Medieval Philosophical Texts in translation No. 21 (Marquette University Press, 1980).

DOMINICAN SPIRITUALITY
Simon Tugwell (ed.), *Early Dominicans: Selected Writings*, CWS (1982).

DONNE
Sir Herbert Grierson (ed.), *Donne: Poetical Works* (1933, 1966).

EASTERN CHURCH
Nicholas Arseniev, *Mysticism and the Eastern Church* (1979).
Sergius Bolshakoff, *Russian Mystics* (1976).

Vladimir Lossky, *The Mystical Theology of the Eastern Church* (1957).
——, *The Vision of God* (1963).

MEISTER ECKHART
Hustache Ancelet, *Master Eckhart and the Rhineland Mystics*, tr. Hilda Graef (1958).
R. P. Blakney (tr.), *Meister Eckhart: A Modern Translation* (1941).
James Clarke, *Meister Eckhart: An Introduction to the Study of his Works, with an Anthology of his Sermons* (1957).
——, *The Great German Mystics* (1949).
Edmund Colledge and Bernard McGinn (tr.), *Meister Eckhart: The Essential Sermons, Commentaries, Treatises, and Defence*, CWS (1981).
M. O'C. Walshe (tr.), *Meister Eckhart: Sermons and Treatises* (2 vols., 1979).

JONATHAN EDWARDS
Works (Yale, 1959–77).

EVAGRIUS
J. E. Bamberger (tr.), *The Praktikos and 153 Chapters on Prayer*, Cistercian Studies, vol. 4 (1970).

FENELON
Michael de la Medoyère, *The Archbishop and the Lady* (1956).
E. K. Sanders, *Fénelon: His Friends and His Enemies 1651–1715* (1901).
Mildred W. Stillman (tr.), *Christian Perfection* (1976).

GEORGE FOX
N. Penney (ed.), *Journal of George Fox* (1911).

ST FRANCIS OF ASSISI
Raphael Brown (tr.), *The Little Flowers of St Francis* (1958).
Benen Fahy and Placid Hermann (tr.), *Writings of Francis of Assisi* (1964).
A. G. Ferrers Howell (tr.), *The Lives of St Francis of Assisi, by Brother Thomas of Celano* (1908).
Regis J. Armstrong and Ignatius C. Brady (tr.), *Francis and Clare: The Complete Works*, CWS (1982).

FRANCISCO DE OSUNA
Mary E. Giles (tr.), *The Third Spiritual Alphabet*, CWS (1981).

ST FRANCIS DE SALES
Henry B. Mackey (tr.), *Treatise on the Love of God* (1942).
John R. Ryan (tr.), *Introduction to the Devout Life* (1950).
E. K. Sanders, *St François de Sales 1567–1622* (1928).
Elisabeth Stopp (ed.), *St Francis de Sales: Selected Letters* (1960).

GNOSTICISM
W. Foerster, *Gnosis: A Selection of Gnostic Texts* (2 vols., 1972, 1974).
Hans Jonas, *The Gnostic Religion* (1958).
Benjamin Walker, *Gnosticism* (1983).

GREGORY OF NAZIANZUS
E. H. Gifford, C. G. Browne and J. E. Swallow (tr.), in NPNF. vol. vii (1894).

GREGORY OF NYSSA
Hilda Graef (tr), *De beatitudinibus* (The Beatitudes) and the *De oratione dominica* (The Lord's Prayer) (1954).
W. Moore and H. A. Wilson (tr.), *De Virginitate* and other tracts, NPNF, vol. v (1893).
Herbert Musurillo (tr.), *From Glory to Glory: Texts from Gregory of Nyssa's Mystical Writings*, from the French of Jean Daniélou (1962).
Abraham J. Malherbe and Everett Ferguson (tr.), *Gregory of Nyssa: The Life of Moses*, CWS (1978).

MADAME GUYON
T. T. Allen (tr.), *Autobiography of Madame Guyon* (2 vols., 1897).
Michael de la Bedoyère, *The Archbishop and the Lady* (1956).

DAG HAMMARSKJÖLD
Leif Sjöberg and W. H. Auden (tr.), *Markings* (1964).

GEORGE HERBERT
John N. Wall (ed.), *The Country Parson; The Temple*, CWS (1981).
F. E. Hutchinson (ed.), *The Works of George Herbert* (1941, 1967).

WALTER HILTON
Helen Gardner, 'Walter Hilton and the Mystical Tradition in England', *Essays and Studies*, XXIII (1937).
Phyllis Hodgson, 'Walter Hilton and *The Cloud of Unknowing*. A Problem of Authorship Reconsidered', *Modern Language Review*, 50 (1955).
Gerard Sitwell (tr.), *The Scale of Perfection* (1953).

HUGH OF ST VICTOR
Hugh of St Victor: Selected Spiritual Writings, tr. a Religious of C.S.M.V., Introduction by Aeldred Squire, OP (1962).

ST IGNATIUS LOYOLA
Thomas Corbishley (tr.), *The Spiritual Exercises* (1963).
D. F. O'Leary (tr.), *Letters and Instructions of St Ignatius Loyola* (1914).
E. M. Rix (tr.), *The Testament of St Ignatius Loyola* (1900).

IGNATIUS OF ANTIOCH
James A. Kleist (tr.), *The Epistles* (1949).
Kirsopp Lake (tr.) in the *Apostolic Fathers*, vol. i, LCL (1930).
C. C. Richardson (tr.), in *Early Christian Fathers*, vol. i, LCC (1953).

JACOPONE DA TODI
Evelyn Underhill, *Jacopone da Todi* (1919).

RICHARD JEFFERIES
The Story of My Heart (1883).

ST JOHN CLIMACUS
Archimandrite Lazarus Moore (tr.), *St John Climacus: The Ladder of Divine Ascent* (1959).

ST JOHN OF THE CROSS
E. Allison Peers (tr.), *John of the Cross: Complete Works* (3 vols., 1934–5).
——, *Spirit of Flame: A Study of St John of the Cross* (1943).
Gerald Brenan, *St John of the Cross: His Life and Poetry* (1973). Translation of the poems by Lynda Nicholson.
Roy Campbell (tr.), *St John of the Cross: Poems* (1960).
E. W. T. Dicken, *The Crucible of Love* (1963).
Edith Stein, *The Science of the Cross* (1960).
R. H. J. Steuart (ed.), *The Mystical Doctrine of St John of the Cross* (1975).
Medieval Mystical Tradition and St John of the Cross (1954), by a Benedictine of Stanbrook Abbey.

JULIAN OF NORWICH
Percy F. Chambers, *Julian of Norwich: An Appreciation and an Anthology* (1955).
P. Molinari, *Julian of Norwich: The Teaching of a Fourteenth-century English Mystic* (1958).

Sister Anna Maria Reynolds (ed.), *A Shewing of God's Love* [shorter version of *Sixteen Revelations of Divine Love*] (1958).
James Walsh (tr.), *The Revelations of Divine Love of Julian of Norwich* (1961).
Edmund Colledge and James Walsh (tr.), *Julian of Norwich: Showings*, CWS (1978).

MARGERY KEMPE
Clarissa W. Atkinson, *Mystic and Pilgrim: The Book and the World of Margery Kempe* (1983).
W. Butler-Bowden (ed.), *The Book of Margery Kempe* (1936).
S. B. Meech and H. E. Allen (eds.), *The Book of Margery Kempe*, Early English Text Society, orig. ser., 212 (1940).

WILLIAM LAW
S. H. Gem, *William Law on Christian Practice and Mysticism* (1905).
Stephen Hobhouse (ed.), *Selected Mystical Writings of William Law* (1948).
Caroline Spurgeon, 'William Law and the English Mystics', in *The Cambridge History of English Literature*.
Paul G. Stanwood (ed.), *A Serious Call to a Devout and Holy Life; The Spirit of Love*, CWS (1978).

BROTHER LAWRENCE
D. Attwater (tr.), *The Practice of the Presence of God* (1926).

LUIS DE LEON
Luis de Leon: The Names of Christ, CWS series (1984).

LUTHER
Theodore G. Tappert (ed.), *Letters of Spiritual Counsel* (1955).

MECHTHILD OF MAGDEBURG
Lucy Menzies (tr.), *The Revelations* (1953).

MEDIEVAL MYSTICISM
Anne Bancroft, *Luminous Vision: Six Medieval Mystics and their Teachings* (1982).
Eric Colledge (ed.), *The Medieval Mystics of England* (1962).
Ray C. Petry (ed.), *Late Medieval Mysticism*, LCC (1957).
Wolfgang Riehle, *Middle English Mystics* (1981).
Ritamary Bradley and Valerie M. Lagorio (eds.), *Fourteenth-century English Mystics: A Comprehensive Annotated Bibliography* (1981).

THOMAS MERTON
Raymond Bailey, *Thomas Merton on Mysticism* (1975).
Monica Furlong, *Thomas Merton: A Biography* (1980).
Thomas Merton, *Contemplative Prayer* (1971).
——, *New Seeds of Contemplation* (1972).
——, *Thomas Merton on St Bernard*, Cistercian Studies (1980).
Michael C. Mott, *The Seven Mountains of Thomas Merton* (1984).
Edward Rice, *The Man in the Sycamore Tree: The Good Times and Hard Life of Thomas Merton* (1970).

GERTRUDE MORE
B. W. Blundell (ed.), *The Inner Life and Writings of Dame Gertrude More* (2 vols., 1910).

NICOLAS OF CUSA
E. Gurney Salter, *Nicolas of Cusa: The Vision of God* (1928).
Karl Jaspers, *Anselm and Nicolas of Cusa* (1966).

ORIGEN
G. W. Butterworth (tr.), *De Principiis* (1936).
Henry Chadwick (tr.), *Contra Celsum* (1953).
Jean Daniélou, *Origen* (1955).
R. P. Lawson (tr.), ACW, 26 (1957). Commentary and sermons on the Song of Songs.
J. E. L. Oulton and Henry Chadwick (eds.), *Alexandrian Christianity*, LCC, vol. ii (1954). Contains the *De oratione*, *Exhortation to Martyrdom* and the *Dialogue with Heracleides*.

ST PAUL
Albert Schweitzer, *The Mysticism of St Paul the Apostle*, tr. William Montgomery (1931).

ST PETER DAMIAN
Patricia McNulty (tr.), *St Peter Damien: Selected Writings on the Spiritual Life* (1959).

SPANISH MYSTICISM
E. Allison Peers, *Spanish Mysticism: A Preliminary Survey* (1924).
Stephen Clissold (ed.), *The Wisdom of the Spanish Mystics* (1977).
E. W. T. Dicken, *The Crucible of Love* (1963).

PIETISM
Peter Erb (ed.), *Pietists: Selected Writings*, CWS (1983).

QUAKERISM
Quaker Spirituality: Selected Writings, CWS series (1984).

RICHARD OF ST VICTOR
Clare Kirchberger (tr.), *Selected Writings on Contemplation* (1957).
Grover A. Zinn (tr.), *The Twelve Patriarchs*, CWS (1979).

RICHARD ROLLE
F. M. Cooper (tr.), *The Fire of Love* (1914).
C. Horstmann, *Richard Rolle and his Followers* (2 vols., 1895–6).
John G. Harrell (tr.), *Richard Rolle: Selected Writings* (1963).

RUYSBROECK
Eric Colledge (tr.), *The Spiritual Espousals* (1952).
F. Sherwood Taylor (tr.), *The Seven Steps of the Ladder of Spiritual Love* (1943).
P. Wynschenk (tr.), *Adornment of the Spiritual Marriage* (1916).
Eric Colledge and Joyce Bazire (tr.), *The Chastening of God's Children and the Treatise of Perfection of the Sons of God* (1957).

SAINTE CHANTAL
E. K. Sanders, *Sainte Chantal 1572–1641: A Study in Vocation* (1918).

ROBERT SOUTHWELL
P. E. Hallett (tr.), *Spiritual Exercises and Devotions* (1975).

SUSO
James M. Clarke (tr.), *The Little Book of Eternal Wisdom and Little Book of Truth* (1953).
——, *Suso: The Life of the Servant* (1952, 1982).
——, *The Great German Mystics* (1949).
T. F. Knox (tr.), *Life of the Blessed Henry Suso, by Himself* (1913).

TAULER
A. W. Hutton (tr.), *The Inner Way* (1909).
Susanna Winkworth, *History and Life of the Reverend Doctor John Tauler, with 25 of his Sermons* (1906).
James M. Clarke, *The Great German Mystics* (1949).
Eric Colledge and M. Janes (tr.), *Tauler: Spiritual Conferences* (1961).

TEILHARD DE CHARDIN
Robert Faricy, *All Things in Christ: Teilhard de Chardin's Spirituality* (1981).

Ursula King, *Towards a New Mysticism: Teilhard de Chardin and Eastern Religions* (1980).
C. F. Mooney, *Teilhard de Chardin and the Mystery of Christ* (1966).
N. M. Wildiers, *An Introduction to Teilhard de Chardin* (1968).

St Teresa of Avila
Collected Works, tr. Keiran Kavanaugh and Otilio Rodriguez, vol. 1 (1976), vol. 2 (1980).
The Interior Castle, tr. K. Kavanaugh and O. Rodriguez (1980).
Letters, tr. E. Allison Peers (2 vols., 1980).
The Way of Perfection, tr. E. Allison Peers (1977).
E. Allison Peers, *Mother of Carmel: A Portrait of St Teresa of Avila* (1945).
—— (tr.), *St Teresa of Avila: Complete Works* (3 vols. 1946).
Stephen Clissold, *St Teresa of Avila* (1979).
J. M. Cohen (tr.), *The Life of St Teresa of Avila, by Herself* (1957).

Theologia Germanica
Susanna Winkworth (tr.), *Theologia Germanica* (1907).

St Therese of Lisieux
R. A. Knox (tr.), *Autobiography of a Saint* (1958).
Ida Friederike Goerres, *The Hidden Face: A Study of St Thérèse of Lisieux* (1958).
F. P. Keyes, *St Teresa of Lisieux* (1972).
James Norbury, *Warrior in Chains: St Thérèse of Lisieux* (1966).
F. J. Sheed (tr.), *Collected Letters of St Thérèse of Lisieux* (1975).
Barry Ulanov, *The Making of a Modern Saint: A Biographical Study of Thérèse of Lisieux* (1967).

Thomas a Kempis
S. Kettlewell, *Thomas à Kempis and the Brothers of the Common Life* (1882).
Leo Sherly-Price (tr.), *The Imitation of Christ* (1952).

Traherne
Anne Ridler (ed.), *Thomas Traherne: Poems, Centuries and Three Thanksgivings* (1966).

Evelyn Underhill
C. J. R. Armstrong, *Evelyn Underhill: An Introduction to her Life and Writings* (1957).
Margaret Cropper, *Evelyn Underhill* (1958).

T. S. Kepler (ed.), *The Evelyn Underhill Reader* (1962).

HENRY VAUGHAN
L. C. Martin (ed.), *Henry Vaughan: Poetry and Selected Prose* (1963).

SIMONE WEIL
Emma Crauford (tr.), *Waiting for God* (n.d.).
Simone Pétrement, *Simone Weil: A Life*, tr. Raymond Rosenthal (1976).

WILLIAM OF ST-THIERRY
Sister Penelope (tr.), *On Contemplating God*, Cistercian Fathers series (1970).

JOHN WOOLMAN
Philips P. Moultin (ed.), *The Journal and Major Essays* (1971).

Index